The Bournemouth Library
22 The Triangle
Bournemouth
BH2 5RQ
Tel: (01202) 454848

D1491553

DORSET COUNTY LIBRARY

201064547 T

0460045873 001
                                      821.008
EVERYMAN BOOK OF LIGHT VERSE;
ED. BY R.ROBINSON 1984

A

The Everyman book of
LIGHT VERSE

The Everyman book of
LIGHT VERSE

Edited by
Robert Robinson

J. M. Dent & Sons Ltd
London & Melbourne

DORSET COUNTY
638 55
-5 JAN 1985
821·008
LIBRARY HQ
LANSDOWNE REFERENCE

First published 1984
Introduction, selection and notes © J. M. Dent & Sons Ltd, 1984

All rights reserved. No part of this publication may be
reproduced, stored in a retrieval system, or transmitted,
in any form or by any means, electronic, mechanical,
photocopying, recording or otherwise, without the prior
permission of J. M. Dent & Sons Ltd

This book is set in 11/12½ VIP Plantin by
D. P. Media Limited, Hitchin, Hertfordshire

Printed in Great Britain by
Richard Clay (The Chaucer Press) Plc, Bungay for
J. M. Dent & Sons Ltd,
Aldine House, 33 Welbeck Street, London W1M 8LX

British Library Cataloguing in Publication Data

The Everyman book of light verse.
  1. Humorous poetry, English
  I. Robinson, Robert, *1927* –
821'.07'08   PR1195.H8

ISBN 0-460-04587-3

Contents

Introduction

Good light verse has a conversational address:

> Revenge Dad or not?
> That's the gist of the plot,
> And he did, nine soliloquies later . . .

– it is the principle of conversational wit, precipitated:

> My lord Archbishop, what a scold you are!
> And when your man is down how bold you are!
> Of charity how oddly scant you are!
> How Lang O Lord, how full of Cantuar!

– a perfect formality of rhyme and scansion vanishing (in the right hands) within an illusion of nonchalance and spontaneity:

> *Is this a milieu where I must*
> How grahamgreeneish! How infra dig!
> *Snatch from the bottle in my bag*
> *An analeptic swig?*

Though the *timbre* varies with the taste, temper and period:

> Stands that great landmark, Lansdowne House—
> O, stands it where it did?
> Yea, as irrefrageably as
> Cheops his pyramid.

– it never (at its best) arouses suspicions that it is not the author's native voice:

> I'll swear, without the risk of perjury,
> It was a snappy bit of surgery.
> My rectum is a serious loss to me,
> But I've a very neat colostomy,
> And hope, as soon as I am able,
> To make it keep a fixed time-table.

Such verse can turn sharp corners and rejoice in the angularity:

> O stalwart SUSSEX postman who is
> Delivering the post from LEWES . . .

– and plays with discords only spectacularly to discount them:

> There first for thee my passion grew,
> Sweet! sweet Matilda Pottingen!
> thou wast the daughter of my Tu—
> —tor, Law Professor at the U—
> —niversity of Gottingen —
> —niversity of Gottingen.

The poetry that doesn't require an adjective like 'light' to warn you not to expect what you aren't going to get can also do all that light verse can do, but when it's any good carries you into a place you didn't know was there. Whereas light verse, like the conversation of which it is the epitome (and also when *it's* any good), freshens up odd corners everyone is familiar with, and sometimes does it well enough to make you smile, mostly in surprise:

I once had the honour of meeting a philosopher called McIndoe
Who had once had the honour of being flung out of an upstairs
    window.
During his flight, he said, he commenced an interesting train
    of speculation
On why there happened to be such a word as defenestration.

Sometimes, just for a moment, light verse repositions the familiar so cunningly that it may seem not to be light verse at all:

> I wrote: in the dark cavern of our birth.
> The printer had it tavern, which seems better:
> But herein lies the subject of our mirth,
> Since on the next page death appears as dearth.
> So it may be that God's word was distraction,
> Which to our strange type appears destruction,
> Which is bitter.

– but if on reflection you decide (as I did) that these ironies of Malcolm Lowry properly qualify for the light verse canon, and embellish it, you will also recognize what a continuous temptation it is to mistake for light verse what you know certainly is not. Very occasionally in this collection I have included poems whose conversational tone has been assumed for other purposes, and which are carrying unexploded material. An example is Philip Larkin's 'I Remember, I Remember', where what the verse contains has its crown-cork lifted off in the last line. But since it's plain enough where I've succumbed I'll just say that I can't imagine anyone not wanting me to have done.

The conversational character of light verse has another dimension, in that some of the best of it has an incidental ring, as though it were not the principal activity in the life of the man who was writing it. No doubt this was literally true of many (politicians like Canning and Praed, dons like Quiller-Couch and A. C. Godley), but the offhand *dégagé* manner of one exercising an accomplishment rather than plying a trade seems to have become something of a hallmark of the *genre* from the nineteenth century onwards: Calverley and Hood and Belloc and Beerbohm, as well as the later *Punch* writers, such as Owen Seaman and E. V. Knox, all lived by the pen, but the tone of their verse – amateur, though of course not amateurish – implied that to be amusing in this way was the business of any cultivated man (rather as in pre-war Vienna journalism wasn't something you devoted yourself to but, doctor, advocate, professor, you did it as well).

I think this hints at the sort of conditions in which this kind of light verse could flourish – the surroundings, social as well as poetic, had to be carefully defined, the pitch very distinctly marked out, the rules understood by everyone (even those who weren't going to benefit from them) if the game was to be played at all. Rain was beginning to stop play round about the Thirties, though there were still those who carried on as though they didn't know the pitch was about to be swamped and the white lines washed away; blurry with nostalgia, their verses conjure up a tuppence-coloured cyclorama of gun-rooms and colonels and maids with cake-frills in their hair that you feel never quite existed for them – a world of pansy poets and parvenus and comic proles and dropped aitches. (I think Auden fingered the wrong man when he said:

Sir Owen Seaman was teaching some swine
To sneer at a char with a washing-line

but he had a nose for what had gone wrong.) It was a far cry from 'The Belle of the Ballroom', and further yet from the metropolitan severities of the seventeenth- and eighteenth-century wits. Here was the paranoid dreamscape of the uneasy middle-class, in which the urbanity of Dryden had disappeared into the suburbanity of the golf-club wag.

It was the end, in short, of a kind of verse conceived in the early nineteenth century as a separate strain, given the name 'light' or 'humorous' or 'comic', and intensively cultivated. Over the hundred or so years of its ascendancy there is a nervous intensity

about the best of it which suggests the practitioners were vibrating
to a frequency rather higher than might have been required if they
had simply been serving a market: Belloc, for instance, and his
curious mandarin demotic, never heard on land or sea before he
made the verses which implied this was the way everyone spoke,
or would like to be thought to speak; and then there was Praed,
giving you the sensation of actually entering those girl-haunted
drawing-rooms; W. S. Gilbert, who extruded rhyme like a
medium constructing an alternative universe; and the smiling
arctic malice of Harry Graham, kept up page after page but always
seeming more of an obsession than a mere formula (a couple of
pieces by A. E. Housman run him close, Housman who would
sometimes take a moment or two off from his own obsessions and
compose light verse that was quite as assured as the poetry that
kept his parodists in business). Special qualities abound, with
here and there towards the end of the period an undertow of the
surreal – I think of R. P. Lister's 'Plumber-Song at Evening',
Patrick Barrington's 'I Was a Bustle-Maker Once, Girls' (touch of
high camp, as well:

> — I put my heart in the bustle-maker's art,
>   And I don't mind saying so.
> I may have had the brain of a dunce, girls;
>   I may have had the mind of a muff;
> I may have been plain and deficient in the brain,
>   But I did know a bustle-maker's stuff.)

– and, above all, J. B. Morton, who actually delivers the laugh:

> Ibsen had a badger
>   He called it Little Nell . . .
> Springtime over Stinkerhjem
>   And April all a-smell.

But all that's done with now. Light verse as a distinct category
isn't produced any more, the patent ran out because the climate
altered, and now light verse is back where it was before Hood,
Praed and Co. so skilfully packaged it, returned to its original
condition as one aspect, one possibility, one mood of the whole,
and thus no longer available to special order.

Betjeman best illustrates the change, his poetry condensing
both the melancholy and the humorous out of a single undivided

4

impulse. But when you've added Auden (succeeding famously in 'Letter to Lord Byron' and 'On the Circuit', but scarcely in the so-called 'Shorts', where he is roguish and condescending), Eliot cutting his solemn capers, the dry perspicuity of William Plomer, and when you've admitted the handful of sparks thrown off from the fiercer flame by contemporaries such as Larkin, Ewart and half a dozen others, Betjeman still remains the only one to have used the powerful single instrument *purposefully* to divert and amuse. Those who might be able to do it don't seem to want to do it, aren't prepared to socialize as once the founding fathers did, and any of them getting down to their version of 'The Essay on Man' are unlikely to follow it with 'The Rape of the Lock'.

Which brings me to the longer poems. I could only have included all those I would have liked to include by leaving out so many of the shorter ones that variety (which is probably the best reason for having anthologies at all) would have been seriously impaired. So you have to look elsewhere for 'The Rape of the Lock' and 'The Hunting of the Snark', though not for 'Verses on the Death of Dr Swift' or 'The Miller's Tale' (the latter in Nevill Coghill's translation, since you need more than a glossary to get as much fun out of the original). I was reluctant to make the choice, but the same unrefined impulse was at work in the selection of the longer pieces as in the choice of all the others – it is whim rather than principle which distinguishes one anthology from the next. But I should say a word about deliberate exclusions: ballads, for instance.

The dark, the sonorous, the romantic, brought into the drawing-room in the eighteenth-century, titillate our sense of a magical mythical past, but the lighter sort, telling stories with the endless repetitions required by an oral tradition, seem unbearably dilute. Perhaps they were better when sung, a proposition certainly true of the modern lyrics which I've also omitted: the words of Noel Coward and Cole Porter should never be deprived of the music without which they would have had to have been a great deal better. There are one or two limericks, but any single limerick you read has the peculiar quality of making you remember a better one, and anyway the best limericks are the rude ones and rude verse is something else I've left out on the grounds that even when it doesn't immediately seem to be it is far too angry for the canon – the dark words aren't light enough. There are no verses by Edward Lear: that first line so fatally repeated in the last is an invitation to tread continuously on a step that isn't there, and in his longer nonsense poems you know his heart is in the right place but (to quote the late John Whiting) it's the tiny pointed little head that worries you.

Further to nonsense verse, I've slipped in a couple of sonnets that came out of the computer – 'How Can the Purple Yeti be So Red' and 'Oh Salamander Tell Me Why the Moon'. They carry a rather more ominous charge than most light verse, but they have an eldritch charm, and whereas in ordinary nonsense rhyming the product is still gripped by ineradicable compulsions to make sense, the computer conjures out of the minds which primed it a pure surreality. I can be pretty sure that these two pieces – both kindly supplied by Dr J. R. Partington of Fitzwilliam College, Cambridge, who tells me I can have another two million, for the trouble of giving his micro-chip kaleidoscope a further shake – will be unfamiliar to the reader of this book, and since the unfamiliar is a piquant ingredient in this sort of mixture I found myself hoping, as I burrowed through to the original sources via the anthologies, that what was unfamiliar to me would be equally so to others. I was greatly helped by correspondents who pointed me in directions I might not otherwise have taken, and among others I should like to thank Margaret Askew, Graham Collier, Jean Foster, Ian Gillies, Lin Hardiman, E. M. Hugh-Jones, Kate Love, Jack Robinson, Violet Rutter and Hugh Williams. I am grateful to Jonathan Barker, Librarian of the Arts Council Poetry Library, for the lines of enquiry he suggested, and in particular for his gift of T. S. Eliot's 'Billy M'Caw: the Remarkable Parrot', verses not (to my knowledge) reprinted since they made their original appearance in *The Queen's Book of the Red Cross* (Hodder, 1939), a source the unadventurous might have overlooked. But it is to the kindness of Mrs Eliot that I owe 'There's No One Left to Press My Pants', a poem by T. S. Eliot never before published, which the poet copied out for his wife in her private notebook. Above the autograph version, Eliot notes: 'Composed about 1910. Still awaiting a musical composer.'

I'm rather against a chronological arrangement of authors in a book like this, since the geological strata so formed do seem to loom up through the actual verse, and when you get the poets coming in layers a century thick there's an exhumatory effect that gives your anthology a touch of the archaeological dig. And let's face it (since nobody's all that open-minded) doesn't the chronological system rather unsportingly give the reader too much of a chance not to come across what he thinks he doesn't like? If his memory of the eighteenth-century satirists invokes (as it easily might) a cramped page, pedestrian with footnotes winding across the graves of topical gags long dead, your stacking them all together in one neat little pile looks like a positive invitation to skip; and if his recollection of nineteenth-century light verse is associated with a feeling – something to do with the mean-spirited typefaces of early cheap editions – that it was sold by the yard, then if you parcel it up it may be ignored:

> As I was laying on the green,
> A small English book I seen.
> Carlyle's *Essay on Burns* was the edition,
> So I left it laying in the same position.

This principle also applies to the other sort of packaging, where the stuff is laid out under categories – parodies, satire, nonsense and so on. That sort of arrangement can seem a bit officious, especially when the categories are given facetious names as though the anthologist felt the verse could do with a bit of a leg-up. So I've adopted the simple expedient of arranging the poems themselves in alphabetical order by first lines. This way each author keeps reappearing, instead of being swallowed whole just once, and the material itself can't form lumps.

The research for this collection was divided equally between myself and Josephine Robinson. I made the choice but, venturing into territory I might have skirted, she ensured an ampler range.

Positive opacities encountered on any given page may be found to have been dealt with in the Notes at the back of the book.

ROBERT ROBINSON

A Classic Waits for Me

(With apologies to Walt Whitman, plus a trial membership in the Classics Club)

A classic waits for me, it contains all, nothing is lacking,
Yet all were lacking if taste were lacking, or if the endorsement of
      the right man were lacking.
O clublife, and the pleasures of membership,
O volumes for sheer fascination unrivalled.
Into an armchair endlessly rocking,
Walter J. Black my president,
I, freely invited, cordially welcomed to membership,
My arm around John Kieran, Hendrik Willem van Loon, Pearl S.
      Buck,
My taste in books guarded by the spirit of William Lyon Phelps
(From your memories, sad brothers, from the fitful risings and
      callings I heard),
I to the classics devoted, brother of rough mechanics,
      beauty-parlor technicians, spot welders, radio-program
      directors
(It is not necessary to have a higher education to appreciate these
      books),
I, connoisseur of good reading, friend of connoisseurs of good
      reading everywhere,
I, not obligated to take any specific number of books,
      free to reject any volume, perfectly free to reject
      Montaigne, Erasmus, Milton,
I, in perfect health except for a slight cold, pressed for
      time, having only a few more years to live,
Now celebrate this opportunity.
Come, I will make the club indissoluble,
I will read the most splendid books the sun ever shone upon,
I will start divine magnetic groups,
  With the love of comrades,
    With the life-long love of distinguished committees.
I strike up for an Old Book.
Long the best-read figure in America, my dues paid, sitter in
      armchairs everywhere, wanderer in populous cities,
      weeping with Hecuba and with the late Willian Lyon
      Phelps,
Free to cancel my membership whenever I wish.

Turbulent, fleshy, sensible,
Never tiring of clublife,
Always ready to read another masterpiece provided it has the
        approval of my president, Walter J. Black,
Me imperturbe, standing at ease among writers,
Raised by a perfect mother and now belonging to a perfect book
        club,
Bearded, sunburnt, gray-neck'd, astigmatic,
Loving the masters and the masters only
(I am mad for them to be in contact with me),
My arm around Pearl S. Buck, only American woman to receive
        the Nobel Prize for Literature,
I celebrate this opportunity.
And I will not read a book nor the least part of a book but has the
        approval of the Committee,
For all is useless without that which you may guess at many times
        and not hit, that which they hinted at,
All is useless without readability.
By God! I will accept nothing which all cannot have their
        counterpart of on the same terms (89¢ for the Regular
        Edition or $1.39 for the De Luxe Edition, plus a few cents
        postage).
I will make inseparable readers with their arms around each
        other's necks,
  By the love of classics,
    By the manly love of classics.

E. B. WHITE

The Bison

A Cockney lady, on a summer cruise
(Miss Hicks, of 47 (c), The Mews)
Had the misfortune to encounter Biscay
When the tormentor's mood was rather frisky.
'Steward,' she cried, 'Oh, Steward! Quick!
  Quick! Quick!
I'm almost sure I'm going to be sick!

Bring me a bison.' He has heard her cries,
And—what is this? Imagine her surprise.
No wonder all the other people stare.
The steward has led a bison to her chair,
And tied it up, and, plain for all to see,
It rubs its massive nose against her knee.
Surprise and shock have quickly done the trick,
And she's forgotten she was feeling sick.
(On every liner that is well-equipped
At least one full-grown bison will be shipped.)

And now the bison's living in her flat,
And sleeps with Rover, on the larder mat.

J. B. MORTON

Miss Robinson's Funeral

A cold afternoon, and death looks prouder
As mourning motors mourning motors follow,
One solemn as another. Lilies shiver,
Carnations also shiver, while the hollow
Seagulls search for offal in the river
And a woman burrows in her bag for powder.

The undertakers don't observe the scenery
And nothing moves them but the wheels they glide on,
The undertakers undertake to bury
(How black the motor cars they ride on),
They are not volatile or sad or merry,
Neither are waxworks going by machinery.

The coffin's full, and the time is after four;
The grave is empty, earth joins earth once more—
But the ghost of the late Miss Robinson is floating
Backside upwards in the air with a smile across her jaw:
She was tickled to death, and is carefully noting
Phenomena she never thought of noticing before.

WILLIAM PLOMER

The Crocodile

A Crocodile once dropped a line
To a Fox to invite him to dine;
    But the Fox wrote to say
    He was dining, that day,
With a Bird friend, and begged to decline.

She sent off at once to a Goat.
'Pray don't disappoint me,' she wrote;
    But he answered too late,
    He'd forgotten the date,
Having thoughtlessly eaten her note.

The Crocodile thought him ill-bred,
And invited two Rabbits instead;
    But the Rabbits replied,
    They were hopelessly tied
By a previous engagement, and fled.

Then she wrote in despair to some Eels,
And begged them to 'drop in' to meals;
    But the Eels left their cards
    With their coldest regards,
And took to what went for their heels.

Cried the Crocodile then, in disgust,
'My motives they seem to mistrust.
    Their suspicions are base,
    Since they don't know their place,—
I suppose if I *must* starve, I *must!*'

OLIVER HERFORD

Dr J. Collis Browne

A crowd there was in Ramsgate town
To honour Dr Collis Browne,
Whose Chlorodyne's saved countless chaps
From having untoward mishaps.
And many other skilled invention
He made, too numerous to mention.
So Collis Browne deserves his plaque
Which Mayor, Mayoress and Town Clerk
With friends and kinsmen by the score
(Although he died in 'eighty-four)
Unveiled, and thus gave him his meed
Which he (or she) who runs may read.

ANON

New-made Honour
(Imitated from Martial)

A friend I met, some half hour since—
    'Good-morrow, Jack!' quoth I;
The new-made knight, like any prince,
    Frowned, nodded, and passed by;
When up came Jem—'Sir John, your slave!'
    'Ah, James! we dine at eight—
Fail not—(low bows the supple knave)
    Don't make my lady wait.'
The king can do no wrong? As I'm a sinner,
He's spoilt an honest tradesman—and my dinner.

R. H. BARHAM

On a Distant Prospect of an Absconding Bookmaker

Alas! what boots it that my noble steed,
Chosen so carefully, the field outran?
I did not reckon, bookie, on *your* speed:
The proper study of mankind is man.

GEORGE ROSTREVOR HAMILTON

'Alfred de Musset'

Alfred de Musset
Used to call his cat 'pusset'
(His accent was affected—
That was to be expected.)

MAURICE HARE

The Place of the Damned

All folks who pretend to religion and grace,
Allow there's a hell, but dispute of the place;
But if hell may by logical rules be defined,
The place of the damned—I will tell you my mind.

Wherever the damned do chiefly abound,
Most certainly there is hell to be found;
Damned poets, damned critics, damned blockheads, damned
    knaves,
Damned senators bribed, damned prostitute slaves;
Damned lawyers and judges, damned lords and damned squires,
Damned spies and informers, damned friends and damned liars;
Damned villains, corrupted in every station,
Damned time-serving priests all over the nation.

And into the bargain I'll readily give you,
Damned ignorant prelates, and councillors privy.
Then let us no longer by parsons be flammed,
For we know by these marks, the place of the damned;
And hell to be sure is at Paris or Rome,
How happy for us, that it is not at home!

JONATHAN SWIFT

Mac Flecknoe

or
A satire upon the true-blue Protestant poet,
Thomas Shadwell

All human things are subject to decay,
And when fate summons, monarchs must obey:
This Flecknoe found, who, like Augustus, young
Was called to empire and had governed long:
In prose and verse was owned, without dispute
Through all the realms of nonsense, absolute.
This aged prince now flourishing in peace,
And blessed with issue of a large increase,
Worn out with business, did at length debate
To settle the succession of the state;
And pondering which of all his sons was fit
To reign, and wage immortal war with wit,
Cried, 'tis resolved; for nature pleads that he
Should only rule, who most resembles me:
Shadwell alone my perfect image bears,
Mature in dullness from his tender years;
Shadwell alone of all my sons is he
Who stands confirmed in full stupidity.
The rest to some faint meaning make pretence,
But Shadwell never deviates into sense.
Some beams of wit on other souls may fall,
Strike through and make a lucid interval;
But Shadwell's genuine night admits no ray,
His rising fogs prevail upon the day:

Besides, his goodly fabric fills the eye
And seems designed for thoughtless majesty:
Thoughtless as monarch oaks that shade the plain,
And, spread in solemn state, supinely reign.
Heywood and Shirley were but types of thee,
Thou last great prophet of tautology:
Even I, a dunce of more renown than they,
Was sent before but to prepare thy way:
And coarsely clad in Norwich drugget came
To teach the nations in thy greater name.
My warbling lute, the lute I whilom strung,
When to King John of Portugal I sung,
Was but the prelude to that glorious day,
When thou on silver Thames did'st cut thy way,
With well timed oars before the royal barge,
Swelled with the pride of thy celestial charge;
And, big with hymn, commander of an host,
The like was ne'er in Epsom blankets tossed.
Methinks I see the new Arion sail,
The lute still trembling underneath thy nail.
At thy well sharpened thumb from shore to shore
The treble squeaks for fear, the basses roar:
Echoes from Pissing-Alley, Shadwell call,
And Shadwell they resound from Aston Hall.
About thy boat the little fishes throng,
As at the morning toast that floats along.
Sometimes, as prince of thy harmonious band,
Thou wield'st thy papers in thy threshing hand.
St André's feet ne'er kept more equal time,
Not even the feet of thy own Psyche's rhyme:
Though they in number as in sense excel,
So just, so like tautology they fell
That, pale with envy, Singleton forswore
The lute and sword which he in triumph bore,
And vowed he ne'er would act Villerius more.
Here stopped the good old sire; and wept for joy,
In silent raptures of the hopeful boy.
All arguments, but most his plays, persuade
That for anointed dullness he was made.
    Close to the walls which fair Augusta bind,
(The fair Augusta much to fears inclined)
An ancient fabric raised to inform the sight,

There stood of yore, and Barbican it hight:
A watch tower once, but now, so fate ordains,
Of all the pile an empty name remains.
From its old ruins brothel-houses rise,
Scenes of lewd loves, and of polluted joys,
Where their vast courts the mother-strumpets keep,
And, undisturbed by watch, in silence sleep.
Near these a Nursery erects its head,
Where queens are formed, and future heroes bred;
Where unfledged actors learn to laugh and cry,
Where infant punks their tender voices try,
And little Maximins the gods defy.
Great Fletcher never treads in buskins here,
Nor greater Johnson dares in socks appear.
But gentle Simkin just reception finds
Amidst this monument of vanished minds;
Pure clinches, the suburbian muse affords;
And Panton waging harmless war with words.
Here Flecknoe, as a place to fame well known,
Ambitiously designed his Shadwell's throne.
For ancient Decker prophesied long since,
That in this pile should reign a mighty prince,
Born for a scourge of wit, and flail of sense,
To whom true dullness should some Psyches owe,
But worlds of misers from his pen should flow;
Humorists and hypocrites it should produce,
Whole Raymond families and tribes of Bruce.
    Now empress fame had published the renown
Of Shadwell's coronation through the town.
Roused by report of fame, the nations meet,
From near Bun-Hill and distant Watling-street.
No Persian carpets spread the imperial way,
But scattered limbs of mangled poets lay;
From dusty shops neglected authors come,
Martyrs of pies and reliques of the bum.
Much Heywood, Shirley, Ogleby there lay,
But loads of Shadwell almost choked the way.
Bilk't stationers for yeomen stood prepared,
And Herringman was captain of the guard.
The hoary prince in majesty appeared,
High on a throne of his own labours reared.
At his right hand our young Ascanius sat,

Rome's other hope and pillar of the state.
His brows thick fogs, instead of glories, grace,
And lambent dullness played around his face,
As Hannibal did to the altars come,
Swore by his sire a mortal foe to Rome;
So Shadwell swore, nor would his vow be vain,
That he till death true dullness should maintain;
And, in his father's right, and realms defence,
Ne'er to have peace with wit, nor truce with sense.
The king himself the sacred unction made,
As king by office, and as priest by trade:
In his sinister hand, instead of ball,
He placed a mighty mug of potent ale;
Love's Kingdom to his right he did convey,
At once his sceptre and his rule of sway;
Whose righteous lore the prince had practised young,
And from whose loins recorded Psyche sprung.
His temples, last, with poppies were o'erspread,
That nodding seemed to consecrate his head:
Just at that point of time, if fame not lie,
On his left hand twelve reverend owls did fly.
So Romulus, 'tis sung, by Tyber's Brook,
Presage of sway from twice six vultures took.
Th' admiring throng loud acclamations make
And omens of his future empire take.
The sire then shook the honours of his head,
And from his brows damps of oblivion shed
Full on the filial dullness: long he stood,
Repelling from his breast the raging God;
At length burst out in this prophetic mood:
    Heavens bless my son, from Ireland let him reign
To far Barbados on the western main;
Of his dominion may no end be known,
And greater than his father's be his throne.
Beyond Love's Kingdom let him stretech his pen;
He paused, and all the people cried amen.
Then thus continued he, my son, advance
Still in new impudence, new ignorance.
Success let others teach, learn thou from me
Pangs without birth, and fruitless industry.
Let Virtuoso's in five years be writ;
Yet not one thought accuse thy toil of wit.

18

Let gentle George in triumph tread the stage,
Make Dorimant betray, and Loveit rage;
Let Cully, Cockwood, Fopling, charm the pit,
And in their folly show the writers wit.
Yet still thy fools shall stand in thy defence
And justify their author's want of sense.
Let 'em be all by thy own model made
Of dullness and desire no foreign aid,
That they to future ages may be known,
Not copies drawn, but issue of thy own.
Nay let thy men of wit too be the same,
All full of thee, and differing but in name;
But let no alien Sedley interpose
To lard with wit thy hungry Epsom prose.
And when false flowers of rhetoric thou would'st cull,
Trust nature, do not labour to be dull;
But write thy best, and top; and in each line
Sir Formal's oratory will be thine.
Sir Formal, though unsought, attends thy quill,
And does thy northern dedications fill.
Nor let false friends seduce thy mind to fame,
By arrogating Johnson's hostile name.
Let father Flecknoe fire thy mind with praise
And uncle Ogleby thy envy raise.
Thou art my blood, where Johnson has no part:
What share have we in nature or in art?
Where did his wit on learning fix a brand
And rail at arts he did not understand?
Where made he love in prince Nicander's vein,
Or swept the dust in Psyche's humble strain?
Where sold he bargains, whip-stitch, kiss my arse,
Promised a play and dwindled to a farce?
When did his muse from Fletcher scenes purloin,
As though whole Etherege dost transfuse to thine?
But so transfused as oils on waters flow,
His always floats above, thine sinks below.
This is thy province, this thy wondrous way,
New humours to invent for each new play:
This is that boasted bias of thy mind,
By which one way, to dullness, 'tis inclined,
Which makes thy writings lean on one side still,
And, in all changes, that way bends thy will.

Nor let thy mountain belly make pretence
Of likeness; thine's a tympany of sense.
A tun of man in thy large bulk is writ,
But sure thou'rt but a kilderkin of wit.
Like mine thy gentle numbers feebly creep;
Thy tragic muse gives smiles, thy comic sleep.
With what'er gall thou settst thy self to write,
Thy inoffensive satires never bite.
In thy felonious heart though venom lies,
It does but touch thy Irish pen, and dies.
Thy genius calls thee not to purchase fame
In keen iambics, but mild anagram:
Leave writing plays, and choose for thy command
Some peaceful province in acrostic land.
There thou may'st wings display, and altars raise,
And torture one poor word ten thousand ways;
Or, if thou would'st thy different talents suit,
Set thy own songs, and sing them to thy lute.
He said, but his last words were scarcely heard,
For Bruce and Longvil had a trap prepared,
And down they sent the yet declaiming bard.
Sinking he left his drugget robe behind,
Borne upwards by a subterranean wind.
The mantle fell to the young prophet's part
With double portion of his father's art.

JOHN DRYDEN

The Little Dog's Day

All in the town were still asleep,
When the sun came up with a shout and a leap.
In the lonely streets unseen by man,
A little dog danced. And the day began.

All his life he'd been good, as far as he could,
And the poor little beast had done all that he should.
But this morning he swore, by Odin and Thor
And the Canine Valhalla—he'd stand it no more!

So his prayer he got granted—to do just what he wanted,
Prevented by none, for the space of one day.
'*Jam incipiebo*,* *sedere facebo*',†
In dog-Latin he quoth, '*Euge! sophos! hurray!*'

He fought with the he-dogs, and winked at the she-dogs,
A thing that had never been *heared* of before.
'For the stigma of gluttony, I care not a button!' he
Cried, and ate all he could swallow—and more.

He took sinewy lumps from the shins of old frumps,
And mangled the errand-boys—when he could get 'em,
He shammed furious *rabies*, and bit all the babies,
And followed the cats up the trees, and then ate 'em!

They thought 'twas the devil was holding a revel,
And sent for the parson to drive him away;
For the town never knew such a hullabaloo
As that little dog raised—till the end of that day.

When the blood-red sun had gone burning down,
And the lights were lit in the little town,
Outside, in the gloom of the twilight grey,
The little dog died when he'd had his day.

RUPERT BROOKE

* *Now we're off.*
† *I'll make them sit up.*

The Playboy of the Demi-World: 1938

Aloft in Heavenly Mansions, Doubleyou One—
Just Mayfair flats, but certainly sublime—
You'll find the abode of D'Arcy Honeybunn,
A rose-red sissy half as old as time.

Peace cannot age him, and no war could kill
The genial tenant of those cosy rooms,
He's lived there always and he lives there still,
Perennial pansy, hardiest of blooms.

There you'll encounter aunts of either sex,
Their jokes equivocal or over-ripe,
Ambiguous couples wearing slacks and specs
And the stout Lesbian knocking out her pipe.

The rooms are crammed with flowers and objets d'art,
A Ganymede still hands the drinks—and plenty!
D'Arcy still keeps a rakish-looking car
And still behaves the way he did at twenty.

A ruby pin is fastened in his tie,
The scent he uses is *Adieu Sagesse*,
His shoes are suède, and as the years go by
His tailor's bill's not getting any less.

He cannot whistle, always rises late,
Is good at indoor sports and parlour tricks,
Mauve is his favourite colour, and his gait
Suggests a peahen walking on hot bricks.

He prances forward with his hands outspread
And folds all comers in a gay embrace,
A wavy toupee on his hairless head,
A fixed smile on his often-lifted face.

'My dear!' he lisps, to whom all men are dear,
'How perfectly enchanting of you!'; turns
Towards his guests and twitters, 'Look who's here!
Do come and help us fiddle while Rome burns!'

'The kindest man alive,' so people say,
'Perpetual youth!' But have you seen his eyes?
The eyes of some old saurian in decay,
That asks no questions and is told no lies.

Under the fribble lurks a worn-out sage
Heavy with disillusion, and alone;
So never say to D'Arcy, 'Be your age!'—
He'd shrivel up at once or turn to stone.

WILLIAM PLOMER

Amelia Mixed the Mustard

Amelia mixed the mustard,
  She mixed it good and thick;
She put it in the custard
  And made her Mother sick,
And showing satisfaction
  By many a loud huzza,
'Observe,' she said, 'the action
  Of mustard on Mamma.'

A. E. HOUSMAN

On the Circuit

Among pelagian travelers,
Lost on their lewd conceited way
To Massachusetts, Michigan,
Miami or L.A.,

An airborne instrument I sit,
Predestined nightly to fulfill
Columbia-Giesen-Management's
Unfathomable will,

By whose election justified,
I bring my gospel of the Muse
To fundamentalists, to nuns,
To Gentiles and to Jews,

And daily, seven days a week,
Before a local sense has jelled,
From talking-site to talking-site
Am jet-or-prop-propelled.

Though warm my welcome everywhere,
I shift so frequently, so fast,
I cannot now say where I was
The evening before last,

Unless some singular event
Should intervene to save the place,
A truly asinine remark,
A soul-bewitching face,

Or blessed encounter, full of joy,
Unscheduled on the Giesen Plan,
With, here, an addict of Tolkien,
There, a Charles Williams fan.

Since Merit but a dunghill is,
I mount the rostrum unafraid:
Indeed, 'twere damnable to ask
If I am overpaid.

Spirit is willing to repeat
Without a qualm the same old talk,
But Flesh is homesick for our snug
Apartment in New York.

A sulky fifty-six, he finds
A change of mealtime utter hell,
Grown far too crotchety to like
A luxury hotel.

The Bible is a goodly book
I always can peruse with zest,
But really cannot say the same
For Hilton's *Be My Guest*,

Nor bear with equanimity
The radio in students' cars,
Muzak at breakfast, or—dear God!—
Girl-organists in bars.

Then, worst of all, the anxious thought,
Each time my plane begins to sink
And the No Smoking sign comes on:
What will there be to drink?

Is this a milieu where I must
How grahamgreeneish! How infra dig!
Snatch from the bottle in my bag
An analeptic swig?

Another morning comes: I see,
Dwindling below me on the plane,
The roofs of one more audience
I shall not see again.

God bless the lot of them, although
I don't remember which was which:
God bless the USA, so large,
So friendly, and so rich.

W. H. AUDEN

Lullaby for a British Prig

A mother sat in the gloaming,
   With her baby at her knee,
And the little child, in accents mild,
   Cried 'Mummy, sing to me.'
Whereat that British matron
   Rose to her fullest height
And a lullaby stole like a sigh,
   Across the tranquil night.

Refrain

Sleep a while, my darling,
   And you shall be bowling lobs
To good Archbishop Jardine,
   Or even to Canon Hobbs.
Angels will bring you wickets
   And sing to you as they bat,
And you shall have tea with the MCC,
   In a little fairy hat.

J. B. MORTON

25

Rhyme on the Road

And is there then no earthly place
  Where we can rest in dream Elysian,
Without some cursed, round English face,
  Popping up near, to break the vision?

Mid northern lakes, mid southern vines,
  Unholy cits we're doomed to meet;
Nor highest Alps nor Apennines
  Are sacred from Threadneedle Street!

If up the Simplon's path we wind,
Fancying we leave this world behind,
Such pleasant sounds salute one's ear
As—'Baddish news from 'Change, my dear—

'The funds—(phew, curse this ugly hill!)
Are lowering fast—(what! higher still?)
And—(zooks, we're mounting up to heaven!)—
Will soon be down to sixty-seven.'

  Go where we may, rest where we will,
  Eternal London haunts us still.
  The trash of Almack's or Fleet-Ditch—
  And scarce a pin's head difference *which*—
  Mixes, though even to Greece we run,
  With every rill from Helicon!
  And, if this rage for travelling lasts,
  If cockneys, of all sects and castes,
  Old maidens, aldermen, and squires,
  Will leave their puddings and coal fires,
  To gape at things in foreign lands
  No soul among them understands—
  If Blues desert their coteries,
  To show off 'mong the Wahabees—
  If neither sex nor age controls,
    Nor fear of Mamelukes forbids
  Young ladies, with pink parasols,
    To glide among the pyramids—
  Why, then, farewell all hope to find
  A spot that's free from London-kind!

Who knows, if to the West we roam,
But we may find some *Blue* 'at home'
  Among the *Blacks* of Carolina—
Or, flying to the eastward, see
Some Mrs Hopkins, taking tea
  And toast upon the Wall of China!

THOMAS MOORE

Epigram

A petty sneaking knave I knew—
O Mr Cromek, how do ye do?

WILLIAM BLAKE

The Python

A Python I should not advise—
It needs a doctor for its eyes
And has the measles yearly.
However, if you feel inclined
To get one (to improve your mind,
And not from fashion merely),
Allow no music near its cage;
And when it flies into a rage
Chastise it, most severely.

I had an aunt in Yucatan
Who bought a Python from a man
  And kept it for a pet.
She died, because she never knew
Those simple little rules and few—
  The Snake is living yet.

HILAIRE BELLOC

27

A Clerical Error

Archbishop (then Mr) Lang
Once let slip 'swing' for 'hang'.
He still got preferment,
But it was a bad merment.

L. E. JONES

Antichrist, or the Reunion of Christendom: an Ode

'A Bill which has shocked the conscience of every Christian
community in Europe'—*Mr F. E. Smith
on the Welsh Disestablishment Bill*

Are they clinging to their crosses,
    F. E. Smith,
Where the Breton boat-fleet tosses,
    Are they Smith?
Do they, fasting, trembling, bleeding,
    Wait the news from this our city?
Groaning 'That's the Second Reading!'
    Hissing 'There is still Committee!'
If the voice of Cecil falters,
    If McKenna's point has pith,
Do they tremble for their altars?
    Do they, Smith?

Russian peasants round their pope
    Huddled, Smith,
Hear about it all, I hope,
    Don't they, Smith?
In the mountain hamlets clothing
    Peaks beyond Caucasian pales,
Where Establishment means nothing
    And they never heard of Wales,
Do they read it all in Hansard
    With a crib to read it with—
'Welsh Tithes: Dr Clifford Answered.'
    Really, Smith?

28

In the lands where Christians were,
   F. E. Smith,
In the little lands laid bare,
    Smith, O Smith!
Where the Turkish bands are busy,
   And the Tory name is blessed
Since they hailed the Cross of Dizzy
   On the banners from the West!
Men don't think it half so hard if
   Islam burns their kin and kith,
Since a curate lives in Cardiff
    Saved by Smith.

It would greatly, I must own,
    Soothe me, Smith!
If you left this theme alone,
    Holy Smith!
For your legal cause or civil
   You fight well and get your fee;
For your God or dream or devil
   You will answer, not to me.
Talk about the pews and steeples
   And the Cash that goes therewith!
But the souls of Christian peoples . . .
    Chuck it, Smith!

       G. K. CHESTERTON

Old Surrey Saws and Sayings

A red sky at night
Is a shepherd's delight,
A red sky at morning
Is a shepherd's warning,
A sky that looks bad
Is a shepherd's plaid,
A good-looking sky
Is a shepherd's pie.

       MAX BEERBOHM

The Yak

As a friend to the children commend me the Yak.
  You will find it exactly the thing:
It will carry and fetch, you can ride on its back,
  Or lead it about with a string.

The Tartar who dwells on the plains of Thibet
  (A desolate region of snow)
Has for centuries made it a nursery pet,
  And surely the Tartar should know!

Then tell your papa where the Yak can be got,
  And if he is awfully rich
He will buy you the creature—or else he will *not*.
  (I cannot be positive which.)

HILAIRE BELLOC

Mr Maxton

As a laddie, Mrr. Maxton
Was apprenticed tae a saxton,
He thot it wid be prime
To hae Socialism in oor time.

E. CLERIHEW BENTLEY

Lines Left at Mr Theodore Hook's House in June 1834

As Dick and I
Were a-sailing by
At Fulham bridge, I cocked my eye,
  And says I, 'Add-zooks!
There's Theodore Hook's,
Whose sayings and doings make such pretty books.

'I wonder,' says I,
Still keeping my eye
On the house, 'if he's in—I should like to try';
    With his oar on his knee,
    Says Dick, says he,
'Father, suppose you land and see!'

    'What land and *sea*,'
    Says I to he,
'Together! why Dick, why how can that be?'
    And my comical son,
    Who is fond of fun,
I thought would have split his sides at the pun.

    So we rows to shore,
    And knocks at the door—
When William, a man I've seen often before,
    Makes answer and says,
    'Master's gone in a chaise
Called a *homnibus*, drawn by a couple of bays.'

    So I says then,
    'Just lend me a pen':
'I will, sir,' says William, politest of men;
    So having no card, these poetical brayings,
    Are the record I leave of my doings and sayings.

                                    R. H. BARHAM

The Death of the Referee

A shroud, a shroud for Spring-Heeled Jack,
The only honest referee,
A crowd to keep the devil back
And sing in tune Abide with Me.

The pit unlocks its cage of doves
To tumble in the dirty air,
And far below the coffin drives
To meet the council and the mayor.

31

The barges drag through stiff canals,
Milky with clay and black with coal,
And as the varnished coffin falls
The mayor proclaims the grave no goal.

The colours of the local club
Flower to hide the yellow clay,
And all the foundry hammers throb
Their solace of the working day.

At home the silver trophies burn
About the mourning company,
And wishing she could be alone
The widow pours out cups of tea.

For Jack is dead, the man on springs,
Whose whistle trapped the wildest ball,
Whose portrait done in oils now hangs
For ever in the Civic Hall.

Burly with cataracts, the eyes,
Are blind at last to local fame
And friends who fail to recognize
A stranger in the golden frame.

But those who know their loss will make
The winter field his funeral,
And peel their caps to Spring-Heeled Jack
While brass bands play the March in Saul.

PHILIP OAKES

Spectator Ab Extra

I

As I sat at the café I said to myself,
They may talk as they please about what they call pelf,
They may sneer as they like about eating and drinking,
But help it I cannot, I cannot help thinking
    How pleasant it is to have money, heigh-ho!
    How pleasant it is to have money.

I sit at my table *en grand seigneur*,
And when I have done, throw a crust to the poor;
Not only the pleasure itself of good living,
But also the pleasure of now and then giving:
    So pleasant it is to have money, heigh-ho!
    So pleasant it is to have money.

They may talk as they please about what they call pelf,
And how one ought never to think of one's self,
How pleasures of thought surpass eating and drinking,—
My pleasure of thought is the pleasure of thinking
    How pleasant it is to have money, heigh-ho!
    How pleasant it is to have money.

II
LE DINER

Come along, 'tis the time, ten or more minutes past,
And he who came first had to wait for the last;
The oysters ere this had been in and been out;
Whilst I have been sitting and thinking about
    How pleasant it is to have money, heigh-ho!
    How pleasant it is to have money.

A clear soup with eggs; *voilà tout*; of the fish
The *filets de sole* are a moderate dish
A là Orly, but you're for red mullet, you say:
By the gods of good fare, who can question today
    How pleasant it is to have money, heigh-ho!
    How pleasant it is to have money.

After oysters, sauterne; then sherry; champagne,
Ere one bottle goes, comes another again;
Fly up, thou bold cork, to the ceiling above,
And tell to our ears in the sound that they love
    How pleasant it is to have money, heigh-ho!
    How pleasant it is to have money.

I've the simplest of palates; absurd it may be,
But I almost could dine on a *poulet-au-riz*,
Fish and soup and omelette and that—but the deuce—
There were to be woodcocks, and not *Charlotte Russe*!
    So pleasant it is to have money, heigh-ho!
    So pleasant it is to have money.

Your chablis is acid, away with the hock,
Give me the pure juice of the purple médoc:
St Peray is exquisite; but, if you please,
Some burgundy just before tasting the cheese.
 So pleasant it is to have money, heigh-ho!
 So pleasant it is to have money.

As for that, pass the bottle, and d——n the expense,
I've seen it observed by a writer of sense,
That the labouring classes could scarce live a day,
If people like us didn't eat, drink, and pay.
 So useful it is to have money, heigh-ho!
 So useful it is to have money.

One ought to be grateful, I quite apprehend,
Having dinner and supper and plenty to spend,
And so suppose now, while the things go away,
By way of a grace we all stand up and say
 How pleasant it is to have money, heigh-ho!
 How pleasant it is to have money.

III
PARVENANT

I cannot but ask, in the park and the streets
When I look at the number of persons one meets,
What e'er in the world the poor devils can do
Whose fathers and mothers can't give them a *sous*.
 So needful it is to have money, heigh-ho!
 So needful it is to have money.

I ride, and I drive, and I care not a d——n,
The people look up and they ask who I am;
And if I should chance to run over a cad,
I can pay for the damage, if ever so bad.
 So useful it is to have money, heigh-ho!
 So useful it is to have money.

It was but this winter I came up to town,
And already I'm gaining a sort of renown;
Find my way to good houses without much ado,
Am beginning to see the nobility too.
 So useful it is to have money, heigh-ho!
 So useful it is to have money.

O dear what a pity they ever should lose it,
Since they are the people that know how to use it;
So easy, so stately, such manners, such dinners,
And yet, after all, it is we are the winners.
    So needful it is to have money, heigh-ho!
    So needful it is to have money.

It's all very well to be handsome and tall,
Which certainly makes you look well at a ball;
It's all very well to be clever and witty,
But if you are poor, why it's only a pity.
    So needful it is to have money, heigh-ho!
    So needful it is to have money.

There's something undoubtedly in a fine air,
To know how to smile and be able to stare,
High breeding is something, but well-bred or not,
In the end the one question is, what have you got.
    So needful it is to have money, heigh-ho!
    So needful it is to have money.

And the angels in pink and the angels in blue,
In muslins and moirés so lovely and new,
What is it they want, and so wish you to guess,
But if you have money, the answer is yes.
    So needful, they tell you, is money, heigh-ho!
    So needful it is to have money.

ARTHUR HUGH CLOUGH

'As I was laying on the green'

As I was laying on the green,
A small English book I seen.
Carlyle's *Essays on Burns* was the edition,
So I left it laying in the same position.

ANON

Sight Unseen

As I was waiting for the bus
   A girl came up the street,
Detectable as double-plus
   At seven hundred feet.

Her head was high, her step was free,
   Her face a lyric blur;
Her waist was narrow, I could see,
   But not the rest of her.

At fifty feet I watched her stop,
   Bite at a glove, then veer
Aside into some pointless shop,
   Never to reappear.

This happens every bloody day:
   They about-turn, they duck
Into their car and drive away,
   They hide behind a truck.

Look, if they knew me, well and good,
   There might be cause to run;
Or even saw me—understood;
   No. Not a peep. Not one.

Love at first sight—by this we mean
   A stellar entrant thrown
Clear on the psyche's radar-screen,
   Recognized before known.

All right: things work the opposite
   Way with the poles reversed;
It's galling, though, when girls omit
   To switch the set on first.

KINGSLEY AMIS

As I was Walking Backwards

As I was walking backwards,
And never looked behind,
I trod upon a lady
Who'd gone out of her mind.
She did not show the least surprise,
She did not howl or hoot,
She only softly and silently
Began chewing my left boot.

In the greatest haste I took it off,
And she chewed it up to rags;
She swallowed all the elastics down,
And the hobnails and the tags.
And I'll never, never, put my foot
In a lady's mouth again,
Unless I'm perfectly certain
She has not gone insane.

A. E. HOUSMAN

There's No One Left to Press My Pants

As I was walking down the street
            upon a winter's day
I saw a man outside a bar,
            his aspect was *distrait*;
His ears were flapping in the breeze,
His pants were baggy at the knees,
He had a baby in his arms
            and thus I heard him sigh:
'If whiskey's 15¢ a drink
            how many can I buy?'

Then soon becoming bolder
I tapped him on the shoulder,
         and I said to him: 'Look here!
Tell me what's the matter, mister,
Has some wretch deceived your sister?
Or can't you find an opener for the beer?'
Then straightway he did turn around
         and I did hear him sigh.
He flipped the ash from his segar
         and to me did reply:

'O there's no one left to press my pants
         since Nellie's went away.
Don't let me hear that stupid joke:
         "Does matrimony pay?"
    Of my eye she was the apple
    When I led her to the chapel,
But the cost of living's risen since our wedding day.
    She took the silver-plated spoons,
         she took the whirling spray,
And all she left me was the kid
         and all the bills to pay.
O there's no one left to mix the drinks,
There's no one left to clean the sinks,
There's no one left to press my pants
         since Nellie's went away!'

                                   T. S. ELIOT

Printer's Error

    As o'er my latest book I pored,
       Enjoying it immensely
    I suddenly exclaimed 'Good Lord!'
       And gripped the volume tensely.
    'Golly!' I cried. I writhed in pain.
    'They've done it on me once again!'
       And furrows creased my brow.
    I'd written (which I thought quite good)
    'Ruth, ripening into womanhood,
    Was now a girl who knocked men flat

And frequently got whistled at,'
And some vile, careless, casual gook
Had spoiled the best thing in the book
   By printing 'not'
   (Yes, 'not', great Scott!)
      When I had written 'now'.

On murder in the first degree
   The Law, I knew, is rigid:
Its attitude, if A kills B,
   To A is always frigid.
It counts it not a trivial slip
If on behalf of authorship
You liquidate compositors.
This kind of conduct it abhors
   And seldom will allow.
Nevertheless, I deemed it best
And in the public interest
To buy a gun, to oil it well,
Inserting what is called a shell,
   And go and pot
     With sudden shot
      This printer who had printed 'not'
       When I had written 'now'.
I tracked the bounder to his den
   Through private information:
I said 'Good afternoon' and then
   Explained the situation:
'I'm not a fussy man,' I said.
'I smile when you put "rid" for "red"
And "bad" for "bed" and "hoad" for "head"
   And "bolge" instead of "bough".
When "wone" appears in lieu of "wine"
Or if you alter "Cohn" to "Schine",
   I never make a row.
I know how easy errors are.
But this time you have gone too far
By printing "not" when you knew what
   I really wrote was "now".
Prepare,' I said, 'to meet your God
Or, as you'd say, your Goo or Bod
   Or possibly your Gow.'

A few weeks later into court
  I came to stand my trial.
The Judge was quite a decent sort,
  He said 'Well, cocky, I'll
Be passing sentence in a jiff,
And so, my poor unhappy stiff,
If you have anything to say,
Now is the moment. Fire away.
    You have?'
      I said 'And how!
Me lud, the facts I don't dispute.
I did, I own it freely, shoot
This printer through the collar stud.
What else could I have done, me lud?
    He's printed "not" . . .'
    The Judge said '*What!*
      When you had written "now"?
God bless my soul! Gadzooks!' said he.
'The blighters did that once to me.
    A dirty trick, I trow.
I hereby quash and override
The jury's verdict. Gosh!' he cried.
'Give me your hand. Yes, I insist,
You splendid fellow! Case dismissed.'
    (Cheers, and a Voice 'Wow-wow!')

A statue stands against the sky,
  Lifelike and rather pretty.
'Twas recently erected by
  The P.E.N committee.
And many a passer-by is stirred,
For on the plinth, if that's the word,
In golden letters you may read
'This is the man who did the deed.
    His hand set to the plough,
He did not sheathe the sword, but got
A gun at great expense and shot
The human blot who'd printed "not"
    When he had written "now".
He acted with no thought of self,
Not for advancement, not for pelf,

But just because it made him hot
To think the man had printed "not"
    When he had written "now".'

P. G. WODEHOUSE

Verses on the Death of Dr Swift

As Rochefoucault his maxims drew
From nature, I believe 'em true:
They argue no corrupted mind
In him; the fault is in mankind.

This maxim more than all the rest
Is thought too base for human breast;
'In all distresses of our friends
We first consult our private ends,
While nature kindly bent to ease us,
Points out some circumstance to please us.'

If this perhaps your patience move
Let reason and experience prove.

We all behold with envious eyes,
Our equal raised above our size;
Who would not at a crowded show,
Stand high himself, keep others low?
I love my friend as well as you,
But would not have him stop my view;
Then let him have the higher post;
I ask but for an inch at most.

If in a battle you should find,
One, whom you love of all mankind,
Had some heroic action done,
A champion killed, or trophy won;
Rather than thus be over-topped,
Would you not wish his laurels cropped?

Dear honest Ned is in the gout,
Lies racked with pain, and you without:
How patiently you hear him groan!
How glad the case is not your own!

What poet would not grieve to see,
His brethren write as well as he?
But rather than they should excel,
He'd wish his rivals all in hell.

Her end when emulation misses,
She turns to envy, stings and hisses:
The strongest friendship yields to pride,
Unless the odds be on our side.

Vain human kind! Fantastic race!
Thy various follies, who can trace?
Self-love, ambition, envy, pride,
Their empire in our hearts divide:
Give others riches, power, and station,
'Tis all on me an usurpation.
I have no title to aspire;
Yet, when you sink, I seem the higher.
In Pope, I cannot read a line,
But with a sigh, I wish it mine:
When he can in one couplet fix
More sense than I can do in six:
It gives me such a jealous fit,
I cry, pox take him, and his wit.

Why must I be outdone by Gay,
In my own humorous biting way?

Arbuthnot is no more my friend,
Who dares to irony pretend;
Which I was born to introduce,
Refined it first, and shewed its use.

St John, as well as Pultney knows,
That I had some repute for prose;

And till they drove me out of date,
Could maul a minister of state:
If they have mortified my pride,
And made me throw my pen aside;
If with such talents heaven hath blest 'em
Have I not reason to detest 'em?

To all my foes, dear fortune, send
Thy gifts, but never to my friend:
I tamely can endure the first,
But, this with envy makes me burst.

Thus much may serve by way of proem,
Proceed we therefore to our poem.

The time is not remote, when I
Must by the course of nature die:
When I foresee my special friends,
Will try to find their private ends:
Tho' it is hardly understood,
Which way my death can do them good;
Yet, thus methinks, I hear 'em speak;
See, how the Dean begins to break:
Poor gentleman, he droops apace,
You plainly find it in his face:
That old vertigo in his head,
Will never leave him, till he's dead:
Besides, his memory decays,
He recollects not what he says;
He cannot call his friends to mind;
Forgets the place where last he dined:
Plies you with stories o'er and o'er,
He told them fifty times before.
How does he fancy we can sit,
To hear his out-of-fashioned wit?
But he takes up with younger folks,
Who for his wine will bear his jokes:
Faith, he must make his stories shorter,
Or change his comrades once a quarter:
In half the time, he talks them round;
There must another set be found.

For poetry, he's past his prime,
He takes an hour to find a rhyme:
His fire is out, his wit decayed,
His fancy sunk, his muse a jade.
I'd have him throw away his pen;
But there's no talking to some men.

And, then their tenderness appears,
By adding largely to my years:
'He's older than he would be reckoned,
And well remembers Charles the Second.

'He hardly drinks a pint of wine;
And that, I doubt, is no good sign.
His stomach too begins to fail:
Last year we thought him strong and hale;
But now, he's quite another thing;
I wish he may hold out till spring.'

Then hug themselves, and reason thus:
'It is not yet so bad with us.'

In such a case they talk in tropes,
And, by their fears express their hopes:
Some great misfortune to portend,
No enemy can match a friend;
With all the kindness they profess,
The merit of a lucky guess,
(When daily howd'y's come of course,
And servants answer: *worse and worse*)
Would please 'em better than to tell,
That, God be praised, the Dean is well.
Then he who prophesied the best,
Approves his foresight to the rest:
'You know, I always feared the worst,
And often told you so at first:'
He'd rather choose, that I should die,
Than his prediction prove a lie.
Not one foretells I shall recover;
But, all agree, to give me over.

Yet should some neighbour feel a pain,
Just in the parts, where I complain;
How many a message would he send?
What hearty prayers that I should mend?
Enquire what regimen I kept;
What gave me ease, and how I slept?
And more lament, when I was dead,
Than all the snivellers round my bed.

My good companions, never fear,
For though you may mistake a year;
Though your prognosticks run too fast,
They must be verified at last.

Behold the fatal day arrive!
'How is the Dean? He's just alive.
Now the departing prayer is read:
He hardly breathes. The Dean is dead.'
Before the passing-bell begun,
The news through half the town has run.
'O, may we all for death prepare!
What has he left? And who's his heir?
I know no more than what the news is,
'Tis all bequeathed to public uses.
To public use! A perfect whim!
What had the public done for him!
Mere envy, avarice, and pride!
He gave it all:—But first he died.
And had the Dean, in all the nation,
No worthy friend, no poor relation?
So ready to do strangers good,
Forgetting his own flesh and blood?'

Now grub-street wits are all employed;
With elegies, the town is cloyed:
Some paragraph in every paper,
To *curse* the *Dean*, or *bless* the *Drapier*.

The doctors tender of their fame,
Wisely on me lay all the blame:
'We must confess his case was nice;
But he would never take advice:
Had he been ruled, for ought appears,
He might have lived these twenty years:
For when we opened him we found,
That all his vital parts were sound.'

From Dublin soon to London spread,
'Tis told at Court, the Dean is dead.

Kind Lady Suffolk in the spleen,
Runs laughing up to tell the queen.
The queen, so gracious, mild, and good.
Cries, 'Is he gone? 'Tis time he should.
He's dead you say; why, let him rot;
I'm glad the medals were forgot.
I promised him, I own, but when?
I only was a princess then;
But now as consort of a king
You know 'tis quite a different thing.'

Now, Chartres at Sir Robert's levee,
Tells, with a sneer, the tidings heavy:
'Why, is he dead without his shoes?'
(Cries Bob) 'I'm sorry for the news;
Oh, were the wretch but living still,
And, in his place my good friend Will;
Or, had a mitre on his head
    Provided Bolingbroke were dead.'

Now, Curll his shop from rubbish drains;
Three genuine tomes of Swift's remains.
And then, to make them pass the glibber,
    Revised by Tibbalds, Moore, and Cibber.
He'll treat me as he does my betters.
    Publish my will, my life, my letters.
Revive the libels born to die;
Which Pope must bear, as well as I.

Here shift the scene, to represent
How those I love, my death lament.
Poor Pope will grieve a month; and Gay
A week; and Arbuthnot a day.

St John himself will scarce forbear,
To bite his pen, and drop a tear.
The rest will give a shrug, and cry,
I'm sorry; but we all must die.
Indifference clad in wisdom's guise,
All fortitude of mind supplies:
For how can stony bowels melt,
In those who never pity felt;
When *we* are lashed, *they* kiss the rod;
Resigning to the will of God.

The fools, my juniors by a year,
Are tortured with suspense and fear.
Who wisely thought my age a screen,
When death approached, to stand between:
The screen removed, their hearts are trembling,
They mourn for me without dissembling.

My female friends, whose tender hearts,
Have better learned to act their parts,
Receive the news in doleful dumps,
'The Dean is dead (and what is trumps?)
Then Lord have mercy on his soul.
(Ladies I'll venture for the vole.)
Six deans they say must bear the pall.
(I wish I knew what king to call.)
Madam, your husband will attend
The funeral of so good a friend.
No madam, 'tis a shocking sight,
And he's engaged tomorrow night!
My lady Club would take it ill,
If he should fail her at quadrill.
He loved the Dean. (I led a heart.)
But dearest friends, they say, must part.
His time was come, he ran his race;
We hope he's in a better place.'

Why do we grieve that friends should die?
No loss more easy to supply.
One year is past; a different scene;
No further mention of the Dean;
Who now, alas, no more is missed,
Than, if he never did exist.
Where's now this favourite of Apollo?
Departed; and his works must follow:
Must undergo the common fate;
His kind of wit is out of date.
Some country squire to Lintot goes,
Enquires for Swift in verse and prose:
Says Lintot, 'I have heard the name:
He died a year ago.' The same.
He searches all his shop in vain;
'Sir you may find them in Duck-lane:
I sent them with a load of books,
Last Monday, to the pastry-cooks.
To fancy they could live a year!
I find you're but a stranger here.
The Dean was famous in his time;
And had a kind of knack at rhyme:
His way of writing now is past;
The town hath got a better taste:
I keep no antiquated stuff;
But, spick and span I have enough.
Pray, do but give me leave to shew 'em,
Here's Colley Cibber's birthday poem.
This ode you never yet have seen,
By Stephen Duck, upon the queen.
Then, here's a letter finely penned
Against the Craftsman and his friend;
It clearly shews that all reflection
On ministers, is disaffection.
   Next, here's Sir Robert's vindication,
   And Mr Henly's last oration:
The hawkers have not got 'em yet,
Your honour please to buy a set?
Here's Woolston's tracts, the twelfth edition;

'Tis read by every politician:
The country members, when in town,
To all their boroughs send them down:
You never met a thing so smart;
The courtiers have them all by heart:
Those maids of honour (who can read)
Are taught to use them for their creed.
The reverend author's good intention,
Hath been rewarded with a pension:
He doth an honour to his gown,
By bravely running priest-craft down:
He shews, as sure as God's in Gloucester,
That Jesus was a grand impostor:
That all his miracles were cheats,
Performed as jugglers do their feats:
The church had never such a writer:
A shame, he hath not got a mitre!'

Suppose me dead; and then suppose
A club assembled at the *Rose*;
Where from discourse of this and that,
I grow the subject of their chat:
And, while they toss my name about,
With favour some, and some without;
One quite indifferent in the cause,
My character impartial draws.

'The Dean, if we believe report,
Was never ill received at court.
As for his works in verse and prose,
I own my self no judge of those:
Nor, can I tell what critics thought 'em;
But, this I know, all people bought 'em;
As with a moral view designed
To cure the vices of mankind:
His vein, ironically grave,
Exposed the fool, and lashed the knave:
To steal a hint was never known,
But what he writ, was all his own.

'He never thought an honour done him
Because a duke was proud to own him:
Would rather slip aside, and choose
To talk with wits in dirty shoes:
Despised the fools with Stars and Garters,
So often seen caressing Chartres:
He never courted men in station,
Nor persons had in admiration;
Of no man's greatness was afraid,
Because he sought for no man's aid.
Though trusted long in great affairs,
He gave himself no haughty airs:
Without regarding private ends,
Spent all his credit for his friends:
And, only chose the wise and good;
No flatterers; no allies in blood;
But succoured virtue in distress,
And seldom failed of good success;
As numbers in their hearts must own,
Who, but for him, had been unknown.

'With princes kept a due decorum,
But never stood in awe before 'em:
He followed David's lesson just,
In princes never put thy trust.
And, would you make him truly sour;
Provoke him with a slave in power:
The Irish senate, if you named,
With what impatience he declaimed!
Fair Liberty was all his cry;
For her he stood prepared to die;
For her he boldly stood alone;
For her he oft exposed his own.
Two kingdoms, just as faction led,
Had set a price upon his head;
But, not a traitor could be found,
To sell him for six hundred pound.

'Had he but spared his tongue and pen,
He might have rose like other men:
But, power was never in his thought;
And, wealth he valued not a groat:
Ingratitude he often found,
And pitied those who meant the wound:
But, kept the tenor of his mind,
To merit well of human kind:
Nor made a sacrifice of those
Who still were true, to please his foes.

He laboured many a fruitless hour
To reconcile his friends in power;
Saw mischief by a faction brewing,
While they pursued each other's ruin.
But, finding vain was all his care,
He left the court in mere despair.

'And, oh! how short are human schemes!
Here ended all our golden dreams.
What St John's skill in state affairs,
What Ormond's valour, Oxford's cares,
To save their sinking country lent,
Was all destroyed by one event.

Too soon that precious life was ended,
On which alone, our weal depended.

'When up a dangerous faction starts,
With wrath and vengeance in their hearts;
By solemn league and covenant bound,
To ruin, slaughter, and confound;
To turn religion to a fable,
And make the government a Babel:
Pervert the law, disgrace the gown,
Corrupt the senate, rob the crown,
To sacrifice old England's glory,
And make her infamous in story.
When such a tempest shook the land,
How could unguarded virtue stand?

'With horror, grief, despair the Dean
Beheld the dire destructive scene:
His friends in exile, or the Tower,
Himself within the frown of power;
Pursued by base envenomed pens,
Far to the land of slaves and fens;
A servile race in folly nursed,
Who truckle most, when treated worst.

'By innocence and resolution,
He bore continual persecution;
While numbers to preferment rose;
Whose merits were, to be his foes.
When, even his own familiar friends
Intent upon their private ends;
Like renegadoes now he feels,
Against him lifting up their heels.

'The Dean did by his pen defeat
An infamous destructive cheat.
Taught fools their interest how to know;
And gave them arms to ward the blow.
Envy hath owned it was his doing,
To save that helpless land from ruin;
While they who at the steerage stood,
And reaped the profit, sought his blood.

'To save them from their evil fate,
In him was held a crime of state.
A wicked monster on the bench,
Whose fury blood could never quench;
As vile and profligate a villain,
As modern Scroggs or old Tressilian;
Who long all justice had discarded,
Nor feared he God, nor man regarded;
Vowed on the Dean his rage to vent,
And make him of his zeal repent;

But heaven his innocence defends,
The grateful people stand his friends:
Not strains of law, nor judges frown,
Nor topics brought to please the crown,
Nor witness hired, nor jury picked,
Prevail to bring him in convict.

'In exile with a steady heart,
He spent his life's declining part;
Where, folly, pride, and faction sway,
Remote from St John, Pope, and Gay.
His friendship there to few confined,
Were always of the middling kind:
No fools of rank, a mongrel breed,
Who fain would pass for lords indeed;
Where titles give no right or power,
And peerage is a withered flower,
He would have held it a disgrace,
If such a wretch had known his face.
On rural squires, that kingdom's bane,
He vented oft his wrath in vain:
Biennial squires, to market brought;
Who sell their souls and votes for naught;
The nation stripped go joyful back,
To rob the church, their tenants rack,
Go snacks with rogues and rapparees
And, keep the peace, to pick up fees:
In every job to have a share,
A jail or barrack to repair;
And turn the tax for public roads
Commodious to their own abodes.

'Perhaps I may allow, the Dean
Had too much satire in his vein;
And seemed determined not to starve it,
Because no age could more deserve it.
Yet, malice never was his aim;

He lashed the vice, but spared the name.
No individual could resent,
Where thousands equally were meant.
His satire points at no defect,
But what all mortals may correct:
For he abhorred that senseless tribe,
Who call it humour when they jibe:
He spared a hump, or crooked nose,
Whose owners set not up for beaux.
True genuine dullness moved his pity,
Unless it offered to be witty.
Those, who their ignorance confessed,
He ne'er offended with a jest;
But laughed to hear an idiot quote,
A verse from Horace, learned by rote.

'He knew an hundred pleasant stories,
With all the turns of Whigs and Tories:
Was cheerful to his dying day,
And friends would let him have his way.

'He gave the little wealth he had,
To build a house for fools and mad:
And shewed by one satiric touch,
No nation wanted it so much:
    That kingdom he hath left his debtor,
I wish it soon may have a better.'

JONATHAN SWIFT

Advice to a Lady in Autumn

Asses' milk, half a pint, take at seven, or before,
Then sleep for an hour or two, and no more.
At nine stretch your arms, and, oh! think when alone
There's no pleasure in bed.—Mary, bring me my gown.
Slip on that ere you rise; let your caution be such;
Keep all cold from your breast, there's already too much;
Your pinners set right, your twitcher tied on,
Your prayers at an end, and your breakfast quite done,

Retire to some author improving and gay,
And with sense like your own, set your mind for the day.
At twelve you may walk, for at this time o' the year,
The sun, like your wit, is as mild as 'tis clear:
But mark in the meadows the ruin of time;
Take the hint, and let life be improved in its prime.
Return not in haste, nor of dressing take heed;
For beauty like yours no assistance can need.
With an appetite thus down to dinner you sit,
Where the chief of the feast is the flow of your wit:
Let this be indulged, and let laughter go round;
As it pleases your mind to your health 'twill redound.
After dinner two glasses at least, I approve;
Name the first to the king, and the last to your love:
Thus cheerful, with wisdom, with innocence, gay,
And calm with your joys, gently glide through the day.
The dews of the evening most carefully shun;
Those tears of the sky for the loss of the sun.
Then in chat, or at play, with a dance or a song,
Let the night, like the day, pass with pleasure along.
All cares, but of love, banish far from your mind;
And those you may end, when you please to be kind.

PHILIP STANHOPE, EARL OF CHESTERFIELD

To Mrs Martha Blount on Her Leaving the Town after the Coronation

As some fond virgin, whom her mother's care
Drags from the town to wholesome country air,
Just when she learns to roll a melting eye,
And hear a spark, yet think no danger nigh;
From the dear man unwilling she must sever,
Yet takes one kiss before she parts for ever:
Thus from the world fair Zephalinda flew,
Saw others happy, and with sighs withdrew;
Not that their pleasures caused her discontent,
She sighed not that they stayed, but that she went.

She went to plain-work, and to purling brooks,
Old-fashioned halls, dull aunts, and croaking rooks:
She went from opera, park, assembly, play,
To morning walks, and prayers three hours a-day;
To part her time 'twixt reading and bohea,
To muse, and spill her solitary tea,
Or o'er cold coffee trifle with the spoon,
Count the slow clock, and dine exact at noon;
Divert her eyes with pictures in the fire,
Hum half a tune, tell stories to the 'squire;
Up to her godly garret after seven,
There starve and pray, for that's the way to Heaven.
　　Some 'squire, perhaps, you take delight to rack;
Whose game is whist, whose treat a toast in sack;
Who visits with a gun, presents you birds,
Then gives a smacking buss and cries,—No words!
Or with his hound comes hallooing from the stable,
Makes love with nods, and knees beneath a table;
Whose laughs are hearty, though his jests are coarse,
And loves you best of all things—but his horse.
　　In some fair evening, on your elbow laid,
You dream of triumphs in the rural shade;
In pensive thought recall the fancied scene,
See coronations rise on every green;
Before you pass the imaginary sights
Of lords, and earls, and dukes, and gartered knights,
While the spread fan o'ershades your closing eyes;
Then give one flirt, and all the vision flies.
Thus vanish sceptres, coronets, and balls,
And leave you in lone woods, or empty walls!
　　So when your slave, at some dear idle time,
(Not plagued with head-aches, or the want of rhyme)
Stands in the streets, abstracted from the crew,
And while he seems to study, thinks of you;
Just when his fancy points your sprightly eyes,
Or sees the blush of soft Parthenia rise,
Gay pats my shoulder, and you vanish quite,
Streets, chairs, and coxcombs rush upon my sight;
Vexed to be still in town, I knit my brow,
Look sour, and hum a tune as you may now.

ALEXANDER POPE

Epigram

As Thomas was cudgelled one day by his wife,
He took to the street, and fled for his life:
Tom's three dearest friends came by in the squabble,
And saved him at once from the shrew and the rabble;
Then ventured to give him some sober advice—
But Tom is a person of honour so nice,
Too wise to take counsel, too proud to take warning,
That he sent to all three a challenge next morning.
Three duels he fought, thrice ventured his life;
Went home, and was cudgelled again by his wife.

JONATHAN SWIFT

The Ballad of Bouillabaisse

A street there is in Paris famous,
   For which no rhyme our language yields,
Rue Neuve des Petits Champs its name is—
   The New Street of the Little Fields.
And here's an inn, not rich and splendid,
   But still in comfortable case;
The which in youth I oft attended,
   To eat a bowl of Bouillabaisse.

This Bouillabaisse a noble dish is—
   A sort of soup, or broth, or brew,
Or hotchpotch of all sorts of fishes,
   That Greenwich never could outdo:
Green herbs, red peppers, mussels, saffron,
   Soles, onions, garlic, roach, and dace:
All these you eat at Terré's tavern
   In that one dish of Bouillabaisse.

Indeed, a rich and savoury stew 'tis;
 And true philosophers, methinks,
Who love all sorts of natural beauties,
 Should love good victuals and good drinks.
And Cordelier or Benedictine
 Might gladly, sure, his lot embrace,
Nor find a fast-day too afflicting,
 Which served him up a Bouillabaisse.

I wonder if the house still there is?
 Yes, here the lamp is, as before;
The smiling red-cheeked *écaillère* is
 Still opening oysters at the door.
Is Terré still alive and able?
 I recollect his droll grimace:
He'd come and smile before your table,
 And hope you liked your Bouillabaisse.

We enter—nothing's changed or older.
 'How's Monsieur Terré, waiter, pray?'
The waiter stares, and shrugs his shoulder—
 'Monsieur is dead this many a day.'
'It is the lot of saint and sinner,
 So honest Terré's run his race.'
'What will Monsieur require for dinner?'
 'Say, do you still cook Bouillabaisse?'

'Oh, oui, Monsieur,' 's the waiter's answer:
 'Quel vin Monsieur désire-t-il?'
'Tell me a good one.'—'That I can, Sir:
 The Chambertin with yellow seal.'
'So Terré's gone,' I say, and sink in
 My old accustomed corner-place;
'He's done with feasting and with drinking,
 With Burgundy and Bouillabaisse.'

My old accustomed corner here is,
　　The table still is in the nook;
Ah! vanished many a busy year is
　　This well-known chair since last I took.
When first I saw ye, *cari luoghi*,
　　I'd scarce a beard upon my face,
And now a grizzled, grim old fogy,
　　I sit and wait for Bouillabaisse.

Where are you, old companions trusty
　　Of early days here met to dine?
Come, waiter! quick, a flagon crusty—
　　I'll pledge them in the good old wine.
The kind old voices and old faces
　　My memory can quick retrace;
Around the board they take their places,
　　And share the wine and Bouillabaisse.

There's Jack has made a wondrous marriage;
　　There's laughing Tom is laughing yet;
There's brave Augustus drives his carriage;
　　There's poor old Fred in the *Gazette*;
On James's head the grass is growing:
　　Good Lord! the world has wagged apace
Since here we set the claret flowing,
　　And drank, and ate the Bouillabaisse.

Ah me! how quick the days are flitting!
　　I mind me of a time that's gone,
When here I'd sit, as now I'm sitting,
　　In this same place—but not alone,
A fair young form was nestled near me,
　　A dear, dear face looked fondly up,
And sweetly spoke and smiled to cheer me
　　—There's no one now to share my cup.

　　　　*　　*　　*　　*　　*

I drink it as the Fates ordain it.
  Come, fill it, and have done with rhymes:
Fill up the lonely glass, and drain it
  In memory of dear old times.
Welcome the wine, whate'er the seal is;
  And sit you down and say your grace
With thankful heart, whate'er the meal is.
  —Here comes the smoking Bouillabaisse!

WILLIAM MAKEPEACE THACKERAY

Delight in Disorder

A sweet disorder in the dress
Kindles in clothes a wantonness;
A lawn about the shoulders thrown
Into a fine distraction;
An erring lace, which here and there
Enthralls the crimson stomacher;
A cuff neglectful, and thereby
Ribbons to flow confusedly;
A winning wave, deserving note,
In the tempestuous petticoat;
A careless shoe-string, in whose tie
I see a wild civility;
Do more bewitch me, than when art
Is too precise in every part.

ROBERT HERRICK

Chard Whitlow

(Mr Eliot's Sunday evening postscript)

As we get older we do not get any younger.
Seasons return, and today I am fifty-five,
And this time last year I was fifty-four,
And this time next year I shall be sixty-two.
And I cannot say I should like (to speak for myself)
To see my time over again—if you can call it time:
Fidgeting uneasily under a draughty stair,
Or counting sleepless nights in the crowded tube.

There are certain precautions—though none of them very
    reliable—
Against the blast from the bombs and the flying splinter,
But not against the blast from heaven, *vento dei venti*,
The wind within a wind unable to speak for wind;
And the frigid burnings of purgatory will not be touched
By any emollient.
              I think you will find this put,
Better than I could ever hope to express it,
In the words of Kharma: 'It is, we believe,
Idle to hope that the simple stirrup-pump
Will extinguish hell.'
            Oh, listeners,
And you especially who have turned off the wireless,
And sit in Stoke or Basingstoke listening appreciatively to the
    silence,
(Which is also the silence of hell) pray, not for your skins, but your
    souls.

And pray for me also under the draughty stair.
As we get older we do not get any younger.

And pray for Kharma under the holy mountain.

                HENRY REED

The Elephant, or the Force of Habit

A tail behind, a trunk in front,
Complete the usual elephant.
The tail in front, the trunk behind,
Is what you very seldom find.

If you for specimens should hunt
With trunks behind and tails in front,
That hunt would occupy you long;
The force of habit is so strong.

A. E. HOUSMAN

Marble-Top

At counters where I eat my lunch
In dim arcades of industry,
I cock my elbows up and munch
Whatever food occurs to me.

By many mirrors multiplied,
My silly face is not exalted;
And when I leave I have inside
An egg-and-lettuce and a malted.

And just to hear the pretty peal
Of merry maids at their pimento
Is more to me than any meal
Or banquet that I ever went to.

E. B. WHITE

Ahkh

At full moon in cold Khamchatka,
   Where the Wheelagheelah flows,
That aquatic fowl, the Vhatka,
   Softly tippets on its toes
(Inebriate with her love-light,
     I suppose).
It is then the astute Khamchatkan
     Fowling goes.

But when her dwindling quarter
   Has to dark her disc resigned,
'Tis a job, by Gob, to slaughter
   A fowl no eye can find—
And his '*Ahkh*', his '*Ahkh*' is nothing
     But a blind.

Now it's nearer, sweeter, clearer;
   Now it wails and wanes and dies;
Now the night-beleaguered hearer
   Hears it *ahkhing* in the skies;
When, in sooth, it's nesting snugly in a nest
     not half its size,
Hidden in the reeds and rushes, scarce a hand's-
     breadth from his eyes!

So the Fowler should go fowling,
   Armed with candle, book, and bell,
When Khamchatka's gleamy crescent
   Casts a beamy, dreamy spell
O'er a forest vaguely pleasant
   With the Oomatonga's smell,
And for leagues around him amorous '*Ahkhs!*'
   Cacophonously swell:
With luck he'll bag a Vhatka!
     Who can tell?

WALTER DE LA MARE

Song

At last the secret is out, as it always must come in the end,
The delicious story is ripe to tell to the intimate friend;
Over the tea-cups and in the square the tongue has its desire;
Still waters run deep, my dear, there's never smoke without fire.

Behind the corpse in the reservoir, behind the ghost on the links,
Behind the lady who dances and the man who madly drinks,
Under the look of fatigue, the attack of migraine and the sigh
There is always another story, there is more than meets the eye.

For the clear voice suddenly singing, high up in the convent wall,
The scent of elder bushes, the sporting prints in the hall,
The croquet matches in summer, the handshake, the cough, the
    kiss,
There is always a wicked secret, a private reason for this.

W. H. AUDEN

Annual Meeting

At the Conway Hall in Holborn
Anti-vaccinators meet:
'Mrs Twemlow, are you comfy?'
'Gladys, darling, here's a seat.'

Greet the lady on the doorway,
Give your name as you go in.
'Are you for us or against us?'
I return a shifty grin,

Walk across the polished parquet,
Hear a deep consensual hum
Fill the radiator-smelling
Churchy auditorium.

Hurry up the centre gangway,
Rather anxious not to meet
Eyes I feel may spot I haven't
Paid what *they* paid for the seat.

Pairs of knees snap sharply sideways—
Are my *bona fides* thin?—
Here's my ticket, but a ticket—
Does it really let you in?

Rows of chairs, all stuck together,
Made of tubes—I sit on one
Feeling that the seats move towards a
Single destination.

'Poisoned food from poisoned farmland!'
How the hall falls silent when
From the tannoy trills the anxious
Fluting voice of Gwendolen.

Tall and pallid on the platform,
Finger raised, Gwen seems to see
Legions of perverted doctors
In some dark conspiracy.

'Vaccination is their idol,
Mercenary quacks! The blind,
Duped by Fleet Street and the City,
Help to keep their pockets lined!

'Devil's brew and witch's potion!'
Clapping. 'Filth pressed through the skin!
Infant children stuck with needles—
Crime's too mild a word. It's *sin*!'

Ah, applause is now tumultuous—
High the note with which she hit
Just the word to make us all am-
Bivalently relish it.

Glancing down, I scan the programme,
Catch a paragraph or two
Telling all about the founder
Who in 1892

Put the hard word on the doctors,
And to show she'd risk her hide
Visited the smallpox victims
Just to prove that science lied.

Right or wrong, you will admit it's
More than you or I would do—
And the thought, I must say, tempered,
Slightly, my agnostic view.

'Nature-cure will bring the good life,
That's the way salvation lies—
I regret', Gwen said, 'there aren't more
Who embrace all that implies.'

Arms unscratched by any needle,
(Snug in puffer-coats they stay)
Hypodermic virgins all, they
Vote the afternoon away.

One young lady—right beside me—
Screwed her nose up, smiled, uncurled—
Round about her all the faithful,
Far outside, the hateful world.

And I thought: she fears the needle—
Or is that a surrogate
For the sudden touch of others
Threatening to penetrate?

Covertly I looked about me,
Spotted, as I hid my stare,
Faces burning with excitement
That I hadn't guessed was there.

'Lies', 'misrepresent', 'gag', 'pressure'—
Voices shook, their edges frayed:
Nor did laughter seem to ease them
When the smallpox jokes were made.

Something unexpressed was moving,
Transferred from its buried site,
To a temporary lodging
Within one obsessive rite.

Stars and tea-leaves, euthanasia,
Is the world we live in flat?
There's a chance it may not turn out
Quite as simple as all that—

More than likely, personal luggage
That from childhood we must hump,
Tiresome as it is to carry
Is impossible to dump.

Stuck with mine, I dodged the hell out
Up the aisle, left 50 pee,
Half-ashamed to feel I hoped I'd
Found a bunch worse off than me.

ROBERT ROBINSON

Geraldine Green

At Worthing, an exile from Geraldine G——,
How aimless, how wretched an exile is he!
Promenades are not even prunella and leather
To lovers, if lovers can't foot them together.

He flies the parade;—by ocean he stands;
He traces a 'Geraldine G.' on the sands;
Only 'G.!' though her loved patronymic is 'Green',—
'I will not betray thee, my own Geraldine.'

The fortunes of men have a time and a tide,
And Fate, the old fury, will not be denied;
That name was, of course, soon wiped out by the sea;
She jilted the exile, did Geraldine G.

They meet, but they never have spoken since that;
He hopes she is happy,—he knows she is fat;
She, woo'd on the shore, now is wed in the Strand,—
And *I*—it was I wrote her name on the sand.

FREDERICK LOCKER

The Elephant

Aunt Mary is my aunt,
    She took me to the Zoo.
She offered to the Elephant
    One bun—it wanted two.

Aunt Mary had a hat
    All cherries on her head.
The beast thought, 'Buns are good, but that
    Will do quite well instead.'

The creature smiled serene,
    And made a little bow . . .
Aunt Mary's never, never seen
    Her hat from then till now.

Aunt Mary danced a jig,
    And wept till she was blind,
And screamed, 'You bad, old, ugly pig!'
    But, it didn't seem to mind.

JOHN JOY BELL

68

Mr Bluefrock Considers It All

Bagpipes, balloons and bubbles, I have blown 'em all,
I have watched them rise and I have watched them fall,
I have heard the mermaids calling, each to each,
I have eaten a peach.

Campbells, Colquhouns and Comyns, I have known 'em all,
I have known the short ones and I have known the tall,
I have seen my second cousin sit in the gorse,
I have ridden a horse.

Sonnets, lampoons, and ballads, I have wrote 'em all,
I have dipped my pen in alternate honey and gall,
I have drunk a great deal of indescribable wine,
I have been down a mine.

Collage, cartoons and crayons, I have done 'em all,
I have drawn on the flagstones and on the kitchen wall,
I have washed my midnight head in the forest pool,
I have played the fool.

Salons, saloons and sawdust, I have paced 'em all,
I have wielded the little stick and chased the ball,
I have eaten a million rounds of buttered toast,
I have seen a ghost.

Gibbons, baboons and lemurs, I have loved 'em all,
I have watched the eagles fly and the lizards crawl,
I have seen the giants sleep and the Muses snore;
Need I say more?

R. P. LISTER

The Waltz

Behold with downcast eyes and modest glance,
In measured step, a well-dressed pair advance,
One hand on hers, the other on her hip,
For thus the law's ordained by Baron Trip.
'Twas in such posture our first parents moved,
When hand in hand through Eden's bowers they roved,
Ere yet the devil, with practice foul and false
Turned their poor heads and taught them how to waltz.

RICHARD BRINSLEY SHERIDAN

May-day Song for North Oxford

(Annie Laurie tune)

Belbroughton Road is bonny, and pinkly bursts the spray
Of prunus and forsythia across the public way,
For a full spring-tide of blossom seethed and departed hence,
Leaving land-locked pools of jonquils by sunny garden fence.

And a constant sound of flushing runneth from windows where
The toothbrush too is airing in this new North Oxford air
From Summerfields to Lynam's, the thirsty tarmac dries,
And a Cherwell mist dissolveth on elm-discovering skies.

Oh! well-bound Wells and Bridges! Oh! earnest ethical search
For the wide high-table λογος of St C. S. Lewis's Church.
This diamond-eyed Spring morning my soul soars up the slope
Of a right good rough-cast buttress on the housewall of my hope.

And open-necked and freckled, where once there grazed the cows,
Emancipated children swing on old apple boughs,
And pastel-shaded book rooms bring New Ideas to birth
As the whitening hawthorn only hears the heart beat of the earth.

JOHN BETJEMAN

70

Beside a Vast and Primal Sea

Beside a vast and primal sea
A solitary savage he,

Who gathered for his tribe's rude need
The daily dole of raw sea-weed.

He watched the great tides rise and fall,
And spoke the truth—or not at all!

Along the awful shore he ran
A simple pre-Pelasgian;

A thing primeval, undefiled,
Straightforward as a little child—

Until one morn he made a grab
And caught a mesozoic crab!

Then—told the tribe at close of day
A bigger one had got away!

From him have sprung (I own a bias
    To ways the cult of rod and fly has)
All fishermen—and Ananias!

PATRICK CHALMERS

Ode to the Human Heart
By Sir Fretful Plagiary

Blind Thamyris, and blind Mæonides,
    Pursue the triumph and partake the gale!
Drop tears as fast as the Arabian trees,
    To point a moral or adorn a tale.*

Full many a gem of purest ray serene,
   Thoughts that do often lie too deep for tears,
Like angels' visits, few and far between,
   Deck the long vista of departed years.

Man never is, but always to be blest,
   The tenth transmitter of a foolish face,
Like Aaron's serpent, swallows up the rest,
   And makes a sunshine in the shady place.

For man the hermit sighed, till woman smiled,
   To waft a feather or to drown a fly,
(In wit a man, simplicity a child),
   With silent finger pointing to the sky.

But fools rush in where angels fear to tread,
   Far out amid the melancholy main;
As when a vulture on Imaus bred,
   Dies of a rose in aromatic pain.

Music hath charms to soothe the savage breast,
   Look on her face, and you'll forget them all;
Some mute inglorious Milton here may rest,
   A hero perish, or a sparrow fall.

My way of life is fall'n into the sere;
   I stood in Venice on the Bridge of Sighs.
Like a rich jewel in an Ethiop's ear,
   Who sees through all things with his half-shut eyes.

Oh! for a lodge in some vast wilderness!
   Full many a flower is born to blush unseen,
Fine by degrees and beautifully less,
   And die ere man can say 'Long live the Queen!'

S. LAMAN BLANCHARD

* The printer's devil has taken upon himself to make the following additions to these lines:

Blind Thamyris, and blind Mæonides (Something like Milton.)
   Pursue the triumph and partake the gale! (Rather like Pope.)
Drop tears as fast as the Arabian trees. (Why, this is Shakespeare!)
   To point a moral or adorn a tale. (Oh, it's Dr Johnson.)

   To the succeeding lines the same authority has added in succession the names of Gray, Wordsworth, Campbell, and so on throughout. What does he mean? Does he mean to say he has ever met with any of these lines before?

Ballade of No Meaning

Blithe adjuvant of unregardful Time,
    Consort of old Alcides' privy play,
Vexing swart noons beneath the quickening lime:
    What shall I say of thee? What *shall* I say?
    Were it not venial in our frantic day
To limn thee (rogue!) unchecked of pedant rhyme?
    Well, where there is a will, there is a way:
This may be Nonsense, but it sounds Sublime.

Or ever Asgard frowned on Jötenheim
    Or bearded statecraft gave the Curds their Whey
Thou only in fastidious pantomine
    Mocked'st the wild Haywain, and the wilder Hay!
    Spoke then the Bells: ere Echo all astray
Malvert our tidings and misprise our chime,
    Let Echo answer: Echo answered Nay:
This may be Nonsense, but it sounds Sublime.

Nimbly remote from Dollar and from Dime,
    Tuning (O deft!) thy febrile roundelay,
Oblivious of the greasy paradigm
    Squat Orchis carved in the insensate clay,
    Queen non-Elect of a too-thrusting May
That roots and wallows in its wormwood prime—
    Thou in thy Tomb promiscuous art alway:
This may be Nonsense, but it sounds Sublime.

    PRINCE, I have heard you grossly overpay
The scribblers who extol your steady climb.
    I might come cheaper; look at this, I pray:
This may be Nonsense, but it sounds Sublime.

W. BRIDGES-ADAMS

Brian

Brian is a baddie,
As nasty as they come.
He terrifies his daddy
And mortifies his mum.

One morning in December
They took him to the zoo,
But Brian lost his temper
And kicked a kangaroo.

And then he fought a lion
Escaping from its pit.
It tried to swallow Brian
Till Brian swallowed it!

Yes, Brian is a devil,
A horrid little curse—
Unlike his brother Neville
Who's infinitely worse!

DOUG MACLEOD

There is No Opera Like 'Lohengrin'

But one Apocalyptic Lion's whelp (in flesh
called William Lyon Phelps) purrs: After all,
there is no opera like 'Lohengrin'!
My father, a Baptist preacher, a good man,
is now with God—and every day is Christmas.
Apart from questions of creative genius,
there are no gooder men than our good writers.
Lyman Abbott and I, who never can read Dante,
still find cathedrals beautifully friendly.
Hell is OK; Purgatory bores me; Heaven's dull.

DORSET COUNTY LIBRARY

There is no opera like 'Lohengrin'!
Miss Lulu Bett's outline is a Greek statue.
Augustus Thomas' 'Witching Hour' 's a masterpiece;
Housman's Second Volume is a masterpiece;
Anglo-Americans well know Olivant's
masterpiece, 'Bob, Son of Battle', that masterpiece!
There is no opera like 'Lohengrin'!
In verse, these masterpieces are worth reading:
'The Jar of Dreams', by Lilla Cabot Perry;
'Waves of Unrest', by Bernice Lesbia Kenyon.
(O Charlotte Endymion Porter! Percy Bysshe Shelley?
Helen Archibald Clark! O women with three names!)
Anna Hempstead Branch read all the Bible
through in a few days. Speaking of Milton,
bad manners among critics are too common,
but gentlemen should not grow obsolete.
Often we fall asleep—not when we're bored,
but when we think we are most interesting.
There is no opera like 'Lohengrin'!
I sometimes think there are no persons who
can do more good than good librarians can.
American books grow easier to hold;
dull paper and light weight is the ideal.

JOHN WHEELWRIGHT

To Charlotte While Shaving

Charlotte: from whose too enterprising womb
    Sprang our dull Edward and our duller Joan,
Twin fruit of sunless days at Ilfracombe—
    O limp coitus when such seed was sown!—

Charlotte: I take small pleasure in our young:
    Do they rejoice? I find it hard to bear;
Do they repine? My withers are not wrung;
    And if you ate them, Charlotte, should I care?

75

The little flat foot slapping on the stair,
  The little muffin face, the sticky kiss—
These joys withheld I doubt if I should miss;
  I might perhaps be glad they were not there.

Charlotte, we do at least know what is what.
  Stand them against the wall, love, side by side;
Snuffling, myopic, cabriole-legged and squat:
  Great heaven, wife, what is there here for pride?

I do not ask for wit, or poise, or beauty—
  Nor could one ask, looking at me and you.
But in God's name, how will they do their duty
  In that dim station He has called them to?

Edward (at Pembroke?) will not get his Blue;
  Joan (at St Hugh's?) may clock a lenient Third:
What can we find the horrid pair to do
  That will not be uncalled-for and absurd?

Edward, BA, games master at The Gables,
  Willing but costive, spotty, not too clean?
Joan, taking notes at rich men's board-room tables,
  Leaving moist handkerchiefs where she has been?

Or shall we launch them on less charted waters
  Where adenoids are looked for and admired?
Shall Edward bleat of art to errant daughters,
  Or Joan dance, puffing, till the Left are tired?

What hope have they, so mothered and so sired,
  But to hand on the ineffectual flame
Of half-lit torches to the dreadful same
  Sort as themselves, virgin and undesired?

If I had had one grand, almighty Beano,
  And had stopped thinking how much one should spend,
If you had been a Whore in a Casino
  (Think of it, Charlotte) and my Lady Friend,

Then these our young, of love and mischance begotten,
    Had stood erect, braced for all winds that blow:
Will you confess that Ilfracombe was rotten?
    Can you deny that I have told you so?

Thus far the might-have-been; but let them go:
    Theirs is the weird, and they can damned well dree it—
Nay, you are dull, sweet Charlotte, as I see it,
    And I am far from being bright, I know.

W. BRIDGES-ADAMS

Tripe

Come, gentle tripe, the hungry carter's joy,
    Drayman's delight, conductor's second course,
Passion and dream of every errand boy,
    Vision of every rogue that holds a horse,
Bane of all titled ladies, bishops' dread,
    Doom of the softly nurtured, peers' despair,
Was it for this the tall Achilles bled,
    For this that Agamemnon tore his hair?
Was this the food that launched a thousand ships
    And tore the heart of Dido, as she stood
Above the feast, wiping her royal lips,
    And called her love again—was this the food?

(The answer is, in a sense, no.)

J. B. MORTON

I Remember, I Remember

Coming up England by a different line
For once, early in the cold new year,
We stopped, and, watching men with number-plates
Sprint down the platform to familiar gates,
'Why, Coventry!' I exclaimed. 'I was born here.'

I leant far out, and squinnied for a sign
That this was still the town that had been 'mine'
So long, but found I wasn't even clear
Which side was which. From where those cycle-crates
Were standing, had we annually departed

For all those family hols? . . . A whistle went:
Things moved. I sat back, staring at my boots.
'Was that,' my friend smiled, 'where you "have your roots"?'
No, only where my childhood was unspent,
I wanted to retort, just where I started:

By now I've got the whole place clearly charted.
Our garden, first: where I did not invent
Blinding theologies of flowers and fruits,
And wasn't spoken to by an old hat.
And here we have that splendid family

I never ran to when I got depressed,
The boys all biceps and the girls all chest,
Their comic Ford, their farm where I could be
'Really myself'. I'll show you, come to that,
The bracken where I never trembling sat,

Determined to go through with it; where she
Lay back, and 'all became a burning mist'.
And, in those offices, my doggerel
Was not set up in blunt ten-point, nor read
By a distinguished cousin of the mayor,

Who didn't call and tell my father *There*
Before us, had we the gift to see ahead—
'You look as if you wished the place in Hell,'
My friend said, 'judging from your face.' 'Oh well,
I suppose it's not the place's fault,' I said.

'Nothing, like something, happens anywhere.'

PHILIP LARKIN

Synopsis of the Great Welsh Novel

Dai K lives at the end of a valley. One is not quite sure
Whether it has been drowned or not. His Mam
Loves him too much and his Dada drinks.
As for his girlfriend Blodwen, she's pregnant. So
Are all the other girls in the village—there's been a Revival.
After a performance of Elijah, the mad preacher
Davies the Doom has burnt the chapel down.
One Saturday night after the dance at the Con Club,
With the Free Wales Army up to no good in the back lanes,
A stranger comes to the village; he is, of course,
God, the well known television personality. He succeeds
In confusing the issue, whatever it is, and departs
On the last train before the line is closed.
The colliery blows up, there is a financial scandal
Involving all the most respected citizens; the Choir
Wins at the National. It is all seen, naturally,
Through the eyes of a sensitive boy who never grows up.
The men emigrate to America, Cardiff and the moon. The girls
Find rich and foolish English husbands. Only daft Ianto
Is left to recite the Complete Works of Sir Lewis Morris
To puzzled sheep, before throwing himself over
The edge of the abandoned quarry. One is not quite sure
Whether it is fiction or not.

HARRI WEBB

The Metamorphosis of Dan Donkin, Collier

Dan Donkin was a Collier,
A man who never smiled,
Of evil words a volleyer,
Intemperate and wild.
But when another Collier
Fell headlong down a shaft,
The evil-minded Collier
Got ever so much jollier,
And read the works of Mollier*
—And actually laughed.

* *Or Molière*

RALPH WOTHERSPOON

The Daniel Jazz

*Let the leader train the audience to roar like lions, and
to join in the refrain 'Go chain the lions down',
before he begins to lead them in this jazz*

Darius the Mede was a king and a wonder. *Beginning*
His eye was proud, and his voice was thunder. *with a strain*
He kept bad lions in a monstrous den. *of 'Dixie'.*
He fed up the lions on Christian men.

Daniel was the chief hired man of the land. *With a touch*
He stirred up the jazz in the palace band. *of 'Alexander's*
He whitewashed the cellar. He shovelled *Ragtime Band'.*
   in the coal.
And Daniel kept a-praying:—'Lord save my soul.'
Daniel kept a-praying 'Lord save my soul.'
Daniel kept a-praying 'Lord save my soul.'

Daniel was the butler, swagger and swell.
He ran up stairs. He answered the bell.
And *he* would let in whoever came a-calling:—
Saints so holy, scamps so appalling.
'Old man Ahab leaves his card.
Elisha and the bears are a-waiting in the yard.
Here comes Pharaoh and his snakes a-calling.
Here comes Cain and his wife a-calling.
Shadrach, Meshach and Abednego for tea.
Here comes Jonah and the whale,
And the *Sea!*
Here comes St Peter and his fishing pole.
Here comes Judas and his silver a-calling.
Here comes old Beelzebub a-calling.'
And Daniel kept a-praying:—'Lord save my soul.'
Daniel kept a-praying:—'Lord save my soul.'
Daniel kept a-praying:—'Lord save my soul.'

His sweetheart and his mother were Christian and meek.
They washed and ironed for Darius every week.
One Thursday he met them at the door:—
Paid them as usual, but acted sore.

He said:—'Your Daniel is a dead little pigeon.
He's a good hard worker, but he talks religion.'
And he showed them Daniel in the lion's cage.
Daniel standing quietly, the lions in a rage.

His good old mother cried:—
'Lord save him.'
And Daniel's tender sweetheart cried:—
'Lord save him.'

And she was a golden lily in the dew.
And she was as sweet as an apple on the tree
And she was as fine as a melon in the corn-field,
Gliding and lovely as a ship on the sea,
Gliding and lovely as a ship on the sea.

And she prayed to the Lord:—
'*Send* Gabriel. *Send* Gabriel.'

King Darius said to the lions:—
'Bite Daniel. Bite Daniel.
Bite him. Bite him. Bite him!'

Thus roared the lions:—
'We want Daniel, Daniel, Daniel,
We want Daniel, Daniel, Daniel.
Grrrrrrrrrrrrrrrrrrrrrrrrrrrrrrrrrrrrrrrrrrrrrrr   *Here the*
Grrrrrrrrrrrrrrrrrrrrrrrrrrrrrrrrrrrrrrrrrrrrrrrr.'   *audience*
                                                       roars with
                                                       the leader.

And Daniel did not frown,
Daniel did not cry.
He kept on looking at the sky.
And the Lord said to Gabriel:—   *The audience*
'Go chain the lions down.   *sings this*
Go chain the lions down.   *with the leader,*
Go chain the lions down.   *to the old*
Go chain the lions down.'   *negro tune.*

And *Gabriel* chained the lions,
And *Gabriel* chained the lions,
And *Gabriel* chained the lions,
And Daniel got out of the den,
And Daniel got out of the den,
And Daniel got out of the den.
And Darius said:—'You're a Christian child,'
Darius said:—'You're a Christian child,'
Darius said:—'You're a Christian child,'
And gave him his job again,
And gave him his job again,
And gave him his job again.

VACHELL LINDSAY

The Talented Man

A letter from a lady in London to a lady at Lausanne

Dear Alice! you'll laugh when you know it,—
　Last week, at the Duchess's ball,
I danced with the clever new poet,—
　You've heard of him,—Tully St Paul.
Miss Jonquil was perfectly frantic;
　I wish you had seen Lady Anne!
It really was very romantic,
　He *is* such a talented man!

He came up from Brazen nose College,
　Just caught, as they call it, this spring;
And his head, love, is stuffed full of knowledge
　Of every conceivable thing.
Of science and logic he chatters,
　As fine and as fast as he can;
Though I am no judge of such matters,
　I'm sure he's a talented man.

His stories and jests are delightful;—
    Not stories or jests, dear, for you;
The jests are exceedingly spiteful,
    The stories not always *quite* true.
Perhaps to be kind and veracious
    May do pretty well at Lausanne;
But it never would answer,—good gracious!
    Chez nous—in a talented man.

He sneers,—how my Alice would scold him!—
    At the bliss of a sigh or a tear;
He laughed—only think!—when I told him
    How we cried o'er Trevelyan last year;
I vow I was quite in a passion;
    I broke all the sticks of my fan;
But sentiment's quite out of fashion,
    It seems, in a talented man.

Lady Bab, who is terribly moral,
    Has told me that Tully is vain,
And apt—which is silly—to quarrel,
    And fond—which is sad—of champagne.
I listened and doubted, dear Alice,
    For I saw, when my Lady began,
It was only the Dowager's malice;—
    She *does* hate a talented man!

He's hideous, I own it. But fame, love,
    Is all that these eyes can adore;
He's lame,—but Lord Byron was lame, love,
    And dumpy,—but so is Tom Moore.
Then his voice,—*such* a voice! my sweet creature,
    It's like your Aunt Lucy's toucan:
But oh! what's a tone or a feature,
    When once one's a talented man?

My mother, you know, all the season,
    Has talked of Sir Geoffrey's estate;
And truly, to do the fool reason,
    He *has* been less horrid of late.
But today, when we drive in the carriage,
    I'll tell her to lay down her plan;—
If ever I venture on marriage,
    It must be a talented man!

PS—I have found, on reflection,
    One fault in my friend,— *entre nous;*
Without it, he'd just be perfection;—
    Poor fellow, he has not a *sou!*
And so, when he comes in September
    To shoot with my uncle, Sir Dan,
I've promised mamma to remember
    He's *only* a talented man!

W. M. PRAED

Epistle from Mr Murray to Dr Polidori

Dear Doctor, I have read your play,
Which is a good one in its way,—
Purges the eyes and moves the bowels,
And drenches handkerchiefs like towels
With tears, that, in a flux of grief,
Afford hysterical relief
To shattered nerves and quickened pulses,
Which your catastrophe convulses.

I like your moral and machinery;
Your plot, too, has such scope for scenery:

Your dialogue is apt and smart:
The play's concoction full of art;
Your hero raves, your heroine cries,
All stab, and everybody dies.
In short, your tragedy would be
The very thing to hear and see:
And for a piece of publication,
If I decline on this occasion,
It is not that I am not sensible
To merits in themselves ostensible,
But—and I grieve to speak it—plays
Are drugs—mere drugs, sir—now-a-days.
I had a heavy loss by 'Manuel',—
Too lucky if it prove not annual,—
And Sotheby, with his 'Orestes',
(Which, by the by, the author's best is,)
Has lain so very long on hand,
That I despair of all demand.
I've advertised, but see my books,
Or only watch my shopman's looks;—
Still Ivan, Ina, and such lumber,
My back-shop glut, my shelves encumber.

There's Byron too, who once did better,
Has sent me, folded in a letter,
A sort of—it's no more a drama
Than Darnley, Ivan, or Kehama:
So altered since last year his pen is,
I think he's lost his wits at Venice.
In short, sir, what with one and t'other,
I dare not venture on another.
I write in haste; excuse each blunder;
The coaches through the street so thunder!
My room's so full—we've Gifford here
Reading MS., with Hookham Frere,
Pronouncing on the nouns and particles
Of some of our forthcoming articles.

The Quarterly—Ah, sir, if you
Had but the genius to review!—
A smart critique upon St Helena,
Or if you only would but tell in a
Short compass what——but to resume:
As I was saying, sir, the room—
The room's so full of wits and bards,
Crabbes, Campbells, Crokers, Freres, and Wards,
And others, neither bards nor wits:—
My humble tenement admits
All persons in the dress of gent,
From Mr Hammond to Dog Dent.

A party dines with me today,
All clever men, who make their way;
Crabbe, Malcolm, Hamilton, and Chantrey,
Are all partakers of my pantry.
They're at this moment in discussion
On poor De Staël's late dissolution.
Her book, they say, was in advance—
Pray Heaven, she tell the truth of France!
Thus run our time and tongues away;—
But, to return, sir, to your play:
Sorry, sir, but I cannot deal,
Unless 'twere acted by O'Neill;
My hands so full, my head so busy,
I'm almost dead, and always dizzy;
And so, with endless truth and hurry,
Dear Doctor, I am yours,
                                    John Murray

                                    LORD BYRON

A Tradesman to a Poet

'Do these things pay—these poems that you write?'
'Oh! yes, so much I am almost ashamed
Of my reward, so very great it is.'
'Then tell me why you are so poorly dressed?'
'I did not know that I was poorly dressed.'
'Indeed you are. And think of how you live.
You should have blooming gardens, houses grand,
If your reward is great as you have said.
I understand you live in three small rooms.'
'And that is two too many, I'm afraid.'
'You do not travel. Do you travel, sir?'
'Oh! yes, I go each week into the woods,
And often sit upon the river bank.'
'You are not loved by any woman, sir,
And have you any children of your own?'
'I love all women, every child is mine.'
'Come, come, these poems do not pay, I know.'
'Oh! yes, they pay me very well indeed.'
'Then what have you been doing with the pay
Received? Have you some secret investments?'
'Yes, yes! I have some secret investments.'
'Oh! that is very different. Oh, yes!'

MAX EHRMANN

Tit-Bittern

'Eena Meena Myna Mo
(Sing hullo, Sing dynamo)
Catch a tit-wit by its toe—
(Silly, silly dynamo)
If it yodels, let it go—
It's not a tit-wit. No!
Ah! No—
(Tell it so)
Heed not then its pretty tweeting
(If 'tis goose, say Bo!)
Journeys end in plovers meeting

(If 'tis raven—Poe!)
Let go! Let go!
Once bittern, woe!
Heigh-ho,
Heigh nonny no,
Heigh nonny nonny nonny nonny . . .'

Buckets without. Enter King Penguin with Girl Guides,
Gamekeepers, Egg-watchers, and two Obsolete Canons. A pearl of
    Ordnance.
The King lays an egg. Sensation.
(Bird-song from Shakespeare, *Nothing Much To Do About*
Anything, Act XXI, Scene XXII, lines 6793–end)

R. J. YEATMAN and W. C. SELLARS

The Post that Fitted

Though tangled and twisted the course of true love,
    This ditty explains,
No tangle's so tangled it cannot improve
    If the Lover has brains.

Ere the steamer bore him Eastward, Sleary was engaged to marry
An attractive girl at Tunbridge, whom he called 'my little Carrie'.
Sleary's pay was very modest; Sleary was the other way.
Who can cook a two-plate dinner on eight poor rupees a day?

Long he pondered o'er the question in his scantly furnished
    quarters—
Then proposed to Minnie Boffkin, eldest of Judge Boffkin's
    daughters.
Certainly an impecunious Subaltern was not a catch,
But the Boffkins knew that Minnie mightn't make another match.

So they recognized the business and, to feed and clothe the bride,
Got him made a Something Something somewhere on the Bombay
    side.
Anyhow, the billet carried pay enough for him to marry—
As the artless Sleary put it:—'Just the thing for me and Carrie.'

Did he, therefore, jilt Miss Boffkin—impulse of a baser mind?
No! He started epileptic fits of an appalling kind.
(Of his *modus operandi* only this much I could gather:—
'Pear's shaving sticks will give you little taste and lots of lather'!)

Frequently in public places his affliction used to smite
Sleary with distressing vigour—always in the Boffkins' sight.
Ere a week was over Minnie weepingly returned his ring,
Told him his 'unhappy weakness' stopped all thought of
    'marrying'.

Sleary bore the information with a chastened holy joy,—
Epileptic fits don't matter in Political employ,—
Wired three short words to Carrie—took his ticket, packed his
    kit—
Bade farewell to Minnie Boffkin in one last, long, lingering fit.

Four weeks later, Carrie Sleary read—and laughed until she
    wept—
Mrs Boffkin's warning letter on the 'wretched epilept'. . . .
Year by year, in pious patience, vengeful Mrs Boffkin sits
Waiting for the Sleary babies to develop Sleary's fits.

RUDYARD KIPLING

A Nocturnal Sketch

Even is come; and from the dark Park, hark
The signal of the setting sun—one gun!
And six is sounding from the chime, prime time
To go and see the Drury-Lane Dane slain,—
Or hear Othello's jealous doubt spout out,—
Or Macbeth raving at that shade-made blade,
Denying to his frantic clutch much touch;—
Or else to see Ducrow with wide stride ride
Four horses as no other man can span;
Or in the small Olympic Pit, sit split
Laughing at Liston, while you quiz his phiz.

Anon Night comes, and with her wings brings things
Such as, with his poetic tongue, Young sung;
The gas up-blazes with its bright white light,
And paralytic watchmen prowl, howl, growl,
About the streets and take up Pall Mall Sal,
Who, hasting to her nightly jobs, robs fobs.

Now thieves to enter for your cash, smash, crash
Past drowsy Charley, in a deep sleep, creep,—
But, frightened by Policeman B. 3, flee
And while they're going, whisper low, 'No go!'

Now puss, while folks are in their beds, treads leads,
And sleepers waking, grumble—'Drat that cat!'
Who in the gutter caterwauls, squalls, mauls
Some feline foe, and screams in shrill ill-will.

Now Bulls of Bashan, of a prize size, rise
In childish dreams, and with a roar gore poor
Georgy, or Charley, or Billy, willy-nilly;—
But Nursemaid in a nightmare rest, chest-pressed,
Dreameth of one of her old flames, James Games,—

And that she hears—what faith is man's! Ann's banns
And his, from Reverend Mr Rice, twice, thrice:
White ribbons flourish, and a stout shout out,
That upward goes, shows Rose knows those bows' woes.

THOMAS HOOD

Factory Windows are Always Broken

Factory windows are always broken.
Somebody's always throwing bricks,
Somebody's always heaving cinders,
Playing ugly Yahoo tricks.

Factory windows are always broken.
Other windows are let alone.
No one throws through the chapel-window
The bitter, snarling, derisive stone.

Factory windows are always broken.
Something or other is going wrong.
Something is rotten—I think, in Denmark.
End of the factory-window song.

VACHELL LINDSAY

A Cockney's Evening Song

Fades into twilight the last golden gleam
Thrown by the sunset on upland and stream;
Glints o'er the Serpentine—tips Notting Hill—
Dies on the summit of proud Pentonville.

Day brought us trouble, but Night brings us peace;
Morning brought sorrow, but Eve bids it cease.
Gaslight and Gaiety, beam for a while;
Pleasure and Paraffin, lend us a smile.

Temples of Mammon are voiceless again—
Lonely policemen inherit Mark Lane,
Silent is Lothbury—quiet Cornhill—
Babel of Commerce, thine echoes are still.

Far to the South—where the wanderer strays
Lost among graveyards and riverward ways,
Hardly a footfall and hardly a breath
Comes to dispute Laurence—Pountney with Death.

Westward the stream of Humanity glides;—
'Busses are proud of their dozen insides.
Put up thy shutters, grim Care, for today—
Mirth and the lamplighter hurry this way.

Out on the glimmer weak Hesperus yields!
Gas for the cities and stars for the fields.
Daisies and buttercups, do as ye list;
I and my friends are for music or whist.

H. D. TRAILL

On the Birth of His Son

Families, when a child is born,
Want it to be intelligent.
I, through intelligence,
Having wrecked my whole life,
Only hope the baby will prove
Ignorant and stupid.
Then he will crown a tranquil life
By becoming a Cabinet Minister.

ARTHUR WALEY

from the Chinese of Su Tung-P'O (1036–1101)

Loo

First let me suppose, what may shortly be true,
The company set, and the word to be Loo;
All smirking and pleasant and big with adventure,
And ogling the stake which is fixed in the centre.
Round and round go the cards, while I inwardly damn
At never once finding a visit from Pam.
I lay down my stake, apparently cool,
While the harpies about me all pocket the pool.
I fret in my gizzard, yet, cautious and sly,
I wish all my friends may be bolder than I.
Yet still they sit snug, not a creature will aim
By losing their money to venture at fame.
'Tis in vain that at niggardly caution I scold,
'Tis in vain that I flatter the brave and the bold:
All play in their own way and think me an ass.
'What does Mrs Bunbury?' 'I, sir? I pass.'
'Pray what does Miss Horneck? Take courage, come do.'
'Who, I? let me see, sir, why I must pass too.'
Mr Bunbury frets, and I fret like the devil,
To see them so cowardly, lucky and civil.
Yet still I sit snug and continue to sigh on,

Till made by my losses as bold as a lion,
I venture at all, while my avarice regards
The whole pool as my own. 'Come, give me five cards.'
'Well done!' cry the ladies; 'Ah, Doctor, that's good!
The pool's very rich. Ah! the Doctor is Loo'd!'
Thus foiled in my courage, on all sides perplexed,
I ask for advice from the lady that's next:
'Pray, ma'am, be so good as to give your advice;
Don't you think the best way is to venture for't twice?'
'I advise,' cries the lady, 'to try it, I own.
Ah! the Doctor is Loo'd! Come, Doctor, put down.'
Thus, playing and playing, I still grow more eager,
And so bold and so bold, I'm at last a bold beggar.
Now, ladies, I ask, if law-matters you're skilled in,
Whether crimes such as yours should not come before Fielding?
For giving advice that is not worth a straw
May well be called picking of pockets in law;
And picking of pockets, with which I now charge ye,
Is, by quinto Elizabeth, Death without Clergy.
What justice, when both to the Old Bailey brought!
By the gods, I'll enjoy it; though 'tis but in thought!
Both are placed at the bar with all proper decorum,
With bunches of fennel and nosegays before 'em;
Both cover their faces with mobs and all that,
But the judge bids them angrily take off their hat.
When uncovered, a buzz of enquiry runs round:
'Pray what are their crimes?'—'They've been pilfering found.'
'But, pray, whom have they pilfered?'—'A Doctor, I hear.'
'What, yon solemn-faced, odd-looking man that stands near?'
'The same.'—'What a pity! how does it surprise one!
Two handsomer culprits I never set eyes on!'
Then their friends all come round me with cringing and leering,
To melt me to pity and soften my swearing.

First Sir Charles advances with phrases well strung:
'Consider, dear Doctor, the girls are but young.'
'The younger the worse,' I return him again;
'It shows that their habits are all dyed in grain.'
'But then they're so handsome, one's bosom it grieves.'
'What signifies handsome, when people are thieves?'
'But where is your justice? Their cases are hard.'

'What signifies justice? I want the reward.
There's the parish of Edmonton offers forty pound;
there's the parish of St Leonard, Shoreditch, offers forty
pound; there's the parish of Tyburn, from the Hog-in-the-Pound
to St Giles's watch-house, offers forty pounds, I shall have all that
if I convict them.'

'But consider their case: it may yet be your own!
And see how they kneel: is your heart made of stone?'
This moves, so at last I agree to relent,
For ten pounds in hand and ten pounds to be spent.
The judge takes the hint, having seen what we drive at,
And lets them both off with correction in private.

OLIVER GOLDSMITH

The Hundred Best Books

First there's the Bible,
   And then the Koran,
Odgers on Libel,
   Pope's Essay on Man,
Confessions of Rousseau,
   The Essays of Lamb,
Robinson Crusoe
   And Omar Khayyám,
Volumes of Shelley
   And Venerable Bede,
Machiavelli
   And Captain Mayne Reid,
Fox upon Martyrs
   And Liddell and Scott,
Stubbs on the Charters,
   The works of La Motte,
The Seasons by Thomson,
   And Paul de Verlaine,
Theodore Mommsen
   And Clemens (Mark Twain),

The Rocks of Hugh Miller,
  The Mill on the Floss,
The Poems of Schiller,
  The Iliados,
Don Quixote (Cervantes),
  La Pucelle by Voltaire,
Inferno (that's Dante's),
  And Vanity Fair,
Conybeare-Howson,
  Brillat-Savarin,
And Baron Munchausen,
  Mademoiselle De Maupin,
The Dramas of Marlowe
  The Three Musketeers,
Clarissa Harlowe,
  And the Pioneers,
Sterne's Tristram Shandy,
  The Ring and the Book,
And Handy Andy,
  And Captain Cook,
The Plato of Jowett,
  And Mill's Pol. Econ.,
The Haunts of Howitt,
  The Encheiridion,
Lothair by Disraeli,
  And Boccaccio,
The Student's Paley,
  And Westward Ho!
The Pharmacopœia,
  Macaulay's Lays,
Of course The Medea,
  And Sheridan's Plays,
The Odes of Horace,
  And Verdant Green,
The Poems of Morris,
  The Faery Queen,
The Stones of Venice,
  Natural History (White's),
And then Pendennis,
  The Arabian Nights,
Cicero's Orations,

Plain Tales from the Hills,
The Wealth of Nations,
    And Byles on Bills,
As in a Glass Darkly,
    Demosthenes' Crown,
The Treatise of Berkeley,
    Tom Hughes's Tom Brown,
The Mahabharata,
    The Humour of Hook,
The Kreutzer Sonata,
    And Lalla Rookh,
Great Battles by Creasy,
    And Hudibras,
And Midshipman Easy,
    And Rasselas,
Shakespeare *in extenso*
    And the Æneid,
And Euclid (Colenso),
    The Woman who Did,
Poe's Tales of Mystery,
    Then Rabelais,
Guizot's French History,
    And Men of the Day,
Rienzi, by Lytton,
    The Poems of Burns,
The Story of Britain,
    The Journey (that's Sterne's),
The House of Seven Gables,
    Carroll's Looking-Glass,
Æsop his Fables
    And Leaves of Grass,
Departmental Ditties,
    The Woman in White,
The Tale of Two Cities,
    Ships that Pass in the Night,
Meredith's Feverel,
    Gibbon's Decline,
Walter Scott's Peveril,
    And—some verses of mine.

MOSTYN T. PIGGOTT

Heaven

Fish (fly-replete, in depth of June,
Dawdling away their wat'ry noon)
Ponder deep wisdom, dark or clear,
Each secret fishy hope or fear.
Fish say, they have their Stream and Pond;
But is there anything Beyond?
This life cannot be All, they swear,
For how unpleasant, if it were!
One may not doubt that, somehow, Good
Shall come of Water and of Mud;
And, sure, the reverent eye must see
A Purpose in Liquidity.
We darkly know, by Faith we cry,
The future is not Wholly Dry.
Mud unto mud!—Death eddies near—
Not here the appointed End, not here!
But somewhere, beyond Space and Time,
Is wetter water, slimier slime!
And there (they trust) there swimmeth One
Who swam ere rivers were begun,
Immense, of fishy form and mind,
Squamous, omnipotent, and kind;
And under that Almighty Fin,
The littlest fish may enter in.
Oh! never fly conceals a hook,
Fish say, in the Eternal Brook,
But more than mundane weeds are there,
And mud, celestially fair;
Fat caterpillars drift around,
And Paradisal grubs are found;
Unfading moths, immortal flies,
And the worm that never dies.
And in that Heaven of all their wish,
There shall be no more land, say fish.

RUPERT BROOKE

Πάντων γλυκύτατον μεταβολή★

Frankly, I do not greatly care
   Always to be my best;
I like sometimes to take the air,
   Sometimes to take a rest.

Sometimes, austere philosopher,
   I seek what thought reveals:
At other times I much prefer
   Silk stockings and high heels.

And sometimes Beauty moves me much,
   And sometimes Pleasure more;
Great art seems sometimes double Dutch
   And Amabel a bore.

Is God's clock always just at noon?
   Is Heaven always fair?
May angels not adore the moon?
   Is there no tea-time there?

Why, then, how blest are we on earth,
   Who know an ampler range,
With blondes and browns and grief and mirth
   And, above all things, Change.

CLIVE BELL

★ *'Change is the sweetest thing of all' or 'Variety is the spice of life'.*

A Song

For my brother Leslie Finch. Upon a punch bowl

From the park and the play,
   And Whitehall come away,
To the punch-bowl, by far more inviting.
   To the fops and the beaux,
   Leave those dull empty shows,
And see here what is truly delighting.

The half globe 'tis in figure,
  (And would it were bigger)
Yet here's the whole universe floating;
  Here's titles and places,
  Rich lands and fair faces,
And all that is worthy our doting.

  'Twas a world like to this
  The hot Grecian did miss,
Of whom histories keep such a pother,
  To the bottom he sunk,
  And when one he had drunk,
Grew maudlin and wept for another.

LADY WINCHILSEA

To the Virgins to Make Much of Time

Gather ye rose-buds while ye may,
  Old Time is still a-flying;
And this same flower that smiles today,
  Tomorrow will be dying.

The glorious lamp of heaven, the Sun,
  The higher he's a-getting,
The sooner will his race be run,
  And nearer he's to setting.

That age is best, which is the first,
  When youth and blood are warmer
But being spent, the worse, and worst
  Times still succeed the former.

Then be not coy, but use your time,
  And while you may, go marry:
For having lost but once your prime,
  You may for ever tarry.

ROBERT HERRICK

George Eliot

George Eliot was so like a horse
That bookies on the Gatwick course
Shouted the odds against her when
She came there with some gentlemen;
And there was always quite a stir
When punters put their shirts on her.

But doubt creeps in. *The Mill on the Floss*
Was never written by a hoss.

J. B. MORTON

Askew, We Ask You

Gertrude—there's a good old scout!
What's it what's it all about?
Hear a tortured hemisphere
Begging you to make it clear.
Drop a clue or slip a hint
Touching on the what-you-print,
What-you-print and what-there's-in't.

Abdicate the role of sibyl,
At your secret let us nibble.
Pray divulge, reveal, disclose
In communicable prose
Why a rose a rose a rose.

Are you wilfully obscure?
Are you puerile or mature?
We are anything but sure.

Are you spoofing or profound?
Is there sense within the sound?
Will you properly expound?

100

Is your highly Orphic text
Meant for this world or the next?
We concede we are perplexed.

Is it genius, is it sham?
Parlor game or cryptogram?
Will you answer kindly, Ma'am?

Are you hollow or a mine?
One remembers Shakespeare's line:
'Sermons lie concealed in Stein.'

Gertrude answers, slightly bored:
'Gertrude is her own reward.'

MELVILLE CANE

Rigid Body Sings

Gin a body meet a body
    Flyin' through the air,
Gin a body hit a body,
    Will it fly? and where?
Ilka impact has its measure,
    Ne'er a' ane hae I,
Yet a' the lads they measure me,
    Or, at least, they try.

Gin a body meet a body
    Altogether free,
How they travel afterwards
    We do not always see.
Ilka problem has its method
    By analytics high;
For me, I ken na ane o' them,
    But what the waur am I?

JAMES CLERK MAXWELL

Zeke

Gnarly and bent and deaf's a post
Pore ole Ezekiel Purvis
Goeth crippin' slowly up the 'ill
To the Commoonion Survis.

And tappy tappy up the haisle
Goeth stick and brassy ferrule:
And Passon 'ath to stoopy down
An' 'olley in ees yerole.

L. A. G. STRONG

Good and Bad Luck

Good Luck is the gayest of all gay girls;
  Long in one place she will not stay:
Back from your brow she strokes the curls,
  Kisses you quick and flies away.

But Madame Bad Luck soberly comes
  And stays—no fancy has she for flitting,—
Snatches of true-love songs she hums,
  And sits by your bed, and brings her knitting.

JOHN HAY

On Mundane Acquaintances

Good morning, Algernon: Good morning, Percy.
Good morning, Mrs Roebeck. Christ have mercy!

HILAIRE BELLOC

Elegy—On the Death of a Mad Dog

Good people all, of every sort,
　Give ear unto my song;
And if you find it wond'rous short,—
　It cannot hold you long.

In Islington there was a man,
　Of whom the world might say,
That still a godly race he ran,—
　Whene'er he went to pray.

A kind and gentle heart he had,
　To comfort friends and foes;
The naked every day he clad,—
　When he put on his clothes.

And in that town a dog was found,
　As many dogs there be,
Both mongrel, puppy, whelp and hound,
　And curs of low degree.

This dog and man at first were friends;
　But when a pique began,
The dog, to gain some private ends,
　Went mad, and bit the man.

Around from all the neighbouring streets
　The wondering neighbours ran,
And swore the dog had lost his wits,
　To bite so good a man.

The wound it seemed both sore and sad
　To every Christian eye;
And while they swore the dog was mad,
　They swore the man would die.

But soon a wonder came to light
　That showed the rogues they lied;
The man recovered of the bite,
　The dog it was that died.

OLIVER GOLDSMITH

An Elegy

On that glory of her sex, Mrs Mary Blaize

Good people all, with one accord,
   Lament for Madam Blaize,
Who never wanted a good word—
   From those who spoke her praise.

The needy seldom passed her door,
   And always found her kind;
She freely lent to all the poor,—
   Who left a pledge behind.

She strove the neighbourhood to please,
   With manners wond'rous winning;
And never followed wicked ways,—
   Unless when she was sinning.

At church, in silks and satins new,
   With hoop of monstrous size,
She never slumbered in her pew,—
   But when she shut her eyes.

Her love was sought, I do aver,
   By twenty beaux and more;
The king himself has followed her,—
   When she has walked before.

But now her wealth and finery fled,
   Her hangers-on cut short all;
The doctors found, when she was dead,—
   Her last disorder mortal.

Let us lament, in sorrow sore,
   For Kent-street well may say,
That had she lived a twelvemonth more,—
   She had not died today.

OLIVER GOLDSMITH

DORSET COUNTY LIBRARY

Great Grandmama

Great Grandmama wore drawers of lace,
She drank her wine at tea,
She put on all her clothes, then went
And sat down in the sea.

She walked on esplanades in gales,
With gentlemen for props,
The wind came down, her hoops went round
Like twirling whipping-tops.

She had fat legs, she had tight boots,
She flirted through the dirt;
Her little Arab horse flew on
Beneath festoons of skirt.

Great-grandmama, you drooped, appealed,
With spaniels' ears for hair;
You were as cunning as a mouse,
As pear-shaped as a pear.

DOROTHY WELLESLEY

Soliloquy of the Spanish Cloister

Gr-r-r—there go, my heart's abhorrence!
  Water your damned flower-pots, do!
If hate killed men, Brother Lawrence,
  God's blood, would not mine kill you!
What? your myrtle-bush wants trimming
  Oh, that rose has prior claims—
Needs its leaden vase filled brimming?
  Hell dry you up with its flames!

At the meal we sit together:
    Salve tibi! I must hear
Wise talk of the kind of weather,
    Sort of season, time of year:
Not a plenteous cork-crop: scarcely
    Dare we hope oak-galls, I doubt:
What's the Latin name for 'parsley'?
    What's the Greek name for Swine's Snout?

Whew! We'll have our platter burnished,
    Laid with care on our own shelf!
With a fire-new spoon we're furnished,
    And a goblet for ourself,
Rinsed like something sacrificial
    Ere 'tis fit to touch our chaps—
Marked with L. for our initial!
    (He, he! There his lily snaps!)

Saint, forsooth! While brown Dolores
    Squats outside the Convent bank,
With Sanchicha, telling stories,
    Steeping tresses in the tank,
Blue-black, lustrous, thick like horsehairs
    —Can't I see his dead eye glow
Bright, as 'twere a Barbary corsair's?
    (That is, if he'd let it show!)

When he finishes refection,
    Knife and fork he never lays
Cross-wise, to my recollection,
    As do I, in Jesu's praise,
I, the Trinity illustrate,
    Drinking watered orange-pulp—
In three sips the Arian frustrate;
    While he drains his at one gulp!

Oh, those melons! If he's able
　　We're to have a feast; so nice!
One goes to the Abbot's table,
　　All of us get each a slice.
How go on your flowers? None double?
　　Not one fruit-sort can you spy?
Strange!—And I, too, at such trouble,
　　Keep 'em close-nipped on the sly!

There's a great text in Galatians,
　　Once you trip on it, entails
Twenty-nine distinct damnations,
　　One sure, if another fails.
If I trip him just a-dying,
　　Sure of Heaven as sure can be,
Spin him round and send him flying
　　Off to Hell, a Manichee?

Or, my scrofulous French novel,
　　On grey paper with blunt type!
Simply glance at it, you grovel
　　Hand and foot in Belial's gripe:
If I double down its pages
　　At the woeful sixteenth print,
When he gathers his greengages,
　　Ope a sieve and slip it in't?

Or, there's Satan!—one might venture
　　Pledge one's soul to him, yet leave
Such a flaw in the indenture
　　As he'd miss till, past retrieve,
Blasted lay that rose-acacia
　　We're so proud of! *Hy, Zy, Hine* . . .
'St, there's Vespers! *Plena gratiâ*
　　Ave, Virgo! Gr-r-r—you swine!

ROBERT BROWNING

Up at a Villa—Down in the City

(As distinguished by an Italian person of quality)

I

Had I but plenty of money, money enough and to spare,
The house for me, no doubt, were a house in the city-square;
Ah, such a life, such a life, as one leads at the window there!

II

Something to see, by Bacchus, something to hear, at least!
There, the whole day long, one's life is a perfect feast;
While up at a villa one lives, I maintain it, no more than a beast.

III

Well now, look at our villa! stuck like the horn of a bull
Just on a mountain-edge as bare as the creature's skull,
Save a mere shag of a bush with hardly a leaf to pull!
—I scratch my own, sometimes, to see if the hair's turned wool.

IV

But the city, oh the city—the square with the houses! Why?
They are stone-faced, white as a curd, there's something to take
   the eye!
Houses in four straight lines, not a single front awry;
You watch who crosses and gossips, who saunters, who hurries
   by;
Green blinds, as a matter of course, to draw when the sun gets
   high;
And the shops with fanciful signs which are painted properly.

V

What of a villa? Though winter be over in March by rights,
'T is May perhaps ere the snow shall have withered well off the
   heights:
You've the brown ploughed land before, where the oxen steam
   and wheeze,
And the hills over-smoked behind by the faint grey olive-trees.

VI

Is it better in May, I ask you? You've summer all at once;
In a day he leaps complete with a few strong April suns.
'Mid the sharp short emerald wheat, scarce risen three fingers
    well,
The wild tulip, at end of its tube, blows out its great red bell
Like a thin clear bubble of blood, for the children to pick and sell.

VII

Is it ever hot in the square? There's a fountain to spout and splash!
In the shade it sings and springs; in the shine such foam-bows flash
On the horses with curling fish-tails, that prance and paddle and
    pash
Round the lady atop in her conch—fifty gazers do not abash,
Though all that she wears is some weeds round her waist in a sort
    of sash.

VIII

All the year long at the villa, nothing to see though you linger,
Except yon cypress that points like death's lean lifted forefinger.
Some think fireflies pretty, when they mix i' the corn and mingle,
Or thrid the stinking hemp till the stalks of it seem a-tingle.
Late August or early September, the stunning cicala is shrill,
And the bees keep their tiresome whine round the resinous firs on
    the hill.
Enough of the seasons,—I spare you the months of the fever and
    chill.

IX

Ere you open your eyes in the city, the blessed church-bells begin:
No sooner the bells leave off than the diligence rattles in:
You get the pick of the news, and it costs you never a pin.
By-and-by there's the travelling doctor gives pills, lets blood,
    draws teeth;
Or the Pulcinello-trumpet breaks up the market beneath.
At the post-office such a scene-picture—the new play, piping hot!
And a notice how, only this morning, three liberal thieves were
    shot.
Above it, behold the Archbishop's most fatherly of rebukes,
And beneath, with his crown and his lion, some little new law of
    the Duke's!

Or a sonnet with flowery marge, to the Reverend Don So-and-so
Who is Dante, Boccaccio, Petrarca, Saint Jerome and Cicero,
'And moreover,' (the sonnet goes rhyming,) 'the skirts of Saint
    Paul has reached,
Having preached us those six Lent-lectures more unctuous than
    ever he preached.'
Noon strikes,—here sweeps the procession! our Lady borne
    smiling and smart
With a pink gauze gown all spangles, and seven swords stuck in
    her heart!
Bang-whang-whang goes the drum, *tootle-te-tootle* the fife;
No keeping one's haunches still: it's the greatest pleasure in life.

X

But bless you, it's dear—it's dear! fowls, wine, at double the rate.
They have clapped a new tax upon salt, and what oil pays passing
    the gate
It's a horror to think of. And so, the villa for me, not the city!
Beggars can scarcely be choosers: but still—ah, the pity, the pity!
Look, two and two go the priests, then the monks with cowls and
    sandals,
And the penitents dressed in white shirts, a-holding the yellow
    candles;
One, he carries a flag up straight, and another a cross with
    handles,
And the Duke's guard brings up the rear, for the better prevention
    of scandals:
Bang-whang-whang goes the drum, *tootle-te-tootle* the fife.
Oh, a day in the city-square, there is no such pleasure in life!

ROBERT BROWNING

To His Coy Mistress

Had we but world enough, and time,
This coyness, Lady, were no crime.
We would sit down, and think which way
To walk, and pass our long love's day.
Thou by the Indian Ganges' side
Should'st rubies find: I by the tide

Of Humber would complain. I would
Love you ten years before the Flood:
And you should if you please refuse
Till the conversion of the Jews.
My vegetable love should grow
Vaster than empires, and more slow.
An hundred years should go to praise
Thine eyes, and on thy forehead gaze.
Two hundred to adore each breast:
But thirty thousand to the rest.
An age at least to every part,
And the last age should show your heart.
For, Lady, you deserve this state;
Nor would I love at lower rate.
   But at my back I always hear
Time's winged chariot hurrying near:
And yonder all before us lie
Deserts of vast eternity.
Thy beauty shall no more be found;
Nor, in thy marble vault, shall sound
My echoing song: then worms shall try
That long preserved virginity:
And your quaint honour turn to dust;
And into ashes all my lust.
The grave's a fine and private place,
But none I think do there embrace.
   Now therefore, while the youthful hue
Sits on thy skin like morning dew,
And while thy willing soul transpires
At every pore with instant fires,
Now let us sport us while we may;
And now, like amorous birds of prey,
Rather at once our time devour,
Than languish in his slow-chapped power.
Let us roll all our strength, and all
Our sweetness, up into one ball:
And tear our pleasures with rough strife,
Thorough the iron gates of life.
Thus, though we cannot make our sun
Stand still, yet we will make him run.

ANDREW MARVELL

111

An Ode to We

(A hackneyed critic)

I

Hail, Plural Unit! who wouldst be
A Junto o'er my Muse and me,
    With dogmas to control us;
Hail mystic WE! grand Next-to-None!
Large body corporate of One!
    Important *OMNES, Solus!*

II

First Person Singular! pray why
Impregnate thus the Pronoun I?
    Of madness what a tissue!
To write as if with passion wild
Thou oft hadst got Thyself with child,
    And thou wert Self and Issue!

III

Thy voice, which counterfeits alone
A score of voices in its own,
    Awhile takes in the many:
Thus a bad one-pound note is passed
For twenty shillings, and at last
    Turns out not worth a penny.

IV

'Tis well for Thee no laws of thine
Can crush vile followers of the Nine.
    Thou *liv'st* upon the sinners;
And if all poets left off writing
Through thy anonymous inditing,
    Why, thou must leave off dinners.

V

For *Thou* couldst ne'er turn poet sure,
Laurels or luncheons to procure—
　　Witness thy present calling;
Else why not write thyself a name
So very humble, e'en in fame,
　　As mine which thou art mauling?

VI

Yet hold. Thou mayst on Pindus' heights
Have far out-soared my lowly flights—
　　No; that's a thought I'll smother:
The meanest bard among the mean,
Can he thus skulk behind a screen
　　And try to stab a brother?

VII

But come, one moment leave thy pen
Stuck in thy gall-bottle, and then
　　Smooth o'er thy forehead's furrow.
Let's chat. Where got'st thou thy employ?
Art thou of Dublin city joy?
　　Or bonny Edinburgh?

VIII

Or art John Bull, in garret crammed?
'Spirit of health, or goblin damned?'
　　Be *something* for thy credit.
Perhaps thou'rt he who (as they say)
Cut up the last successful play,
　　And never saw nor read it?

IX

Be what thou wilt; when all is done,
To me thou'rt (like Thyself) *All One*.
　　Thou'rt welcome still to flog on;
For till one addled egg's a brood,
Or twenty WEs a multitude,
　　My Muse and I will jog on.

X

Now shouldst thou *praise* me after all,
Though that indeed were comical,
   What honour could I pin to't?
If porridge were my only cheer,
Thy praise or blame must both appear
   Two tasteless chips thrown into't.

XI

Then, WE, shake hands, and part! No breach,
No *difference* 'twixt us I beseech!
   Although our *business varies:*
Thine is detraction, mine is jest—
Which occupation pray is best,
   Thy spite or my 'Vagaries?'*

GEORGE COLMAN THE YOUNGER

* *The collection of Colman's work in which these verses appeared was entitled* Poetical Vagaries.

On the Death of a Female Officer of the Salvation Army

'Hallelujah!' was the only observation
That escaped Lieutenant-Colonel Mary Jane,
When she tumbled off the platform in the station,
And was cut in little pieces by the train.
   Mary Jane, the train is through yer,
   Hallelujah, Hallelujah!
We will gather up the fragments that remain.

A. E. HOUSMAN

from A Review of Schools

Hark! how the sire of chits, whose future share
Of classic food begins to be his care,
With his own likeness placed on either knee,
Indulges all a father's heartfelt glee;

114

And tells them, as he strokes their silver locks,
That they must soon learn Latin, and to box:
Then turning, he regales his listening wife
With all the adventures of his early life;
His skill in coachmanship, or driving chaise,
In bilking tavern bills, and spouting plays;
What shifts he used, detected in a scrape,
How he was flogged, or had the luck to escape;
What sums he lost at play, and how he sold
Watch, seals, and all—till all his pranks are told.
Retracing thus his *frolics* ('tis a name
That palliates deeds of folly and of shame),
He gives the local bias all its sway;
Resolves that where he played his sons shall play,
And destines their bright genius to be shown
Just in the scene where he displayed his own.
The meek and bashful boy will soon be taught
To be as bold and forward as he ought;
The rude will scuffle through with ease enough,
Great schools suit best the sturdy and the rough.
Ah, happy designation, prudent choice,
The event is sure; expect it, and rejoice!
Soon see your wish fulfilled in either child,
The pert made perter, and the tame made wild. . . .

The father who designs his babe a priest,
Dreams him episcopally such at least;
And, while the playful jockey scours the room
Briskly, astride upon the parlour broom,
In fancy sees him more superbly ride
In coach with purple lined, and mitres on its side.
Events improbable and strange as these,
Which only a parental eye foresees,
A public school shall bring to pass with ease.
But how? resides such virtue in that air,
As must create an appetite for prayer?
And will it breathe into him all the zeal,
That candidates for such a prize should feel;
To take the lead, and be the foremost still
In all true worth and literary skill?
'Ah, blind to bright futurity, untaught
The knowledge of the world, and dull of thought!

Church leaders are not always mounted best
By learned clerks, and Latinists professed.
The exalted prize demands an upward look.
Not to be found by poring on a book.
Small skill in Latin, and still less in Greek,
Is more than adequate to all I seek.
Let erudition grace him, or not grace,
I give the bauble but the second place;
His wealth, fame, honours, all that I intend,
Subsist and centre in one point—a friend.
A friend, whate'er he studies or neglects,
Shall give him consequence, heal all defects.
His intercourse with peers and sons of peers—
There dawns the splendour of his future years;
In that bright quarter his propitious skies
Shall blush betimes, and there his glory rise.
Your Lordship, and *Your Grace!* what school can teach
A rhetoric equal to those parts of speech?
What need of Homer's verse, or Tully's prose,
Sweet interjections! if he learn but those?
Let reverend churls his ignorance rebuke,
Who starve upon a dog's-eared Pentateuch,
The parson knows enough who knows a duke.'

WILLIAM COWPER

The Brewer's Man

Have I a wife? Bedam I have!
But we was badly mated.
I hit her a great clout one night,
And now we're separated.
And mornings going to me work
I meets her on the quay:
'Good mornin' to ye, ma'm!' says I,
'To hell with ye!' says she.

L. A. G. STRONG

116

He Lived Amidst Th'Untrodden Ways

(*Wordsworth*)

He lived amidst th'untrodden ways
  To Rydal Lake that lead;
A bard whom there were none to praise,
  And very few to read.

Behind a cloud his mystic sense,
  Deep hidden, who can spy?
Bright as the night when not a star
  Is shining in the sky.

Unread his works—his 'Milk White Doe'
  With dust is dark and dim;
It's still in Longman's shop, and oh!
  The difference to him!

HARTLEY COLERIDGE

Henry VIII

Henry the Eighth
Took a thuctheththion of mateth,
He inthithted that the monkth
Were a lathy lot of thkunkth.

E. CLERIHEW BENTLEY

The Roadmender

Here be an old man crackin' stones,
And the damp is in his bones.
His conduct don't at all agree
With story-book philosophy.

117

I've seed en stoopy for his shoes
And hurt his ancient creaky thews;
And strings of spittin' swears 'e said,
And clipped his grandchild 'cross the 'ead.

L. A. G. STRONG

Jesse Welch

Here be the bones of Jesse Welch,
Who died of keeping back a belch;
Which same did in his pipes expand
And blew him to the Heavenly Band.

L. A. G. STRONG

On the University Carrier

*who sickened in the time of his vacancy, being forbid to go to
London by reason of the plague*

Here lies old Hobson. Death hath broke his girt,
And here, alas, hath laid him in the dirt;
Or else the ways being foul, twenty to one,
He's here stuck in a slough and overthrown.
'Twas such a shifter that, if truth were known,
Death was half glad when he had got him down;
For he had any time this ten years full
Dodged with him betwixt Cambridge and *The Bull*.
And surely, Death could never have prevailed,
Had not his weekly course of carriage failed;
But lately, finding him so long at home,
And thinking now his journey's end was come,
And that he had ta'en up his latest inn,
In the kind office of a chamberlin
Shewed him his room where he must lodge that night,
Pulled off his boots, and took away the light.
If any ask for him, it shall be said,
'Hobson has supped, and's newly gone to bed.'

JOHN MILTON

118

Ephibol on My Dear Love Isabella

Here lies sweet Isabel in bed,
With a nightcap on her head.
Her skin is soft, her face is fair,
And she has very pretty hair.
She and I in bed lies nice,
And undisturbed by rats and mice.
She is disgusted with Mr Wurgan,
Though he plays upon the organ.
A knot of ribbons on her head,
Her cheek is tinged with conscious red.
Her head it rests upon a pilly,
And she is not so very silly.
Her nails are neat, her teeth are white,
Her eyes are very, very bright.
In a conspicuous town she lives,
And to the poor her money gives.
Here ends sweet Isabella's story—
And may it be much to her glory.

MARJORIE FLEMING (aged 8)

Stairs

Here's to the man who invented stairs
And taught our feet to soar!
He was the first who ever burst
Into a second floor.

The world would be downstairs today
Had he not found the key;
So let his name go down to fame,
Whatever it may be.

OLIVER HERFORD

Chocolates

Here the seats are; George, old man,
Get some chocolates while you can.

Quick, the curtain's going to rise
(Either Bradbury's or Spry's).

'The Castle ramparts, Elsinore'
(That's not sufficient, get some more).

There's the *Ghost*: he does look wan
(Help yourself, and pass them on).

Doesn't *Hamlet* do it well?
(This one is a caramel).

Polonius's beard is fine
(Don't you grab; that big one's mine).

Look, the *King* can't bear the play
(Throw that squashy one away).

Now the *King* is at his prayers
(Splendid, there are two more layers).

Hamlet's going for his mother
(Come on, Tony, have another).

Poor *Ophelia*! Look, she's mad
(However many's Betty had?).

The *Queen* is dead, and so's the *King*
(Keep that lovely silver string).

Now even *Hamlet* can no more
(Pig! You've dropped it on the floor).

That last Act's simply full of shocks
(There's several left, so bring the box).

GUY BOAS

Her Voice

'Her voice was darker than it was'—*James Huneker*

Her voice was darker than of old;
    Her hair lacked melody;
Her feet at times were shrill and cold,
    And wandered from the key.

Her gown was tuneful, sweet, and low,
    Cut scherzo to the waist,
With semi-quavers row on row
    In soft, melodious taste.

Her pale rendition failed to show
    The shading of the score.
Her colour scheme was pitched too low,
    And bounded on the floor.

Her gestures were inclined to flat,
    Regardless of their hue.
Her trills were ambidextrous, fat
    And slightly tinged with blue.

Her phrasing was a shade too brown,
    And though superbly placed,
Her smile was loud enough to drown
    The roses at her waist.

The programme was perhaps a bit
    Too blonde for her ambition—
Only one number scored a hit,
    And that was *Intermission*.

OLIVER HERFORD

121

A Window Cleaner

He's gone and we are left to see
Through a glass darkly—not so he.
By Henry's death we lose, he gains.
He's gone where there are no more pains.

GEORGE ROSTREVOR HAMILTON

Peace

A study

He stood, a worn-out city clerk—
  Who'd toiled, and seen no holiday,
For forty years from dawn to dark—
  Alone beside Cærmarthen Bay.

He felt the salt spray on his lips;
  Heard children's voices on the sands;
Up the sun's path he saw the ships
  Sail on and on to other lands;

And laughed aloud. Each sight and sound
  To him was joy too deep for tears;
He sat him on the beach, and bound
  A blue bandana round his ears:

And thought how, posted near his door,
  His own green door on Camden Hill,
Two bands at least, most likely more,
  Were mingling at their own sweet will

Verdi with Vance. And at the thought
  He laughed again, and softly drew
That *Morning Herald* that he'd bought
  Forth from his breast, and read it through.

CHARLES STUART CALVERLEY

The Mad Gardener's Illusions

He thought he saw an Elephant,
  That practised on a fife:
He looked again, and found it was
  A letter from his wife.
'At length I realize,' he said,
  'The bitterness of life.'

He thought he saw a Banker's Clerk
  Descending from the bus:
He looked again, and found it was
  A Hippopotamus:
'If this should stay to dine,' he said,
  'There won't be much for us!'

He thought he saw a Rattlesnake
  That questioned him in Greek:
He looked again and found it was
  The Middle of Next Week.
'The one thing I regret,' he said,
  'Is that it cannot speak!'

He thought he saw an Albatross
  That fluttered round the lamp:
He looked again, and found it was
  A Penny-Postage-Stamp.
'You'd best be getting home,' he said:
  'The nights are very damp!'

He thought he saw a Buffalo
  Upon the chimney-piece:
He looked again, and found it was
  His Sister's Husband's Niece.
'Unless you leave this house,' he said
  'I'll send for the Police!'

He thought he saw a Coach-and-Four
    That stood beside his bed:
He looked again and found it was
    A Bear without a Head.
'Poor thing,' he said, 'poor silly thing!
    It's waiting to be fed!'

LEWIS CARROLL

Autumn

He told his life story, to Mrs Courtly
Who was a widow. 'Let us get married shortly,'
He said. 'I am no longer passionate,
But we can have some conversation before it is too late.'

STEVIE SMITH

On the Death of a German Philosopher

He wrote *The I and the It*
He wrote *The It and the Me*
He died at Marienbad
And now we are all at sea.

STEVIE SMITH

Emphatics

Ho! Miss Perkins, ring the clarion,
Call the lodgers home to tea.
Hark, the telephone is ringing
Bow the head and bend the knee.

124

DORSET COUNTY LIBRARY

Lemonade and soda water,
Gramophones all painted new
In the rocking-chair are waiting
For their turn at Irish stew.

On the wings of evening wafting,
Cupboards play at hide and seek,
Wardrobes in their narrow setting
Hide a turnip and a leek.

Pins and needles clutch a thimble,
In a basin stamps are wet;
From a musty brown potato
Voices tell us not to fret.

On a low and drooping willow
Water cans all bathed in dew
Sing in weak and trembling accents
Metaphors to me and you.

Soap and suds all wildly clamouring
Wash the flannel on its nose,
While the elephant and weasel
Give the shoelift half a rose.

Paperweights complain and whimper
To a top-hat standing by;
And a bluebottle of learning
Shows a tadpole how to fly.

Motor-cars with perforation
Chase a mangle round a bed.
One small hen encased in marble
Wraps a doyley round her head.

Ha! Miss Perkins, stay thy clanging,
On the stairs the lodgers kneel.
While in dainty linen jerseys
Calves' heads dine on tripe and heel.

'ELECTROPLATE'

To Dr D

Honoured Doctor Dryasdust,
Look to your laurels: you really *must*.
You seem so very moist indeed
When one compares you with Herbert Read.

MAX BEERBOHM

Two Sonnets Composed by a Computer

I

How can the purple yeti be so red,
Or chestnuts, like a widgeon, calmly groan?
No sheep is quite as crooked as a bed,
Though chickens ever try to hide a bone.
I grieve that greasy turnips slowly march:
Indeed, inflated is the icy pig:
For as the alligator strikes the larch,
So sighs the grazing goldfish for a wig.
Oh, has the pilchard argued with a top?
Say never that the parsnip is too weird!
I tell thee that a wolf-man will not hop
And no man ever praised the convex beard.
Effulgent is the day when bishops turn:
So let not then the doctor wake the urn!

II

Oh salamander, tell me why the moon
Should be outrageous when the salmon march:
A chuckling damsel never cleans a prune,
Although 'tis true that maidens wake a larch.
My heart is eerie, likewise is it smug,
When e'er I see the reckless carrots talk;
I praised the spectral pirate—for a bug
Had foully gibbered as it stroked a stork.
Alas! the days of nose-flute, crab and shoe
Are gone, and now the tragic ospreys turn;

Outrageous was the ostrich, now so true
And chickens cannot heat the blushing urn.
Inflated is the day when bishops scream:
So let not then the teapot squash the bream!

Lines to Ralph Hodgson Esqre

How delightful to meet Mr Hodgson!
    (Everyone wants to know *him*)
With his musical sound
And his Baskerville Hound
Which, at just one word from his master
Will follow you faster and faster
And tear you limb from limb.
How delightful to meet Mr Hodgson!
Who is worshipped by all waitresses
(They regard him as something apart)
While on his palate fine he presses
The juice of the gooseberry tart.
How delightful to meet Mr Hodgson!
    (Everyone wants to know *him*).
He has 999 canaries
And round his head finches and fairies
In jubilant rapture skim.
How delightful to meet Mr Hodgson!
    (Everyone wants to meet *him*).

T. S. ELIOT

How Doth . . .

How doth the little crocodile
Improve his shining tail,
And pour the waters of the Nile
On every golden scale!

How cheerfully he seems to grin,
How neatly spreads his claws,
And welcomes little fishes in
With gently smiling jaws!

LEWIS CARROLL

An Old Pocket-book

How fast the years go! Here's a book
  I haven't seen for ages;
I'll open it, and have a look—
  How yellow are the pages!
'Belinda B——!' Belinda B——!
  I recognize the writing,
I recollect the early tea,
  The time, and the inditing.

I recollect the tea and toast,
  The larking and the laughter,
The moonlit stroll to see the ghost,
  The rheumatism after:
I recollect the rustic seat—
  'Your friends,' you feared, 'had missed you'—
I recollect you looked so sweet,
  Belinda, that I kissed you.

And then, this pocket-book of mine—
  How well I recollect it!
It just had cost me one-and-nine,—
  You wanted to inspect it;
And then you said you'd write your name—
  'That is, if you will let me.'
You wrote 'Belinda B——', the same,
  Then said, 'You'll soon forget me.'

Ah, yes, Belinda B——, my rhymes
    Have sung of pretty faces,
And fortune's self has set my times
    In very pleasant places;
But still, Belinda, I must own
    Our younger days were jolly,
Though now we think we should have known
    It was but children's folly.

How far by simply musing thus
    One's thoughts are backward carried!
The gout has tortured one of us,
    And you've been ten years married.
This pocket-book of mine—let's see—
    The years have gone in plenty;
Last year I owned to forty-three,
    Then I was one-and-twenty.

                              GORDON CAMPBELL

Eye-opener

How like a man, is Man, who rises late
And gazes on his unwashed dinner plate
And gazes on the bottles, empty too,
All gulphed in last night's loud long how-do-you-do,
—Although one glass yet holds a gruesome bait—
How like to Man is this man and his fate,
Still drunk and stumbling through the rusty trees
To breakfast on stale rum, sardines and peas.

                              MALCOLM LOWRY

To Mr John Moore

Author of the celebrated worm-powder

How much, egregious Moore, are we
   Deceived by shows and forms!
Whate'er we think, whate'er we see,
   All human kind are worms.

Man is a very worm by birth,
   Vile reptile, weak and vain:
Awhile he crawls upon the earth,
   Then shrinks to earth again.

That woman is a worm, we find
   E'er since our grandame's evil;
She first conversed with her own kind,
   That ancient worm, the devil.

The learned themselves we book-worms name,
   The blockhead is a slow-worm;
The nymph whose tail is all on flame,
   Is aptly termed a glow-worm.

The fops are painted butterflies,
   That flutter for a day;
First from a worm they take their rise,
   And in a worm decay.

The flatterer an earwig grows;
   Thus worms suit all conditions;
Misers are muck-worms, silk-worms beaus,
   And death-watches physicians.

That statesmen have the worm, is seen
   By all their winding play;
Their conscience is a worm within,
   That gnaws them night and day.

Ah, Moore! thy skill were well employed,
    And greater gain would rise,
If thou coulds't make the courtier void
    The worm that never dies!

O learned friend of Abchurch Lane,
    Who sett'st our entrails free;
Vain is thy art, thy powder vain,
    Since worms shall eat e'en thee.

Our fate thou only canst adjourn
    Some few short years, no more!
Ev'n Button's wits to worms shall turn,
    Who maggots were before.

ALEXANDER POPE

Poeta Fit, Non Nascitur

'How shall I be a poet?
    How shall I write in rhyme?
You told me once the very wish
    Partook of the sublime:
Then tell me how. Don't put me off
    With your "another time".'

The old man smiled to see him,
    To hear his sudden sally;
He liked the lad to speak his mind
    Enthusiastically,
And thought, 'There's no hum-drum in him,
    Nor any shilly-shally.'

'And would you be a poet
    Before you've been to school?
Ah well! I hardly thought you
    So absolute a fool.
First learn to be spasmodic—
    A very simple rule.

'For first you write a sentence,
     And then you chop it small!
Then mix the bits, and sort them out
     Just as they chance to fall:
The order of the phrases makes
     No difference at all.

'Then, if you'd be impressive,
     Remember what I say,
That abstract qualities begin
     With capitals alway:
The True, the Good, the Beautiful,
     These are the things that pay!

'Next, when you are describing
     A shape, or sound, or tint;
Don't state the matter plainly,
     But put it in a hint;
And learn to look at all things
     With a sort of mental squint.'

'For instance, if I wished, Sir,
     Of mutton-pies to tell,
Should I say "Dreams of fleecy flocks
     Pent in a wheaten cell"?'
'Why, yes,' the old man said: 'that phrase
     Would answer very well.

'Then, fourthly, there are epithets
     That suit with any word—
As well as Harvey's Reading Sauce
     With fish, or flesh, or bird—
Of these "wild", "lonely", "weary", "strange",
     Are much to be preferred.'

'And will it do, O will it do
     To take them in a lump—
As "the wild man went his weary way
     To a strange and lonely pump"?'
'Nay, nay! You must not hastily
     To such conclusions jump.

'Such epithets, like pepper,
    Give zest to what you write,
And, if you strew them sparely,
    They whet the appetite:
But if you lay them on too thick,
    You spoil the matter quite!

'Last, as to the arrangement;
    Your reader, you should show him,
Must take what information he
    Can get, and look for no im-
mature disclosure of the drift
    And purpose of your poem.

'Therefore, to test his patience—
    How much he can endure—
Mention no places, names, nor dates,
    And evermore be sure
Throughout the poem to be found
    Consistently obscure.

'First fix upon the limit
    To which it shall extend:
Then fill it up with "padding",
    (Beg some of any friend):
Your great *sensation-stanza*
    You place towards the end.

'Now try your hand, ere Fancy
    Have lost its present glow——'
'And then,' his grandson added,
    'We'll publish it, you know:
Green cloth—gold-lettered at the back,
    In duodecimo!'

Then proudly smiled the old man
    To see the eager lad
Rush madly for his pen and ink
    And for his blotting-pad—
But when he thought of *publishing*,
    His face grew stern and sad.

LEWIS CARROLL

To the Not Impossible Him

How shall I know, unless I go
    To Cairo and Cathay,
Whether or not this blessèd spot
    Is blest in every way?

Now it may be, the flower for me
    Is this beneath my nose;
How shall I tell, unless I smell
    The Carthaginian rose?

The fabric of my faithful love
    No power shall dim or ravel
Whilst I stay here,—but oh, my dear,
    If I should ever travel!

EDNA ST VINCENT MILLAY

Sheep

How unconcerned the grazing sheep
Behaving in such manner;
They stand upon their breakfast, they
Lie down upon their dinner.

This would not seem so strange to us
If fish grew round our legs,
If we had floors of marmalade
And beds of buttered eggs.

DOROTHY WELLESLEY

A Portrait of the Author

How unmemorable to meet Mr Fuller
With his eyes of piercing blue,
His talk getting duller and duller,
His eyes piercing all except you!

Was he, then, ever worth meeting,
Perhaps in his far-off youth?
No, after his amiable greeting
He soon appeared somewhat uncouth.

He has managed to carry on singing
In a voice rather trembly and harsh,
Like a rook that goes garglingly winging
Over rubbish dump, factory and marsh.

He hopes that the world will be thumbing
His works when he's no longer there.
What a hope, when those seeing him coming
Cross the street with a ruminant air!

There leap on his lap feline friskers
And assume a leonine pose;
Babies meditate over his whiskers
And pull his unaquiline nose.

But only a few adults mutter:
'We must have old Fuller to dine.
We might get him actually to utter
If we ply him with plenty of wine.'

ROY FULLER

Lines for Cuscuscaraway and Mirza Murad Ali Beg

How unpleasant to meet Mr Eliot!
With his features of clerical cut,
And his brow so grim
And his mouth so prim
And his conversation, so nicely
Restricted to What Precisely
And If and Perhaps and But.
How unpleasant to meet Mr Eliot!
With a bobtail cur
In a coat of fur
And a porpentine cat
And a wopsical hat:
How unpleasant to meet Mr Eliot!
    (Whether his mouth be open or shut.)

T. S. ELIOT

To Mr Hodgson

From on Board the Lisbon Packet

Huzza! Hodgson, we are going,
  Our embargo's off at last;
Favourable breezes blowing
  Bend the canvas o'er the mast.
From aloft the signal's streaming,
  Hark! the farewell gun is fired;
Sailors swearing, women screaming,
  Tell us that our time's expired.
     Here's a rascal
     Come to task all,
Prying from the Custom-house;

Trunks unpacking,
Cases cracking:
Not a corner for a mouse
'Scapes unsearched amid the racket,
Ere we sail on board the packet.

Now our boatmen quit their mooring,
And all hands must ply the oar;
Baggage from the quay is lowering,
We're impatient—push from shore.
'Have a care! that case holds liquor—
Stop the boat—I'm sick—O lord!'
'Sick, ma'am, hang it, you'll be sicker
Ere you've been an hour on board.'
Thus are screaming
Men and women,
Gemmen, ladies, servants, Jacks;
Here entangling,
All are wrangling,
Stuck together close as wax,—
Such the general noise and racket,
Ere we reach the Lisbon Packet.

Now we've reached her, lo! the Captain,
Gallant Kidd commands the crew;
Passengers their berths are clapped in,
Some to grumble—some to spew.

'Heyday! call you that a cabin?
Why 'tis hardly three feet square;
Not enough to stow Queen Mab in—
Who the deuce can harbour there?'
'Who, sir?—plenty—
Nobles twenty
Did at once my vessel fill.'
'Did they? Bacchus,
How you pack us!
Would to heaven they did so still:
Then I'd 'scape the heat and racket
Of the good ship, Lisbon Packet.'

Fletcher! Murray! Bob! where are you
    Stretched along the deck like logs—
Bear a hand you jolly tar, you!
    Here's a rope's-end for the dogs.
Hobhouse, muttering fearful curses
    As the hatchway down he rolls,
Now his breakfast, now his verses,
    Vomits forth—and d—s our souls.
        'Here's a stanza
        On Braganza——
Help!'—'A couplet?'—'No, a cup
        Of warm water'—
        'What's the matter?'
'Zounds, my liver's coming up;
I shall not survive the racket
Of this brutal Lisbon Packet.'

Now at length we're off for Turkey,
    Lord knows when we shall come back!
Breezes foul and tempests murky
    May unship us in a crack.
But, since life at most a jest is,
    As philosophers allow,
Still to laugh by far the best is,
    Then laugh on—as I do now.
        Laugh at all things,
        Great and small things,
    Sick or well, at sea or shore;
        While we're quaffing
        Let's have laughing—
Who the devil cares for more?

Some good wine! and who would lack it,
Even on board the Lisbon Packet?

                        LORD BYRON

Latter-Day Love-Song

I am the miser in the madhouse garden
singing and throwing pennies over the wall,
I am the man who lived with Dolly Varden,
sometime butler to the apostle Paul.
I met you in the crush, we heard the trumpets,
I wooed you through the winter and the spring,
when summer came with tea and buttered crumpets
I shot the bird of love upon the wing.

    I remember September, our days on the coast.
    Seedsmen's catalogues congested the post.

    October was sober, a time of renewal,
    the nights still cold, and a shortage of fuel.

    I remember November, strange doings at the rectory,
    and the issue of a brave new telephone directory.

    I remember December. I wrote to my Member
    and suggested something I can't quite remember.

I am the miser in the madhouse garden,
your hands were gentle, your prognosis bridal,
heads grow soft but hearts will ever harden,
the moon was waning, your affection tidal.
We tried to live like lovers in a novel,
we lunched at three and dined on bread and butter,
after a month in our romantic hovel
your eyes were full of thoughts you could not utter.

Turn to me now, like a reluctant statue
swivelling on its pedestal of granite,
write to me now, for there's no getting at you,
my bicycle can't cross the sea, now can it?
Here in my pocket-book with chits and papers
and licences to drive and fish and listen
I carry a memento of our capers—
this faded photograph, with eyes that glisten.

A. R. D. FAIRBAIRN

'I asked a thief to steal me a peach'

I asked a thief to steal me a peach;
He turned up his eyes.
I asked a lithe lady to lie her down,
'Holy and meek!' she cries.

As soon as I went
An angel came;
He winked at the thief
And smiled at the dame—

And without one word said
Had a peach from the tree,
And still as a maid
Enjoyed the lady.

WILLIAM BLAKE

Homage à Ibsen

Ibsen had a badger
    He called it Little Nell . . .
Springtime over Stinkerhjem
    And April all a-smell.

J. B. MORTON

Bunyan

I do not extenuate Bunyan's
Intemperate use of onions,
But if I knew a wicked ogress
I would lend her The Pilgrim's Progress.

E. CLERIHEW BENTLEY

The Parterre

I don't know any greatest treat
As sit him in a gay parterre,
And sniff one up the perfume sweet
Of every roses buttoning there.

It only want my charming miss
Who make to blush the self red rose;
Oh! I have envy of to kiss
The end's tip of her splendid nose.

Oh! I have envy of to be
What grass 'neath her pantoffle push,
And too much happy seemeth me
The margaret which her vestige crush.

But I will meet her nose at nose,
And take occasion for her hairs,
And indicate her all my woes,
That she in fine agree my prayers.

I don't know any greatest treat
As sit him in a gay parterre,
With Madame who is too more sweet
Than every roses buttoning there.

E. H. PALMER

To Alfred Tennyson

I entreat you, Alfred Tennyson,
Come and share my haunch of venison.
I have too a bin of claret,
Good, but better when you share it.
Though 'tis only a small bin,
There 's a stock of it within.
And as sure as I'm a rhymer
Half a butt of Rudesheimer.
Come: among the sons of men is one
Welcomer than Alfred Tennyson?

WALTER SAVAGE LANDOR

The —— Hotel

If ever you go to Dolgelley,
   Don't stay at the —— HOTEL;
There's nothing to put in your belly,
   And no one to answer the bell.

THOMAS HUGHES

Written after Swimming from Sestos to Abydos

If, in the month of dark December,
   Leander, who was nightly wont
(What maid will not the tale remember?)
   To cross thy stream, broad Hellespont!

If, when the wintry tempest roared,
   He sped to Hero, nothing loth,
And thus of old thy current poured,
   Fair Venus! how I pity both!

For *me*, degenerate modern wretch,
   Though in the genial month of May,
My dripping limbs I faintly stretch,
   And think I've done a feat today.

But since he crossed the rapid tide,
   According to the doubtful story,
To woo,—and—Lord knows what beside,
   And swam for Love, as I for Glory;

'Twere hard to say who fared the best:
   Sad mortals! thus the gods still plague you!
He lost his labour, I my jest;
   For he was drowned, and I've the ague.

LORD BYRON

142

So Many Caesars

If Jones were dictator of England
  (As I think that he ought to be)
He would cut off the heads of the principal Reds
  And drown all the rest in the sea.
If Jones were dictator of England
  We should all have plenty of coal;
The land would be void of its unemployed
  And no one would be on the dole.

If Brown were dictator of England
  (And he hasn't refused it yet)
He would levy a tax on these Oxford 'slacks'
  And pay the American debt.
If Brown were dictator of England
  He would stop this shingled hair,
For he thinks that girls ought to keep the curls
  That Grandmother used to wear.

If Smith were dictator of England
  (As no doubt he will be soon)
He would end this craze for unpleasant plays
  That shame the face of the moon.
If Smith were dictator of England
  He would lock up the men with kinks,
The critics and writers and smug first-nighters,
  In a home for missing links.

If Snooks were dictator of England
  (Which he ought to be made at once)
There would be no jams between buses and trams,
  Which are simply the work of a dunce.
If Snooks were dictator of England
  He would build a road through the sky
And pull up the Strand and have it replanned
  And plant it at Peckham Rye.

If Bloggs were dictator of England
  (And I think he should have the chance)
The Poles and the Germans would all read sermons
  And so would the boys in France.
If Bloggs were dictator of England
  The rumours of war would cease,
And the instant dawn would blush like a prawn
  With the roseate hues of peace.

But if I were dictator of England,
  Though people exist in swarms
Who could remedy things, if we made them kings,
  By carrying out reforms—
If I were dictator of England
  I'll tell you what I would do—
I would sell you the job for fifteen bob
  And throw in the hat-stand too.

                                        E. V. KNOX

The Antelope

If you go out alone, I hope
You will not meet the Antelope.

No other beast is half so vicious,
So false, so cruel, so malicious.

It would be wrong for me to write
The sort of things he does at night.

Nor dare I in plain language say
The sort of thing he does by day.

His acts recall, they are so serious,
Those of the Emperor Tiberius.

                              ALFRED DOUGLAS

144

DORSET COUNTY LIBRARY

My Rival

I go to concert, party, ball—
    What profit is in these?
I sit alone against the wall
    And strive to look at ease.
The incense that is mine by right
    They burn before Her shrine;
And that's because I'm seventeen
    And She is forty-nine.

I cannot check my girlish blush,
    My colour comes and goes.
I redden to my finger-tips,
    And sometimes to my nose.
But She is white where white should be,
    And red where red should shine.
The blush that flies at seventeen
    Is fixed at forty-nine.

I wish *I* had her constant cheek:
    I wish that I could sing
All sorts of funny little songs,
    Not quite the proper thing.
I'm very *gauche* and very shy,
    Her jokes aren't in my line;
And, worst of all, I'm seventeen
    While She is forty-nine.

The young men come, the young men go,
    Each pink and white and neat,
She's older than their mothers, but
    They grovel at Her feet.
They walk beside Her *'rickshaw*-wheels—
    None ever walk by mine;
And that's because I'm seventeen
    And She is forty-nine.

She rides with half a dozen men
    (She calls them 'boys' and 'mashes'),
I trot along the Mall alone;
    My prettiest frocks and sashes
Don't help to fill my programme-card,
    And vainly I repine
From ten to two A.M. Ah me!
    Would I were forty-nine.

She calls me 'darling', 'pet', and 'dear',
    And 'sweet retiring maid'.
I'm always at the back, I know—
    She puts me in the shade.
She introduces me to men—
    'Cast' lovers, I opine;
For sixty takes to seventeen,
    Nineteen to forty-nine.

But even She must older grow
    And end Her dancing days,
She can't go on for ever so
    At concerts, balls, and plays.
One ray of priceless hope I see
    Before my footsteps shine;
Just think, that She'll be eighty-one
    When I am forty-nine!

RUDYARD KIPLING

Platypus

I had a duck-billed platypus when I was up at Trinity,
With whom I soon discovered a remarkable affinity.
He used to live in lodgings with myself and Arthur Purvis,
And we all went up together for the Diplomatic Service.
I had a certain confidence, I own, in his ability;
He mastered all the subjects with remarkable facility;

And Purvis, though more dubious, agreed that he was clever,
But no one else imagined he had any chance whatever.

I failed to pass the interview. The Board with wry grimaces
Objected to my boots and took exception to my braces;
And Purvis too was failed by an intolerant examiner,
Who said he had his doubts as to his sock-suspenders' stamina.
Our summary rejection, though we took it with urbanity,
Was naturally wounding in some measure to our vanity.
The bitterness of failure was considerably mollified,
However, by the ease with which our platypus had qualified.

The wisdom of the choice, it soon appeared, was undeniable.
There never was a diplomat more thoroughly reliable,
The creature never acted with undue precipitation O,
But gave to every question his mature consideration O,
He never made rash statements that his enemies might hold him
    to;
He never stated anything, for no one ever told him to;
And soon he was appointed, so correct was his behaviour,
Our Minister (without portfolio) in Trans Moravia.

My friend was loved and honoured from the Andes to Esthonia;
He soon achieved a pact between Peru and Patagonia;
He never vexed the Russians or offended the Rumanians;
He pacified the Letts and he appeased the Lithuanians.
No Minister has ever worked more cautiously or slowly O;
In fact they had decided to award him a portfolio,
When, on the anniversary of Greek Emancipation,
Alas! he laid an egg in the Bulgarian Legation.

This unexpected action caused unheard-of inconvenience.
A breach at once occurred between the Turks and the Armenians;
The Greeks poured ultimata, quite unhinged by the mishap, at
    him;
The Poles began to threaten and the Finns began to flap at him;
The Swedes withdrew entirely from the Anglo-Saxon dailies
The right of photographing the Aurora Borealis;
And, all attempts to come to a *rapprochement* proving barren,
The Japanese in self-defence annexed the Isle of Arran.

My platypus, once thought to be more cautious and more tentative
Than any other living diplomatic representative,
Was now a sort of warning to all diplomatic students—
The perfect incarnation of the perils of imprudence.
Beset and persecuted by the forces of reaction O,
He reaped the consequences of his ill-considered action O;
And, branded in the Honours List as Platypus, Dame Vera,
Retired, a lonely figure, to lay eggs at Bordighera.

PATRICK BARRINGTON

Plumber-Song at Evening

I heard the plumber calling to his mate
    At eventide, when bats were on the wing;
Still was the air, and it was ten past eight—
Thursday it was, but I forget the date—
    And O! I heard a plumber sing.

I listened with my finger to my lip,
    As burglar strains to hear the fell police;
Sweet came his song, that seemed a golden drip,
'Jug-jug!' he cried, and then again, 'Pip-pip!'
    And all the world was peace.

But where his mate? Still, still he silent seemed,
    As plumber cried, 'Tu-whoo!'—a silvery tone.
And still the summer world in silence dreamed.
A distant boiler burst, a woman screamed,
    And O! I fear his mate had flown.

Long, long ago it seems, and long it is,
    Yet still I think I hear that plumber call
At evening, when the leaky faucets fizz,
And Mrs Figgins shrieks at little Liz
    Across the garden wall.

R. P. LISTER

A Perfect Lady

I knew a girl who was so pure
She couldn't say the word Manure.
Indeed, her modesty was such,
She wouldn't pass a rabbit-hutch;
And butterflies upon the wing
Would make her blush like anything.

That lady is a gardener now,
And all her views have changed, somehow,
She squashes greenfly with her thumb,
And knows how little snowdrops come:
In fact, the garden she has got,
Has broadened out her mind a lot.

REGINALD ARKELL

Un Jeune Homme de Dijon

Il y avait un jeune homme de Dijon
Qui n'avait pas trop de religion.
    Il disait 'Ma foi!
      Ils m'embetent, tous les trois,
Et le Père, et le Fils, et le Pigeon.'

ANON

On a Curate's Complaint of Hard Duty

I marched three miles through scorching sand,
With zeal in heart, and notes in hand;
I rode four more to Great St Mary,
Using four legs, when two were weary:
To three fair virgins I did tie men,
In the close bands of pleasing Hymen;
I dipped two babes in holy water,
And purified their mother after.
Within an hour and eke a half,
I preached three congregations deaf;
Where, thundering out, with lungs long-winded,
I chopped so fast, that few there minded.
My emblem, the laborious sun,
Saw all these mighty labours done
Before one race of his was run.
All this performed by Robert Hewit:
What mortal else could e'er go through it!

JONATHAN SWIFT

Only Seven

A pastoral story after Wordsworth

I marvelled why a simple child,
    That lightly draws its breath,
Should utter groans so very wild,
    And look as pale as Death.

Adopting a parental tone,
    I asked her why she cried;
The damsel answered with a groan,
    'I've got a pain inside!

'I thought it would have sent me mad
    Last night about eleven.'
Said I, 'What is it makes you bad?
How many apples have you had?'
    She answered, 'Only seven!'

'And are you sure you took no more,
    My little maid?' quoth I;
'Oh, please, sir, mother gave me four,
    But *they* were in a pie!'

'If that's the case,' I stammered out,
    'Of course you've had eleven.'
The maiden answered with a pout,
    'I ain't had more nor seven!'

I wondered hugely what she meant,
    And said, 'I'm bad at riddles;
But I know where little girls are sent
    For telling taradiddles.

'Now, if you won't reform,' said I,
    'You'll never go to Heaven.'
But all in vain; each time I try,
That little idiot makes reply,
    'I ain't had more nor seven!'

Postscript

To borrow Wordsworth's name was wrong,
    Or slightly misapplied;
And so I'd better call my song,
    'Lines after Ache-Inside'.

HENRY S. LEIGH

I'm a Shrimp! I'm a Shrimp!

I'm a shrimp! I'm a shrimp! Of diminutive size.
Inspect my antennae, and look at my eyes;
I'm a natural syphon, when dipped in a cup,
For I drain the contents to the latest drop up.
I care not for craw-fish, I heed not the prawn,
From a flavour especial my fame has been drawn;
Nor e'en to the crab or the lobster do yield,
When I'm properly cooked and efficiently peeled.
Quick! quick! pile the coals—let your saucepan be deep,
For the weather is warm, and I'm sure not to keep;
Off, off with my head—split my shell into three—
I'm a shrimp! I'm a shrimp—to be eaten with tea.

ROBERT BROUGH

Only a Second Trombone

I'm only a Second Trombone,
　　But whatever the world may say,
I'm bent upon playing a trombone's part
　　In a kind and courageous way.
What matters it if my tone is weak
　　And some of my notes are flat?
Though I'm only a Second Trombone, girls,
　　I'm not any the worse for that.

I'm only a Second Trombone,
　　And nobody seems to care
If half of the time it is pointed out
　　That I'm playing the oboe's air;
But I'm more of a man than a million men
　　Whom frivolous girls admire;
My face is the face of a trombone, girls,
　　But my heart is a heart of fire.

I'm only a Second Trombone,
   But one of these days you'll find
Some hint of the passionate human thoughts
   That burn in a trombone's mind.
They're thoughts that would stultify a bassoon
   And stagger a clarinet;
But they're only a Second Trombone's, girls,
   And nobody knows them yet.

PATRICK BARRINGTON

Translations from the Chinese
Studies in Dry Vermouth

'I'm terrified,' she said,
'When you do something really unselfish,
For I know too well
That the next time you lose your temper
Either you'll brag about it
Or else curse *me*
For having let you do it.'

CHRISTOPHER MORLEY

Time Like an Ever-rolling Stream

I must confess that often I'm
   A prey to melancholy
Because I do not work on *Time*.
   Golly, it must be jolly.
No other bliss, I hold, but pales
   Beside the feeling that you're
One of nine hundred—is it?—males
   And females of such stature.

How very much I would enjoy,
To call Roy Alexander 'Roy'
And hear him say 'Hullo, dear boy!'

Not to mention mixing on easy terms with

Louis Banks
Richard Oulahan Jr
Edward O. Cerf
Estelle Dembeck
Cecilia I. Dempster
Ed. Ogle
Robert Ajemian
Honor Balfour
Dorothy Slavin Haystead
Mark Vishniak
  Old Uncle Fuerbringer and all.

The boys who run the (plural) *Times*
  Are carefully selected;
Chaps who make puns or Cockney rhymes
  Are instantly rejected.
Each day some literary gem
  By these fine lads is written,
And everyone considers them
  A credit to Great Britain.

But dash it all—let's face it, what?—
Though locally esteemed as hot
For all their merits they are not,

  Well, to take an instance at random,

Robert W. Boyd Jr
Lester Bernstein
Gilbert Cant
Edwin Copps
Henry Bradford Darrach Jr
William Forbis
Barker T. Hartshorn
Roger S. Hewlett
Carl Solberg

154

Jonathan Norton Leonard
  Old Uncle Fuerbringer and all.

Alas, I never learned the knack
  (And on *Time's* staff you need it)
Of writing English front to back
  Till swims the mind to read it.
Tried often I've my darnedest, knows
  Goodness, but with a shock I'd
Discover that once more my prose
  Had failed to go all cockeyed.

So, though I wield a gifted pen,
There'll never be a moment when
I join that happy breed of men.

I allude to (among others)

  Douglas Auchincloss
  Louis Kronenherger
  Champ Clark
  Alton J. Klingen
  Michael Demarest
  Bernard Frizell
  Theodore E. Kalem
  Carter Harman
  Robert Shnayerson
  Harriet Bachman
  Margaret Quimby
  Elsie Ann Brown
  Shirley Estabrook
  Marion Hollander Sanders
  Danuta Reszke-Birk
  Deirdre Mead Ryan
  F. Sydnor Trapnell
  Yi Ying Sung
  Content Peckham
  Quinera Sarita King
    Old Uncle Fuerbringer and all,
    Old Uncle Fuerbringer and all.

P. G. WODEHOUSE

Letter to Lord Byron (II)

I'm writing this in pencil on my knee,
  Using my other hand to stop me yawning,
Upon a primitive, unsheltered quay
  In the small hours of a Wednesday morning.
  I cannot add the summer day is dawning;
In Seythisfjördur every schoolboy knows
That daylight in the summer never goes.

To get to sleep in latitudes called upper
  Is difficult at first for Englishmen.
It's like being sent to bed before your supper
  For playing darts with father's fountain-pen,
  Or like returning after orgies, when
Your breath's like luggage and you realize
You've been more confidential than was wise.

I've done my duty, taken many notes
  Upon the almost total lack of greenery,
The roads, the illegitimates, the goats:
  To use a rhyme of yours, there's handsome scenery
  But little agricultural machinery;
And with the help of Sunlight Soap the Geysir
Affords to visitors le plus grand plaisir.

The North, though, never was your cup of tea;
  'Moral' you thought it so you kept away.
And what I'm sure you're wanting now from me
  Is news about the England of the day,
  What sort of things *La Jeunesse* do and say.
Is Brighton still as proud of her pavilion,
And is it safe for girls to travel pillion?

I'll clear my throat and take a Rover's breath
  And skip a century of hope and sin—
For far too much has happened since your death.
  Crying went out and the cold bath came in,
  With drains, bananas, bicycles, and tin,
And Europe saw from Ireland to Albania
The Gothic revival and the Railway Mania.

156

We're entering now the Eotechnic Phase
    Thanks to the Grid and all those new alloys;
That is, at least, what Lewis Mumford says.
    A world of Aertex underwear for boys,
    Huge plate-glass windows, walls absorbing noise,
Where the smoke nuisance is utterly abated
And all the furniture is chromium-plated.

Well, you might think so if you went to Surrey
    And stayed for week-ends with the well-to-do,
Your car too fast, too personal your worry
    To look too closely at the wheeling view.
    But in the north it simply isn't true.
To those who live in Warrington or Wigan,
It's not a white lie, it's a whacking big 'un.

There on the old historic battlefield,
    The cold ferocity of human wills,
The scars of struggle are as yet unhealed;
    Slattern the tenements on sombre hills,
    And gaunt in valleys the square-windowed mills
That, since the Georgian house, in my conjecture
Remain our finest native architecture.

On economic, health, or moral grounds
    It hasn't got the least excuse to show;
No more than chamber pots or otter hounds;
    But let me say before it has to go,
    It's the most lovely country that I know;
Clearer than Scafell Pike, my heart has stamped on
The view from Birmingham to Wolverhampton.

Long, long ago, when I was only four,
    Going towards my grandmother, the line
Passed through a coal-field. From the corridor
    I watched it pass with envy, thought 'How fine!
    Oh how I wish that situation mine.'
Tramlines and slagheaps, pieces of machinery,
That was, and still is, my ideal scenery.

Hail to the New World! Hail to those who'll love
   Its antiseptic objects, feel at home.
Lovers will gaze at an electric stove,
   Another *poésie de départ* come
   Centred round bus-stops or the aerodrome.
But give me still, to stir imagination
The chiaroscuro of the railway station.

Preserve me from the Shape of Things to Be;
   The high-grade posters at the public meeting,
The influence of Art on Industry,
   The cinemas with perfect taste in seating;
   Preserve me, above all, from central heating.
It may be D. H. Lawrence hocus-pocus,
But I prefer a room that's got a focus.

But you want facts, not sights. I'll do my best
   To give a few; you can't expect them all.
To start with, on the whole we're better dressed;
   For chic the difference today is small
   Of barmaid from my lady at the Hall.
It's sad to spoil this democratic vision
With millions suffering from malnutrition.

Again, our age is highly educated;
   There is no lie our children cannot read,
And as MacDonald might so well have stated
   We're growing up and up and up indeed.
   Advertisements can teach us all we need;
And death is better, as the millions know,
Than dandruff, night-starvation, or BO.

We've always had a penchant for field sports,
   But what do you think has grown up in our towns?
A passion for the open air and shorts;
   The sun is one of our emotive nouns.
   Go down by chara' to the Sussex Downs,
Watch the manoeuvres of the week-end hikers
Massed on parade with Kodaks or with Leicas.

These movements signify our age-long rule
     Of insularity has lost its powers;
The cult of salads and the swimming pool
     Comes from a climate sunnier than ours,
     And lands which never heard of licensed hours.
The south of England before very long
Will look no different from the Continong.

You lived and moved among the best society
     And so could introduce your hero to it
Without the slightest tremor of anxiety;
     Because he was your hero and you knew it,
     He'd know instinctively what's done, and do it.
He'd find our day more difficult than yours
For industry has mixed the social drawers.

We've grown, you see, a lot more democratic,
     And Fortune's ladder is for all to climb;
Carnegie on this point was most emphatic.
     A humble grandfather is not a crime,
     At least, if father made enough in time!
Today, thank God, we've got no snobbish feeling
Against the more efficient modes of stealing.

The porter at the Carlton is my brother,
     He'll wish me a good evening if I pay,
For tips and men are equal to each other.
     I'm sure that *Vogue* would be the first to say
     Que le Beau Monde is socialist today;
And many a bandit, not so gently born
Kills vermin every winter with the Quorn.

Adventurers, though, must take things as they find them
     And look for pickings where the pickings are.
The drives of love and hunger are behind them,
     They can't afford to be particular:
     And those who like good cooking and a car,
A certain kind of costume or of face,
Must seek them in a certain kind of place.

Don Juan was a mixer and no doubt
  Would find this century as good as any
For getting hostesses to ask him out,
  And mistresses that need not cost a penny.
  Indeed our ways to waste time are so many,
Thanks to technology, a list of these
Would make a longer book than *Ulysses*.

Yes, in the smart set he would know his way
  By second nature with no tips from me.
Tennis and Golf have come in since your day;
  But those who are as good at games as he
  Acquire the back-hand quite instinctively,
Take to the steel-shaft and hole out in one,
Master the books of Ely Culbertson.

I see his face in every magazine.
  'Don Juan at lunch with one of Cochran's ladies.'
'Don Juan with his red setter May MacQueen.'
  'Don Juan, who's just been wintering in Cadiz,
  Caught at the wheel of his maroon Mercedes.'
'Don Juan at Croydon Aerodrome.' 'Don Juan
Snapped in the paddock with the Aga Khan.'

But if in highbrow circles he would sally
  It's just as well to warn him there's no stain on
Picasso, all-in wrestling, or the Ballet.
  Sibelius is the man. To get a pain on
  Listening to Elgar is a sine qua non.
A second-hand acquaintance of Pareto's
Ranks higher than an intimate of Plato's.

The vogue for Black Mass and the cult of devils
  Has sunk. The Good, the Beautiful, the True
Still fluctuate about the lower levels.
  Joyces are firm and there there's nothing new.
  Eliots have hardened just a point or two.
Hopkins are brisk, thanks to some recent boosts.
There's been some further weakening in Prousts.

I'm saying this to tell you who's the rage,
  And not to loose a sneer from my interior.
Because there's snobbery in every age,
  Because some names are loved by the superior,
  It does not follow they're the least inferior:
For all I know the Beatific Vision's
On view at all Surrealist Exhibitions.

Now for the spirit of the people. Here
  I know I'm treading on more dangerous ground:
I know there're many changes in the air,
  But know my data too slight to be sound,
  I know, too, I'm inviting the renowned
Retort of all who love the Status Quo:
'You can't change human nature, don't you know!'

We've still, it's true, the same shape and appearance,
  We haven't changed the way that kissing's done;
The average man still hates all interference,
  Is just as proud still of his new-born son:
  Still, like a hen, he likes his private run,
Scratches for self-esteem, and slyly pecks
A good deal in the neighbourhood of sex.

But he's another man in many ways:
  Ask the cartoonist first, for he knows best.
Where is the John Bull of the good old days,
  The swaggering bully with the clumsy jest?
  His meaty neck has long been laid to rest,
His acres of self-confidence for sale;
He passed away at Ypres and Passchendaele.

Turn to the work of Disney or of Strube;
  There stands our hero in his threadbare seams;
The bowler hat who strap-hangs in the tube,
  And kicks the tyrant only in his dreams,
  Trading on pathos, dreading all extremes;
The little Mickey with the hidden grudge;
Which is the better, I leave you to judge.

Begot on Hire Purchase by Insurance,
　　Forms at his christening worshipped and adored;
A season ticket schooled him in endurance,
　　A tax collector and a waterboard
　　Admonished him. In boyhood he was awed
By a matric, and complex apparatuses
Keep his heart conscious of Divine Afflatuses.

'I am like you,' he says, 'and you, and you,
　　I love my life, I love the home-fires, have
To keep them burning. Heroes never do.
　　Heroes are sent by ogres to the grave.
　　I may not be courageous, but I save.
I am the one who somehow turns the corner,
I may perhaps be fortunate Jack Horner.

'I am the ogre's private secretary;
　　I've felt his stature and his powers, learned
To give his ogreship the raspberry
　　Only when his gigantic back is turned.
　　One day, who knows, I'll do as I have yearned.
The short man, all his fingers on the door,
With repartee shall send him to the floor.'

One day, which day? O any other day,
　　But not today. The ogre knows his man.
To kill the ogre—that would take away
　　The fear in which his happy dreams began,
　　And with his life he'll guard dreams while he can.
Those who would really kill his dream's contentment
He hates with real implacable resentment.

He dreads the ogre, but he dreads yet more
　　Those who conceivably might set him free,
Those the cartoonist has no time to draw.
　　Without his bondage he'd be all at sea;
　　The ogre need but shout 'Security',
To make this man, so lovable, so mild,
As madly cruel as a frightened child.

162

Byron, thou should'st be living at this hour!
    What would you do, I wonder, if you were?
Britannia's lost prestige and cash and power,
    Her middle classes show some wear and tear,
    We've learned to bomb each other from the air;
I can't imagine what the Duke of Wellington
Would say about the music of Duke Ellington.

Suggestions have been made that the Teutonic
    Führer-Prinzip would have appealed to you
As being the true heir to the Byronic—
    In keeping with your social status too
    (It has its English converts, fit and few),
That you would, hearing honest Oswald's call,
Be gleichgeschaltet in the Albert Hall.

'Lord Byron at the head of his storm-troopers!'
    Nothing, says science, is impossible:
The Pope may quit to join the Oxford Groupers,
    Nuffield may leave one farthing in his Will,
    There may be someone who trusts Baldwin still,
Someone may think that Empire wines are nice,
There may be people who hear Tauber twice.

You liked to be the centre of attention,
    The gay Prince Charming of the fairy story,
Who tamed the Dragon by his intervention.
    In modern warfare, though it's just as gory,
    There isn't any individual glory;
The Prince must be anonymous, observant,
A kind of lab-boy, or a civil servant.

You never were an Isolationist;
    Injustice you had always hatred for,
And we can hardly blame you, if you missed
    Injustice just outside your lordship's door:
    Nearer than Greece were cotton and the poor.
Today you might have seen them, might indeed
Have walked in the United Front with Gide,

Against the ogre, dragon, what you will;
 His many shapes and names all turn us pale,
For he's immortal, and today he still
 Swinges the horror of his scaly tail.
 Sometimes he seems to sleep, but will not fail
In every age to rear up to defend
Each dying force of history to the end.

Milton beheld him on the English throne,
 And Bunyan sitting in the Papal chair;
The hermits fought him in their caves alone,
 At the first Empire he was also there,
 Dangling his Pax Romana in the air:
He comes in dreams at puberty to man,
To scare him back to childhood if he can.

Banker or landlord, booking-clerk or Pope,
 Whenever he's lost faith in choice and thought,
When a man sees the future without hope,
 Whenever he endorses Hobbes' report
 'The life of man is nasty, brutish, short',
The dragon rises from his garden border
And promises to set up law and order.

He that in Athens murdered Socrates,
 And Plato then seduced, prepares to make
A desolation and to call it peace
 Today for dying magnates, for the sake
 Of generals who can scarcely keep awake,
And for that doughy mass in great and small
That doesn't want to stir itself at all.

Forgive me for inflicting all this on you,
 For asking you to hold the baby for us;
It's easy to forget that where you've gone, you
 May only want to chat with Set and Horus,
 Bored to extinction with our earthly chorus:
Perhaps it sounds to you like a trunk-call,
Urgent, it seems, but quite inaudible.

Yet though the choice of what is to be done
    Remains with the alive, the rigid nation
Is supple still within the breathing one;
    Its sentinels yet keep their sleepless station,
    And every man in every generation,
Tossing in his dilemma on his bed,
Cries to the shadows of the noble dead.

We're out at sea now, and I wish we weren't;
    The sea is rough, I don't care if it's blue;
I'd like to have a quick one, but I daren't.
    And I must interrupt this screed to you,
    For I've some other little jobs to do;
I must write home or mother will be vexed,
So this must be continued in our next.

W. H. AUDEN

From Martial

In all thy humours, whether grave or mellow,
Thou'rt such a touchy, testy, pleasant fellow,
Hast so much wit and mirth and spleen about thee,
There is no living with thee or without thee.

JOSEPH ADDISON

Aly Khan

In Bakerloo did Aly Khan
A stately Hippodrome decree:
Where Alf the bread delivery man
Collided with a draper's van
        While doing sixty-three.
So half a mile of tidy ground
With cakes and clothes was littered round:
And here were undies white with gorgeous frills,
Which brought on many a manly blush to see,
And here were rock-cakes ancient as the hills,
Enfolding sundry lots of masonry.

But oh! that deep traumatic scar which slanted
Down Alf's left cheek, that whisker could not cover!
'A horrid trace; as ugly and unwanted
As e'er upon a human face was planted
By Fortune!' said the surgeon, Mr Glover.

JOHN D. McINTOSH

Mamble

I never went to Mamble
That lies above the Teme,
So I wonder who's in Mamble,
And whether people seem
Who breed and brew along there
As lazy as the name,
And whether any song there
Sets alehouse wits aflame.

The finger-post says Mamble,
And that is all I know
Of the narrow road to Mamble,
And should I turn and go
To that place of lazy token
That lies above the Teme,
There might be a Mamble broken
That was lissom in a dream.

So leave the road to Mamble
And take another road
To as good a place as Mamble
Be it lazy as a toad;
Who travels Worcester county
Takes any place that comes
When April tosses bounty
To the cherries and the plums.

JOHN DRINKWATER

166

The Vicar of Bray

In good King Charles's golden days
   When loyalty no harm meant
A zealous high-churchman was I
   And so I got preferment.
To teach my flock I never missed
   Kings were by God appointed;
And damned are those that dare resist
   Or touch the Lord's anointed.

And this is law I will maintain
   Unto my dying day, sir,
That whatsoever king shall reign
   Still I'll be the Vicar of Bray, sir.

When royal James obtained the crown,
   And popery came in fashion,
The penal laws I hooted down
   And read the Declaration.
The Church of Rome I found would fit
   Full well my constitution
And had become a Jesuit
   But for the Revolution.
       And this is law, etc.

When William was our king declared
   To ease a nation's grievance
With this new wind about I steered
   And swore to him allegiance.
Old principles I did revoke
   Set conscience at a distance.
Passive obedience was a joke
   A jest was non-resistance.
       For this is law, etc.

When gracious Anne became our queen,
   The Church of England's glory,
Another face of things was seen
   And I became a Tory.

Occasional conformists base
   I damned their moderation
And thought the Church in danger was
   From such prevarication.
         And this is law, etc.

When George in pudding-time* came o'er
   And moderate men looked big, sir,
I turned a cat in the pan once more
   And so became a Whig, sir.
And thus preferment I procured
   From our new Faith's Defender,
And almost every day abjured
   The Pope and the Pretender.
         This is law, etc.

The illustrious House of Hanover
   And Protestant succession,
To these I do allegiance swear,
   While they can keep possession.
And in my faith and loyalty
   I never more will falter
And George my lawful king shall be
   Until the times do alter.

ANON

* *in a lucky time.*

'In Heaven there'll be no algebra'

In Heaven there'll be no algebra,
No learning dates or names,
But only playing golden harps
And reading Henry James.

ANON

Strike among the Poets

In his chamber, weak and dying,
　　While the Norman baron lay,
Loud, without, his men were crying
　　'Shorter hours and better pay.'

Know you why the ploughman, fretting,
　　Homeward plods his weary way
Ere his time? He's after getting
　　Shorter hours and better pay.

See! the *Hesperus* is swinging
　　Idle in the wintry bay,
And the skipper's daughter's singing
　　'Shorter hours and better pay.'

Where's the Minstrel Boy? I've found him
　　Joining in the labour fray
With his placards slung around him,
　　'Shorter hours and better pay.'

Oh, young Lochinvar is coming;
　　Though his hair is getting grey,
Yet I'm glad to hear him humming
　　'Shorter hours and better pay.'

E'en the Boy upon the Burning
　　Deck has got a word to say,
Something rather cross concerning
　　Shorter hours and better pay.

Lives of great men all remind us
　　We can make as much as they,
Work no more, until they find us
　　Shorter hours and better pay.

ANON

169

Fish

In June it must be very nice
To bask about a block of ice—
And watch the World go broiling by
Under a hot and windless sky;
Then turn aside, and, sniffing, see
Perennial mounds of shrimps for tea;
How genial, too, when fancying dab,
To slip one from one's marble slab;
Or, when the stars begin to twinkle,
To broach an unofficial winkle;
Or to descend in morning slipper
And not to have to *buy* a kipper.
This must be very pleasant, and
As pleasant, too, to understand,
When you have cod—are dining off it—
You're only eating so much profit.
Solacing thoughts like these must stir
The musings of the Fishmonger.

WALTER DE LA MARE

Cologne

In Köhln, a town of monks and bones,
And pavements fanged with murderous stones
And rags, and hags, and hideous wenches;
I counted two and seventy stenches,
All well defined, and several stinks!
Ye Nymphs that reign o'er sewers and sinks,
The river Rhine, it is well known,
Doth wash your city of Cologne;
But tell me, Nymphs, what power divine
Shall henceforth wash the river Rhine?

On My Joyful Departure

(From the same city)

As I am a Rhymer,
And now at least a merry one,
Mr Mum's Rudesheimer
And the church of St Geryon
Are the two things alone
That deserve to be known
In the body-and-soul-stinking town of Cologne.

SAMUEL TAYLOR COLERIDGE

The Contrast

In London I never know what I'd be at,
Enraptured with this, and enchanted with that;
I'm wild with the sweets of variety's plan,
And Life seems a blessing too happy for man.

But the country, Lord help me! sets all matters right,
So calm and composing from morning to night;
Oh! it settles the spirits when nothing is seen
But an ass on a common, a goose on a green.

In town if it rain, why it damps not our hope,
The eye has her choice, and the fancy her scope;
What harm though it pour whole nights or whole days?
It spoils not our prospects, or stops not our ways.

In the country what bliss, when it rains in the fields,
To live on the transports that shuttlecock yields;
Or go crawling from window to window, to see
A pig on a dunghill, or crow on a tree.

In London, if folks ill together are put,
A bore may be dropt, and a quiz may be cut;
We change without end; and if lazy or ill,
All wants are at hand, and all wishes at will.

171

In the country you're nailed, like a pale in the park,
To some *stick* of a neighbour that's crammed in the ark;
And 'tis odd, if you're hurt, or in fits tumble down,
You reach death ere the doctor can reach you from town.

In London how easy we visit and meet,
Gay pleasure's the theme, and sweet smiles are our treat:
Our morning's a round of good-humoured delight,
And we rattle, in comfort, to pleasure at night.

In the country, how sprightly! our visits we make
Through ten miles of mud, for formality's sake;
With the coachman in drink, and the moon in a fog,
And no thought in our head but a ditch or a bog.

In London the spirits are cheerful and light,
All places are gay and all faces are bright;
We've ever new joys, and revived by each whim,
Each day on a fresh tide of pleasure we swim.

But how gay in the country! what summer delight
To be waiting for winter from morning to night!
Then the fret of impatience gives exquisite glee
To relish the sweet rural subjects we see.

In town we've no use for the skies overhead,
For when the sun rises then we go to bed;
And as to that old-fashioned virgin the moon,
She shines out of season, like satin in June.

In the country these planets delightfully glare
Just to show us the object we want isn't there;
O, how cheering and gay, when their beauties arise,
To sit and gaze round with the tears in one's eyes!

But 'tis in the country alone we can find
That happy resource, that relief of the mind,
When, drove to despair, our last efforts we make,
And drag the old fish-pond, for novelty's sake:

Indeed I must own, 'tis a pleasure complete
To see ladies well draggled and wet in their feet;
But what is all that to the transport we feel
When we capture, in triumph, two toads and an eel?

I have heard tho', that love in a cottage is sweet,
When two hearts in one link of soft sympathy meet:
That's to come—for as yet I, alas! am a swain
Who require, I own it, more links to my chain.

Your magpies and stock-doves may flirt among trees,
And chatter their transports in groves, if they please:
But a house is much more to my taste than a tree,
And for groves, O! a good grove of chimneys for me.

In the country, if Cupid should find a man out,
The poor tortured victim mopes hopeless about;
But in London, thank Heaven! our peace is secure,
Where for one eye to kill, there's a thousand to cure.

I know love's a devil, too subtle to spy,
That shoots through the soul, from the beam of an eye;
But in London these devils so quick fly about,
That a new devil still drives an old devil out.

In town let me live then, in town let me die,
For in truth I can't relish the country, not I.
If one must have a villa in summer to dwell,
O, give me the sweet shady side of Pall Mall!

CHARLES MORRIS

The Puritans

Instead of the Puritans landing on Plymouth Rock
(Said Jo Davidson, the delightful sculptor)
How much pleasanter this country would have been
If Plymouth Rock
Had landed on the Puritans.

CHRISTOPHER MORLEY

The Licorice Fields at Pontefract

In the licorice fields at Pontefract
   My love and I did meet
And many a burdened licorice bush
   Was blooming round our feet;
Red hair she had and golden skin,
Her sulky lips were shaped for sin,
Her sturdy legs were flannel-slack'd,
The strongest legs in Pontefract.

The light and dangling licorice flowers
   Gave off the sweetest smells;
From various black Victorian towers
   The Sunday evening bells
Came pealing over dales and hills
And tanneries and silent mills
And lowly streets where country stops
And little shuttered corner shops.

She cast her blazing eyes on me
   And plucked a licorice leaf;
I was her captive slave and she
   My red-haired robber chief.
Oh love! For love I could not speak,
It left me winded, wilting, weak
And held in brown arms strong and bare
And wound with flaming ropes of hair.

JOHN BETJEMAN

A Shot in the Park

(Based upon an incident in the memoirs of the Edwardian hostess, Mrs Hwfa Williams)

I

In the light beneath the leafage
In the afternoon in May
In the Park and near the Row
Gracefully from Hwfa*
Mrs Hwfa Williams turned away,
Saying 'Hwfa, I must go,
I expect a mob for tea;
Such fun, but I must fly—
You dine, I think with me?
Till then, my dear, goodbye!'

Mrs Hwfa Williams
Twirled and furled her parasol,
Lightly stepped into her carriage,
Thinking it was all such fun—
Life, and May, and marriage.
Such a pretty moment—
How were they to figure
Fate in ambush, taking aim
Finger on the trigger?

Later in a tea-gown talking
Over twinkling tea-things on a tray
(Hwfa in the Park still walking)
She was heard to say:

'When my husband and I gave it out
We should move to Great Cumberland Place
My sister-in-law gave a shriek—
"My dears, you'll be lost without trace!"
    And she said it with such a grimace!

---

* *Pronounced Hoover.*

' "It's so utterly out of the world!
So fearfully wide of the mark!
A Robinson Crusoe existence will pall
On that unexplored side of the Park—
    Not a soul will be likely to call!"

'Disparaging all one adores,
Relations are such a disgrace;
They gossip, as bluebottles buzz,
They deplore what one is and one does—
    But they call at Great Cumberland Place!'

II

At home the tea-time tittle-tattle; in the Mall
Two different orbits about to intersect:
That a poor clerk and Mr Hwfa Williams
Should there converge nobody could expect
And only a clairvoyant could foretell.

Gravely conferring with a crony, Hwfa
On one side saunters; on the other glares
A young man, seemingly a loafer,
Whose small brain, infinitely busier than theirs,
Has been inflamed by Post Office affairs.

He sends the telegrams that other people write;
From overwork a breakdown now impends;
Abrupt, elliptic phrases day and night he sends,
Recurring in his fevered brain all day
To be reiterated in his brain all night.

Now all's confused, things are not what they seem,
He stands bemused, as if he had been drinking;
Life is a cryptic, an intolerable dream—
RETURN TONIGHT AUNT HENRIETTA SINKING:
CONGRATULATIONS DEAR FROM ALL AT CHEAM.
GLOXINIA WILTING ORDER PINK GERANIUM:
TEN THOUSAND OFFERED SILLY NOT TO SELL:
Telegraphese tattoos upon his eardrums,
Like red-hot tintacks drives into his cranium
The public syntax of his private hell—

THANK YOU BOTH ENCHANTED:
OIL CONCESSION GRANTED:
HOPE ARRIVE NUNEATON TEN TO EIGHT:
ARRIVING SEVEN MABEL STOP:
DON'T SELL REFECTORY TABLE STOP:
CAT OUT OF BAG YOUR TELEGRAM TOO LATE.

Suddenly he sees two frock-coats passing,
Two top-hats tilted in tête-à-tête—
These are to blame! Revenge upon the senders
Of countless telegrams! He feels the uprush
Of a delayed explosive charge of hate.

He draws and points a pistol, then he shoots.
'Ouch!' cries Hwfa. Something has distressed him.
He stumbles, mutters 'Somebody has shot me!'
He falls. Blood falls upon his patent-leather boots,
And cries go up, 'A murderer! Arrest him!'

III

In the light beneath the leafage
Late that afternoon in May,
In the Mall and on the ground
Mr Hwfa Williams lay,
Happily not dead, but wounded.

'How do you feel?' they asked.
'Injured,' he said, 'and quite astounded.'

Mr Hwfa Williams
Was attended by a Dr Fletcher,
And vexed, but bravely bland,
Was carried home upon a stretcher;
And
On Mr Hwfa Williams' forehead
Mrs Hwfa Williams laid a
Ministering angel's hand.

Later 'Hwfa,' Mrs Hwfa Williams said,
'Do you prefer the sofa to your bed?'

'My dear, I don't mind *where* I lie;
What *does* it signify
When not a living soul can tell me why,
About to cross St James's Park
I'm picked on like a sitting pheasant
By, so they tell me, a demented clerk,
A truant from the GPO, Mount Pleasant?
Too many wires, they say, had turned his brain—
But why he turned on *me*—no, *that* they can't explain.'

IV

'Good morning, have you heard the news?
You'll be amazed!' 'Well, what?'
'I nearly fainted when I read
That Hwfa Williams has been shot.'

'My dear, your coffee's getting cold—'
'Well, does it matter in the least?'
All over London in the morning
Breakfast was a headline feast.

'Now here is what the paper says:
*A dastardly assault . . . the crime
Seems without motive . . . an arrest was made . . .
Alleged . . . admitted . . . passing at the time . . .*

'*A grudge . . . dispatch of telegrams . . .
Pistol discarded, lying in the mud . . .
Enquiries made at Mr Williams' home . . .
Life not in danger . . . shock and loss of blood.*

'No one is safe, it seems, these days:
To stroll across St James's Park
Is to receive a bullet in the leg
From some unhinged, ferocious clerk:

'A little learning, as our fathers knew,
Is certainly a dangerous thing;
The lower orders have been spoilt,
And now they mean to have their fling;

'But though the world's all upside down
And England hastening to decay,
Ring for the carriage; we'll enquire
How Hwfa Williams is today.'

V

'Crikey!' said the butler, Crichton,
'Blocking up the blooming street
All these callers keep on calling—
No one thinks of my poor feet!

'All the toffs with all their questions,
Leaving cards you can't refuse;
These reporters, nosy parkers,
Proper sharks they are for news.

'I was not engaged to answer
Bells that jangle all the time,
These enquiries well might drive a
Better man than me to crime:

'*How's your master? Is he better?*
Is his life in danger still?
Is it true a gang attacked him?
Do you think they shot to kill?
Can you tell us why they did it?
Anarchists? A Fenian plot?
More of this and I'll go barmy,
Like the lad that fired the shot.'

Carriage after carriage crowding,
Kind enquirers choke the street:
How is Mr Hwfa Williams?
'No one thinks of MY POOR FEET!'

VI

'And so,' said Mrs Hwfa Williams,
Telling the story after years had passed,
'It seemed that half of London came to call.
Fruit, game and flowers came crowding thick and fast,

Cards like confetti rained into the hall—
Such a great fuss, poor Hwfa was aghast
Yet pleased, I think, at such extreme concern,
More pleased than our old butler with it all—
Poor Crichton hardly knew which way to turn.

'The street was jammed, the knocker and the bell
Clamoured together like two fiends in hell—
And where was Crichton? Nobody could tell!
At twelve o'clock my maid rushed in and said
"Oh, ma'am, he's drinking quarts of brandy neat—
Crichton's gone mad! I'll see to the front door!"
Not mad but drunk I found him. Bursting into song
With "Home Sweet Home", he lurched and hit the floor.
Abject when sober, Crichton said his feet
Had driven him off his head, nor had he known
That Hwfa's best old brandy was so strong . . .
Hwfa forgave him, he had been with us so long.

'He stayed for years . . . Poor man, his race is run . . .
I also soon shall hear the sunset gun—
But in between times life has been *such fun*!'

WILLIAM PLOMER

The Flying Bum: 1944

In the vegetarian guest-house
All was frolic, feast and fun,
Eager voices were enquiring
'Are the nettle cutlets done?'
Peals of vegetarian laughter,
Husky wholesome wholemeal bread,
Will the evening finish with a
Rush of cocoa to the head?

Yes, you've guessed; it's Minnie's birthday,
Hence the frolic, hence the feast.
Are there calories in custard?
There are vitamins in yeast.
Kate is here and Tom her hubby,
Ex-commissioner for oaths,
She is mad on Christian Science,
Parsnip flan he simply loathes.

And Mr Croaker, call him Arthur,
Such a keen philatelist,
Making sheep's-eyes at Louisa
(After dinner there'll be whist)—
Come, sit down, the soup is coming,
All of docks and darnels made,
Drink a health to dear old Minnie
In synthetic lemonade.

Dentures champing juicy lettuce,
Champing macerated bran,
Oh the imitation rissoles!
Oh the food untouched by man!
Look, an imitation sausage
Made of monkey-nuts and spice,
Prunes tonight and semolina,
Wrinkled prunes, unpolished rice.

Yards of gut absorbing jellies,
Bellies filling up with nuts,
Carbohydrates jostling proteins
Out of intestinal ruts;
Peristalsis calls for roughage,
Haulms and fibres, husks and grit,
Nature's way to open bowels,
Maybe—let them practise it.

'Hark, I hear an air-raid warning!'
'Take no notice, let 'em come.'
'Who'll say grace?' 'Another walnut?'
'Listen, what's that distant hum?'
'Bomb or no bomb,' stated Minnie,
'Lips unsoiled by beef or beer
We shall use to greet our Maker
When he sounds the Great All-Clear.'

When the flying bomb exploded
Minnie's wig flew off her pate,
Half a curtain, like a tippet,
Wrapped itself round bony Kate,
Plaster landed on Louisa,
Tom fell headlong on the floor,
And a spurt of lukewarm custard
Lathered Mr Croaker's jaw.

All were spared by glass and splinters
But, the loud explosion past,
Greater was the shock impending
Even than the shock of blast—
Blast we veterans know as freakish
Gave this feast its final course,
Planted bang upon the table
A lightly roasted rump of horse.

WILLIAM PLOMER

Our Lady of Letters

In T. Square Mrs Bassett Hounde
Keeps books luxuriously bound,
As other ladies are to please
With chows or poms or pekinese.
She reads, though on the other hand
She simply cannot understand;
And drives, with neither frowns nor smiles,
Across the print for miles and miles,
Those eyes so charming and myopic.

Whate'er the treatment or the topic,
She still reads on, because she knows
That whether verse or whether prose,
There is somewhere a *quelquechose*;
She is aware it hovers near
But cannot spy it out, poor dear!
Yet there is one thing she can do—
By no means to be winked at too—
To show her reverence for the Word;
And though perhaps it sounds absurd
To say it of the lovely doxy,
She is an authoress by proxy.
For when her dinner-cards she writes,
Our well-known authors she invites,
And by her famous cellar's lures
The best of sellers she secures,
While masters of the dialogue
Hie up and stuff them like the hog.

So, when their hostess proudly looks
On all her rows and rows of books,
She feels that each high, noble thought
May be the outcome of her port,
Each paragraph an avatar
Of her foie gras and caviare,
While Mr X's rythmic line
Is her own truffles, in white wine.

                                              T. W. EARP

Old Folks at the Home

I often say to an elderly man,
    'What, sir, have *you* found out?'
I whisper it into his hearing aid;
    Sometimes I have to shout.

'I have found out,' says an elderly man,
    'Three ways of darning socks.'
Another replies, 'My message is: Never
    Invest in streetcar stocks.'

Another has learned why elderly men
    Sigh when they sit; or maybe
One has discovered why women laugh
    Whenever they see a baby.

Mostly, however, an elderly man
    Huddles within his shawl,
And all he can say to my question is
    'Nothing. Nothing at all.'

MORRIS BISHOP

Defenestration

I once had the honour of meeting a philospher called McIndoe
Who had once had the honour of being flung out of an upstairs
    window.
During his flight, he said, he commenced an interesting train
    of speculation
On why there happened to be such a word as defenestration.

There is not, he said, a special word for being rolled down a roof
    into the gutter;
There is no verb to describe the action of beating a man to death
    with a putter;
No adjective exists to qualify a man bound to the buffer of the
    12.10 to Ealing,
No abstract noun to mollify a man hung upside down by his
    ankles from the ceiling.

Why, then, of all the possible offences so distressing to
    humanitarians,
Should this one alone have caught the attention of the
    verbarians?
I concluded (said McIndoe) that the incidence of logodaedaly
    was purely adventitious.
About a thirtieth of a second later, I landed in a bush that my
    great-aunt brought back from Mauritius.

184

I am aware (he said) that defenestration is not limited to the
  flinging of men through the window.
On this occasion, however, it was so limited, the object
  defenestrated being I, the philosopher, McIndoe.

R. P. LISTER

Parodies of Bishop Percy's
Hermit of Warkworth

I put my hat upon my head
  And walked into the Strand,
And there I met another man
  Whose hat was in his hand.

The tender infant, meek and mild,
  Fell down upon the stone;
The nurse took up the squealing child,
  But still the child squealed on.

I therefore pray thee, Renny dear,
  That thou wilt give to me,
With cream and sugar softened well,
  Another dish of tea.

Nor fear that I, my gentle maid,
  Shall long detain the cup,
When once unto the bottom I
  Have drank the liquor up.

Yet hear, alas! this mournful truth,
  Nor hear it with a frown;—
Thou canst not make the tea so fast
  As I can gulp it down.

SAMUEL JOHNSON

Domestic Asides; or, Truth in Parentheses

'I really take it very kind,
This visit, Mrs Skinner!
I have not seen you such an age—
(The wretch has come to dinner!)

'Your daughters, too, what loves of girls—
What heads for painters' easels!
Come here and kiss the infant, dears,—
(And give it p'rhaps the measles!)

'Your charming boys I see are home
From Reverend Mr Russel's;
'Twas very kind to bring them both,—
(What boots for my new Brussels!)

'What! little Clara left at home?
Well now I call that shabby:
I should have loved to kiss her so,—
(A flabby, dabby, babby!)

'And Mr S., I hope he's well,
Ah! though he lives so handy,
He never now drops in to sup,—
(The better for our brandy!)

'Come, take a seat—I long to hear
About Matilda's marriage;
You're come, of course, to spend the day!—
(Thank Heaven, I hear the carriage!)

'What! must you go? next time I hope
You'll give me longer measure;
Nay—I shall see you down the stairs—
(With most uncommon pleasure!)

'Goodbye! goodbye! remember all
Next time you'll take your dinners!
(Now, David, mind I'm not at home
In future to the Skinners!)'

THOMAS HOOD

A Terrible Infant

I recollect a nurse called Ann,
    Who carried me about the grass,
And one fine day a fine young man
    Came up, and kissed the pretty lass.
She did not make the least objection!
    Thinks I, *'Aha!*
    When I can talk I'll tell Mamma!'
—And that's my earliest recollection.

FREDERICK LOCKER

My First Love

I recollect in early life,
I loved the local doctor's wife.

I ate an apple ev'ry day
To keep the doctor far away!
Alas! he was a jealous man
And grew suspicious of my plan.

He'd noticed sev'ral pips about,
When taking my appendix out,
(A circumstance that must arouse
Suspicion in the blindest spouse).

And though I squared the thing somehow,
I always eat bananas now!

HARRY GRAHAM

How I Brought the Good News from Aix to Ghent (or Vice Versa)

It runs (or rather gallops) roughly as follows, we quote from memory (having no book of reference at hand)

I sprang to the rollocks and Jorrocks and me,
And I galloped, you galloped, he galloped, we galloped all three . . .
Not a word to each other; we kept changing place,
Neck to neck, back to front, ear to ear, face to face;
And we yelled once or twice, when we heard a clock chime,
'Would you kindly oblige us, *Is that the right time?*'
As I galloped, you galloped, he galloped, we galloped, ye
      galloped, they two shall have galloped; *let us trot*.

I unsaddled the saddle, unbuckled the bit,
Unshackled the bridle (the thing didn't fit)
And ungalloped, ungalloped, ungalloped, ungalloped a bit.
Then I cast off my bluff-coat, let my bowler hat fall,
Took off both my boots and my trousers and all—
Drank off my stirrup-cup, felt a bit tight,
And unbridled the saddle: it still wasn't right.

Then all I remember is, things reeling round
As I sat with my head 'twixt my ears on the ground—
For imagine my shame when they asked what I meant
And I had to confess that I'd been, gone and went
And *forgotten the news* I was bringing to Ghent,
Though I'd galloped and galloped and galloped and galloped and
      galloped
And galloped and galloped and galloped. (Had I not would have
      been galloped?)

Envoi

So I sprang to a taxi and shouted 'To Aix!'
And he blew on his horn and he threw off his brakes,
And all the way back till my money was spent
We rattled and rattled and rattled and rattled and rattled
And rattled and rattled—
And eventually sent a telegram.

R. J. YEATMAN and W. C. SELLARS

188

Poem by a Perfectly Furious Academician

I takes and paints,
Hears no complaints,
And sells before I'm dry;
'Till savage Ruskin
He sticks his tusk in,
Then nobody will buy.

SHIRLEY BROOKS

The Busy Man's 'Ancient Mariner'

'It is the Ancient Mariner, he stoppeth one of three . . .'
A *devastating* 'Raconteur' and Travel-Bore was he;
His victim was a Wedding-Guest who listened while he told
A story that went on for hours and never *did* unfold.
The A.M.'s tale described a trip around Cape Horn and back:
He worked aboard a sailing ship (I think he got the sack);
With nothing but a crossbow-shaft he killed an albatross,
His shipmates did not praise this feat, but were extremely cross;
They hung the bird around his neck (which must have been
    unpleasant,
For when an albatross gets 'high' it's not like grouse or pheasant).
The Ancient M. went off his head, had sunstroke or D.T.s,
A guilt-complex afflicted him which nothing could appease,
He saw the sun and moon behave most oddly in the sky,
He thought he saw the ship break up and all his shipmates die;
Thirst, heat and cold, dead men and ghosts beset the luckless ship
And every kind of *contretemps* combined to spoil the trip.
How he got home he can't recall (on foot? by boat? by carriage?).
The Wedding-Guest who heard all this was stunned and missed
    the marriage.

Moral
Don't let yourself be buttonholed when you have got a date;
Don't travel in a sailing ship (they're nearly always late);
Avoid Old Salts, especially those who have a glittering eye;
Above all don't shoot albatross (or is it albat*ri*?).

189

PS
(The 'Ancient M.' is far too good for usages so vile
And if you read the whole damn thing you'll find it well worth
      while.)

                                    H. S. MACKINTOSH

Suppose I Darken Your Door

It seems to me that if you must be sociable it is better to go and see
      people than to have people come and see you,
Because then you can leave when you are through.
Yes, the moment you begin to nod
You can look at your watch and exclaim Goodness gracious, it is
      ten o'clock already, I had no idea it was so late, how very
      odd!
And you politely explain that you have to get up early in the morn-
      ing to keep an important engagement with a man from
      Alaska or Siam,
And you politely thank your host and hostess for the lovely time
      and politely say goodnight and politely scram,
But when you yourself are the home team and the gathering is un-
      der your own roof,
You haven't got a Manchurian's chance of being aloof.
If you glance at your watch it is a grievous breach of hospitality and
      a disgrace,
And if you are caught in the midst of a yawn you have to pretend
      you were making a face and say Come on everybody, let's see
      who can make the funniest face.
Then as the evening wears on you feel more and more like an un-
      successful gladiator,
Because all the comfortable places to sit in are being sat in by
      guests and you have to repose on the window sill or the
      chandelier or the radiator,
And somebody has always brought along a girl who looks like a
      loaf of raisin bread and doesn't know anybody else in the
      room,

190

And you have to go over to the corner where she is moping and
    try to disperse her gloom,
And finally at last somebody gets up and says they have to get back
    to the country or back to town again,
And you feebly say Oh it's early, don't go yet, so what do they do
    but sit down again,
And people that haven't said a word all evening begin to get lively
    and people that have been lively all evening get their second
    wind and somebody says Let's all go out in the kitchen and
    scramble some eggs,
And you have to look at him or her twice before you can convince
    yourself that anybody who would make a suggestion like that
    hasn't two heads or three legs,
And by this time the birds are twittering in the trees or looking
    in the window and saying Boo,
But nobody does anything about it and as far as I know they're all
    still here, and that's the reason I say that it is better to go and
    see people than to have people come and see you.

OGDEN NASH

Bagpipe Music

It's no go the merrygoround, it's no go the rickshaw,
All we want is a limousine and a ticket for the peepshow.
Their knickers are made of crêpe-de-chine, their shoes are made
    of python,
Their halls are lined with tiger rugs and their walls with heads of
    bison.

John MacDonald found a corpse, put it under the sofa,
Waited till it came to life and hit it with a poker,
Sold its eyes for souvenirs, sold its blood for whisky,
Kept its bones for dumb-bells to use when he was fifty.

It's no go the Yogi-Man, it's no go Blavatsky,
All we want is a bank balance and a bit of skirt in a taxi.

Annie MacDougall went to milk, caught her foot in the heather,
Woke to hear a dance record playing of Old Vienna.
It's no go your maidenheads, it's no go your culture,
All we want is a Dunlop tyre and the devil mend the puncture.

The Laird o' Phelps spent Hogmanay declaring he was sober,
Counted his feet to prove the fact and found he had one foot over.
Mrs Carmichael had her fifth, looked at the job with repulsion,
Said to the midwife 'Take it away; I'm through with
        over-production'.

It's no go the gossip column, it's no go the Ceilidh,
All we want is a mother's help and a sugar-stick for the baby.

Willie Murray cut his thumb, couldn't count the damage,
Took the hide of an Ayrshire cow and used it for a bandage.
His brother caught three hundred cran when the seas were lavish,
Threw the bleeders back in the sea and went upon the parish.

It's no go the Herring Board, it's no go the Bible,
All we want is a packet of fags when our hands are idle.

It's no go the picture palace, it's no go the stadium,
It's no go the country cot with a pot of pink geraniums,
It's no go the Government grants, it's no go the elections,
Sit on your arse for fifty years and hang your hat on a pension.

It's no go my honey love, it's no go my poppet;
Work your hands from day to day, the winds will blow the profit.
The glass is falling hour by hour, the glass will fall for ever,
But if you break the bloody glass you won't hold up the weather.

                                        LOUIS MACNEICE

Number One

(Versified from the prose of a young lady)

It's very hard!—and so it is—
To live in such a row,
And witness this, that every Miss
But me, has got a beau.
For love goes calling up and down,
But here he seems to shun;
I'm sure he has been asked enough
To call at Number One!

I'm sick of all the double knocks
That come to Number Four!
At Number Three, I often see
A lover at the door;
And one in blue at Number Two
Calls daily like a dun,—
It's very hard they come so near
And not to Number One!

Miss Bell, I hear, has got a dear
Exactly to her mind,—
By sitting at the window pane
Without a bit of blind;
But I go in the balcony,
Which she has never done,
Yet arts that thrive at Number Five
Don't take at Number One!

'Tis hard with plenty in the street,
And plenty passing by,—
There's nice young men at Number Ten,
But only rather shy;
And Mrs Smith, across the way,
Has got a grown-up son,
But la! he hardly seems to know
There is a Number One!

There's Mr Wick at Number Nine,
But he's intent on pelf,
And—though he's pious—will not love
His neighbour as himself.
At Number Seven there was a sale—
The goods had quite a run!
And here I've got my single lot
On hand at Number One!

My mother often sits at work
And talks of props and stays,
And what a comfort I shall be
In her declining days:
The very maids about the house
Have set me down a nun,
The sweethearts all belong to them
That call at Number One.

Once only when the flue took fire,
One Friday afternoon,
Young Mr Long came kindly in
And told me not to swoon:
Why can't he come again, without
The Phœnix and the Sun!
We cannot always have a flue
On fire at Number One!

I am not old! I am not plain!
Nor awkward in my gait—
I am not crooked like the bride
That went from Number Eight:
I'm sure white satin made her look
As brown as any bun—
But even beauty has no chance,
I think, at Number One!

At Number Six, they say, Miss Rose
Has slain a score of hearts,
And Cupid, for her sake, has been
Quite prodigal of darts.
The Imp they show with bended bow,
I wish he had a gun!
But if he had, he'd never deign
To shoot with Number One!

It's very hard and so it is
To live in such a row!
And here's a ballad singer come
To aggravate my woe:
O take away your foolish song,
And tones enough to stun—
There is 'Nae luck about the house',
I know, at Number One!

THOMAS HOOD

Divided Destinies

It was an artless *Bandar** and he danced upon a pine,
And much I wondered how he lived, and where the beast might
    dine,
And many other things, till, o'er my morning smoke,
I slept the sleep of idleness and dreamt that *Bandar* spoke.

He said:—'O man of many clothes! Sad crawler on the Hills!
Observe, I know not Ranken's shop, nor Ranken's monthly bills!
I take no heed to trousers or the coats that you call dress;
Nor am I plagued with little cards for little drinks at Mess.

'I steal the bunnia's grain at morn, at noon and eventide.
(For he is fat and I am spare), I roam the mountain-side.
I follow no man's carriage, and no, never in my life
Have I flirted at Peliti's with another *Bandar's* wife.

* *Monkey.*

195

'O man of futile fopperies—unnecessary wraps;
I own no ponies in the hills, I drive no tallwheeled traps.
I buy me not twelve-button gloves, "short-sixes" eke, or rings,
Nor do I waste at Hamilton's my wealth on "pretty things".

'I quarrel with my wife at home, we never fight abroad;
But Mrs B. has grasped the fact I *am* her only lord.
I never heard of fever—dumps nor debts depress my soul;
And I pity and despise you!' Here he pouched my breakfast-roll.

His hide was very mangy and his face was very red,
And ever and anon he scratched with energy his head.
His manners were not always nice, but how my spirit cried
To be an artless *Bandar* loose upon the mountain-side!

So I answered:—'Gentle *Bandar*, an inscrutable Decree,
Makes thee a gleesome fleasome Thou, and me a wretched Me.
Go! Depart in peace, my brother, to thy home amid the pine;
Yet forget not once a mortal wished to change his lot with thine.'

RUDYARD KIPLING

The Everlasting Percy

(After John Masefield's 'The Everlasting Mercy')

I used to be a fearful lad,
The things I did were downright bad;
And worst of all were what I done
From seventeen to twenty-one
On all the railways far and wide
From sinfulness and shameful pride.

For several years I was so wicked
I used to go without a ticket,
And travelled underneath the seat
Down in the dust of people's feet,
Or else I sat as bold as brass
And told them 'Season', in first-class.

In 1921, at Harwich,
I smoked in a non-smoking carriage;
I never knew what Life nor Art meant,
I wrote 'Reserved' on my compartment,
And once (I was a guilty man)
I swopped the labels in guard's van.

From 1922 to 4
I leant against the carriage door
Without a-looking at the latch;
And once, a-leaving Colney Hatch,
I put a huge and heavy parcel
Which I were taking to Newcastle,
Entirely filled with lumps of lead,
Up on the rack above my head;
And when it tumbled down, oh Lord!
I pulled communication cord.
The guard came round and said, 'You mule!
What have you done, you dirty fool?'
I simply sat and smiled, and said
'Is this train right for Holyhead?'
He said, 'You blinking blasted swine,
You'll have to pay the five-pound fine.'
At Bickershaw and Strood and Staines
I've often got on moving trains,
And once alit at Norwood West
Before my coach had come to rest.
A window and a lamp I broke
At Chipping Sodbury and Stoke
And worse I did at Wissendine:
I threw out bottles on the line
And other articles as be
Likely to cause grave injury
To persons working on the line—
That's what I did at Wissendine.
I grew so careless what I'd do
Throwing things out, and dangerous too,
That, last and worst of all I'd done,
I threw a great sultana bun
Out of the train at Pontypridd—
It hit a platelayer, it did.

I thought that I should have to swing
And never hear the sweet birds sing.
But Judge he turned and said to Jury,
'Did Prisoner in a fit of fury
Remember as a bun so hard
Was like to kill at fifteen yard?
If not, you fellows may decide
'Twas accidental homicide.'
The Jury thinks the Judge half-witted,
And, come a month, I were acquitted.

E. V. KNOX

An Idle Word

I used to wear a diamond ring,
A small but valuable thing,
A souvenir of how and when
I had succeeded up till then.
I used to wear it day and night.
I polished it to keep it bright.
I never took it off. I'd sit
For hours at home and look at it.
For years and years I'd had to wait
To make it mine. It kept me straight.

When, too, in shops I've sat at tea,
People would stare at it, and me—
Not knowing *who* I might not be.
I'd just call, 'Miss!'—the waitress would
Scamper to bring me drink and food.
Then with my hand I'd smooth my hair,
Knowing my diamond safely there.

198

Often, when walking in the street,
'Aha!' I've thought (the thought was sweet),
'They little guess what's lying hid
Beneath this glove!' (of suède or kid).
If only I'd been let alone,
I'd have stayed happy with that stone.
But no. In this world there are them
   Who envy even a gem.
One day I heard a lady say—
And as she spoke, she looked my way:
'A diamond is a vulgar thing
To see corusking in a ring;
And, like as not, as I've been told,
They're only glass—in brass: not gold.'

I rose. I felt, without a doubt,
My very life-blood trickling out.
I sold the ring, at awful loss,
To one I knew named Isaac Moss.
And now in life no hope I see;
Its bottom's fallen out for me.

My situation's gone; I owe
Not less than twenty pounds or so;
Outside a Public House I stand,
With loafers upon either hand;
And if a Constable draws near,
My skin goes cold and stiff with fear;
He knows I know he's but to wait
And some dark cell will be my fate.

It only proves—what good men teach—
We should be cautious in our speech.
If that proud lady had not said
My diamond of glass was made,
Should I be drifting in my prime
Into a cul-de-sac of crime?
One heedless, scoffing word—and see!
What the old vixen's done for me!

WALTER DE LA MARE

199

The Plaint of the Middlebrow Novelist

I've written my dozens of novels
I've signed autographs by the score
(and my portrait in oils and my photo at Foyles)
—and I've spoken at Harrods at four;
The money is never a problem
I sell like the proverbial hot cake;
And the libraries fight for each word that I write,
Yet I have this incurable ache:—

Refrain
I wanna be known as a Highbrow.
I want my prestige to go up;
I don't want romance—I want Mr Gollancz
And a par in the dear old *Lit. Sup*.
To hell with my library public;
To hell with a cheaper edition;
A sentence or two in a weekly review
Remains my unswerving ambition.
OH!—
I wanna turn into a Classic
—I'm as good as the next on the list—
I want *some* indication, from the *Statesman and Nation*
That I—as an author—exist.
To hell with the Book of the Month club;
And my serial rights in Cathay—
I wanna be known as a Highbrow
And I don't care what Hutchinsons say!

PHOEBE FENWICK GAYE

Moan in the Form of a Ballade

I went to someone's dinner and a play,
  And supper, with a man whose name was Duff,
Or Herbert Spencer, or the poet Gray.
  I felt inclined to chatter like a chough.
  The Cardinal, whose health I drank, was Puff,
When all at once the wine went to my head,
  I felt as if at sea about to luff.
I can't remember how I went to bed.

The chairs and tables glimmered far away;
  I thought I heard Sir William Wellenough
Remark upon the road to Mandalay,
  How much he liked a little bit of fluff.
  Then everybody played at Blind Man's Buff;
It must have been, I think, my nose that bled.
  I heard a player shout 'I'll call the bluff.'
I can't remember how I went to bed.

I'm feeling very far from well today;
  I cannot bear the taste of smoke or snuff,
Nor anything that's brought upon a tray,
  My brow is fevered and my voice is gruff.
  I've taken what is called a *Quantum Suff*,
Or *Nisi prius* as the lawyer said.
  The doctor came and left me in a huff.
I can't remember how I went to bed.

Envoy
  Prince, have you heard of that tremendous stuff
That startles into life the quiet dead?
  I drank it till I felt I'd had enough.
I can't remember how I went to bed.

MAURICE BARING

The Cockney of the North

(*W. B. Yeats*)

I will arise and go now, and go to Inverness,
   And a small villa rent there, of lath and plaster built;
Nine bedrooms will I have there, and I'll don my native dress,
   And walk about in a d—— loud kilt.

And I will have some sport there, when grouse come driven slow,
   Driven from purple hilltops to where the loaders quail;
While midges bite their ankles, and shots are flying low,
   And the air is full of the grey-hen's tail.

I will arise and go now, for ever, day and night,
   I hear the taxis bleating and the motor-'buses roar,
And over tarred macadam and pavements parched and white
   I've walked till my feet are sore!

For it's oh, to be in Scotland! now that August's nearly there,
   Where the capercailzie warble on the mountain's rugged brow;
There's pleasure and contentment, there's sport and bracing air,
   In Scotland—now!

HARRY GRAHAM

Ringsend

(*After reading Tolstoi*)

I will live in Ringsend
With a red-headed whore,
And the fan-light gone in
Where it lights the hall-door;
And listen each night
For her querulous shout,
As at last she streels in
And the pubs empty out.

To soothe that wild breast
With my old-fangled songs,
Till she feels it redressed
From inordinate wrongs,
Imagined, outrageous,
Preposterous wrongs,
Till peace at last comes,
Shall be all I will do,
Where the little lamp blooms
Like a rose in the stew;
And up the back-garden
The sound comes to me
Of the lapsing, unsoilable,
Whispering sea.

OLIVER ST JOHN GOGARTY

Cancer's a Funny Thing

I wish I had the voice of Homer
To sing of rectal carcinoma,
Which kills a lot more chaps, in fact,
Than were bumped off when Troy was sacked.
Yet, thanks to modern surgeons' skills,
It can be killed before it kills
Upon a scientific basis
In nineteen out of twenty cases.
I noticed I was passing blood
(Only a few drops, not a flood).
So pausing on my homeward way
From Tallahassee to Bombay
I asked a doctor, now my friend,
To peer into my hinder end,
To prove or to disprove the rumour
That I had a malignant tumour.
They pumped in Ba S O$_4$
Till I could really stand no more,
And, when sufficient had been pressed in,
They photographed my large intestine.
In order to decide the issue
They next scraped out some bits of tissue.

203

(Before they did so, some good pal
Had knocked me out with pentothal,
Whose action is extremely quick,
And does not leave me feeling sick.)
The microscope returned the answer
That I had certainly got cancer.
So I was wheeled into the theatre
Where holes were made to make me better.
One set is in my perineum
Where I can feel, but can't yet see 'em.
Another made me like a kipper
Or female prey of Jack the Ripper.
Through this incision, I don't doubt,
The neoplasm was taken out,
Along with colon, and lymph nodes
Where cancer cells might find abodes.
A third much smaller hole is meant
To function as a ventral vent:
So now I am like two-faced Janus
The only* god who sees his anus.
I'll swear, without the risk of perjury,
It was a snappy bit of surgery.
My rectum is a serious loss to me,
But I've a very neat colostomy,
And hope, as soon as I am able,
To make it keep a fixed time-table.
So do not wait for aches and pains
To have a surgeon mend your drains;
If he says 'cancer' you're a dunce
Unless you have it out at once,
For if you wait it's sure to swell,
And may have progeny as well.
My final word, before I'm done,
Is 'Cancer can be rather fun'.
Thanks to the nurses and Nye Bevan
The NHS is quite like heaven
Provided one confronts the tumour
With a sufficient sense of humour.

---

*In India there are several more
With extra faces, up to four,
But both in Brahma and in Shiva
I own myself an unbeliever.*

DORSET COUNTY LIBRARY

I know that cancer often kills,
But so do cars and sleeping pills;
And it can hurt one till one sweats,
So can bad teeth and unpaid debts.
A spot of laughter, I am sure,
Often accelerates one's cure;
So let us patients do our bit
To help the surgeons make us fit.

J. B. S. HALDANE

Wishes of an Elderly Man

I wish I loved the Human Race;
I wish I loved its silly face;
I wish I liked the way it walks;
I wish I liked the way it talks;
And when I'm introduced to one
I wish I thought *What Jolly Fun!*

WALTER RALEIGH

Strange Type

I wrote: in the dark cavern of our birth.
The printer had it tavern, which seems better:
But herein lies the subject of our mirth,
Since on the next page death appears as dearth.
So it may be that God's word was distraction,
Which to our strange type appears destruction,
Which is bitter.

MALCOLM LOWRY

Jenny Kissed Me

Jenny kissed me when we met,
   Jumping from the chair she sat in;
Time, you thief! who love to get
   Sweets into your list, put that in.
Say I'm weary, say I'm sad;
   Say that health and wealth have missed me;
Say I'm growing old, but add—
      Jenny kissed me!

LEIGH HUNT

A Novel

Joseph Conrad's *'Chance'*
Shows you (not exactly at a glance)
How Captain Anthony
Sees snags where there aren't any.

L. E. JONES

Karl Marx

Karl Marx
Was completely wrapped up in his sharks.
The poor creatures seriously missed him
When he was attacking the capitalist system.

E. CLERIHEW BENTLEY

206

Gas from a Burner

(As from the mouth of George Roberts, the Dublin publisher who wanted Joyce to bowdlerize Dubliners *and change all the proper names. Roberts's printer destroyed – Joyce said, by burning – the proofs of the book, claiming the stories offended his patriotism)*

Ladies and gents, you are here assembled
To hear why earth and heaven trembled
Because of the black and sinister arts
Of an Irish writer in foreign parts.
He sent me a book ten years ago;
I read it a hundred times or so,
Backwards and forwards, down and up,
Through both ends of a telescope.
I printed it all to the very last word
But by the mercy of the Lord
The darkness of my mind was rent
And I saw the writer's foul intent.
But I owe a duty to Ireland:
I hold her honour in my hand,
This lovely land that always sent
Her writers and artists to banishment
And in a spirit of Irish fun
Betrayed her own leaders, one by one.
'Twas Irish humour, wet and dry,
Flung quicklime into Parnell's eye . . .
To show you for strictures I don't care a button
I printed the poems of Mountainy Mutton
And a play he wrote (you've read it, I'm sure)
Where they talk of 'bastard', 'bugger' and 'whore',
And a play on the Word and Holy Paul
And some woman's legs that I can't recall,
Written by Moore, a genuine gent
That lives on his property's ten per cent:
I printed mystical books in dozens:
I printed the table-book of Cousins
Though (asking your pardon) as for the verse
'Twould give you a heartburn on your arse:
I printed folklore from North and South
By Gregory of the Golden Mouth:
I printed poets, sad silly and solemn:

I printed Patrick What-do-you-Colm:
I printed the great John Milicent Synge
Who soars above on an angel's wing
In the playboy shift that he pinched as swag
From Maunsel's manager's travelling-bag.*
But I draw the line at that bloody fellow
That was over here dressed in Austrian yellow,
Spouting Italian by the hour
To O'Leary Curtis and John Wyse Power
And writing of Dublin, dirty and dear,
In a manner no blackamoor printer could bear.
Shite and onions! Do you think I'll print
The name of the Wellington Monument,
Sydney Parade and Sandymount tram,
Downes's cakeshop and Williams's jam?
I'm damned if I do—I'm damned to blazes!
Talk about *Irish Names of Places*!
It's a wonder to me, upon my soul,
He forgot to mention Curly's Hole.
No, ladies, my press shall have no share in
So gross a libel on Stepmother Erin,†
I pity the poor—that's why I took
A red-headed Scotchman to keep my book.‡
Poor sister Scotland! Her doom is fell;
She cannot find any more Stuarts to sell.
My conscience is fine as Chinese silk:
My heart is as soft as buttermilk.
Colm can tell you I made a rebate
Of one hundred pounds on the estimate
I gave him for his *Irish Review*.
I love my country—by herrings I do!

      *   *   *

Who was it said: Resist not evil?
I'll burn that book, so help me devil!
I'll sing a psalm as I watch it burn
And the ashes I'll keep in a one-handled urn.
I'll penance do with farts and groans
Kneeling upon my marrowbones.

---

* '*A reference both to Roberts's claim to intrepidity for having published Synge and to his former profession of traveller for ladies' underwear*' (*Ellman*, James Joyce).
† *Roberts was an Ulster Scot.*
‡ *Roberts was his own book-keeper.*

This very next lent I will unbare
My penitent buttocks to the air
And sobbing beside my printing press
My awful sin I will confess.
My Irish foreman from Bannockburn
Shall dip his right hand in the urn
And sign crisscross with reverent thumb
Memento homo upon my bum.

JAMES JOYCE

Twelve Articles

1   Lest it may more quarrels breed
    I will never hear you read.
2   By disputing I will never
    To convince you, once endeavour.
3   When a paradox you stick to,
    I will never contradict you.
4   When I talk, and you are heedless,
    I will show no anger needless.
5   When your speeches are absurd,
    I will ne'er object one word.
6   When you furious argue wrong,
    I will grieve, and hold my tongue.
7   Not a jest, or humorous story,
    Will I ever tell before ye:
    To be chidden for explaining
    When you quite mistake the meaning.
8   Never more will I suppose
    You can taste my verse or prose:
9   You no more at me shall fret,
    While I teach, and you forget;
10 You shall never hear me thunder,
    When you blunder on, and blunder.
11 Show your poverty of spirit,
    And in dress place all your merit;
    Give yourself ten thousand airs
    That with me shall break no squares.

12   Never will I give advice
       Till you please to ask me thrice;
       Which, if you in scorn reject,
       'Twill be just as I expect.

    Thus we both shall have our ends,
And continue special friends.

JONATHAN SWIFT

Let Us Play on the Pianner

Let us play on the pianner in a melancholy manner,
Drinking ipecacuanha while you listen to my songs;
Let us play the bagpipes mellow, and the flute and violoncello,
And the tea-tray and the bellows, and the poker and the tongs.

His dancing made me giddy, and I said 'Oh, do be steady,
Or your wife will be a widdy, and the tears will fill my eyes':
But in spite of all my cautions, he continued his contortions,
Till he broke himself in portions of an unimportant size.

Oh, goodbye! goodbye for ever! You were truly, truly clever
Though you never, never, never did appreciate my songs;
But it didn't make me jealous, and I'll dig your grave most
    zealous,
With the pick-axe and the bellows, and the poker and the tongs.

A. E. HOUSMAN

Song of the Ballet

    Lift her up tenderly,
    Raise her with care,
    Catch hold of one leg,
    And a handful of hair;
    Swing her round savagely,
    And when this palls,
    Heave-Ho! Away with her
    Into the stalls.

J. B. MORTON

'Lips that touch wine jelly'

Lips that touch wine jelly
Will never touch mine, Nellie.

ANON

Contentment

'Man wants but little here below'

Little I ask; my wants are few;
　　I only wish a hut of stone,
(A *very plain* brown stone will do,)
　　　　That I may call my own;
And close at hand is such a one,
In yonder street that fronts the sun.

Plain food is quite enough for me;
　　Three courses are as good as ten;—
If nature can subsist on three,
　　　　Thank heaven for three. Amen!
I always thought cold victual nice;—
My *choice* would be vanilla-ice.

I care not much for gold or land;
　　Give me a mortgage here and there,—
Some good bank-stock,—some note of hand,
　　　　Or trifling railroad share;—
I only ask that fortune send
A *little* more than I shall spend.

Honors are silly toys, I know,
　　And titles are but empty names;—
I would, *perhaps*, be plenipo,—
　　　　But only near St James;—
I'm very sure I should not care
To fill our gubernator's chair.

Jewels are baubles; 'tis a sin
  To care for such unfruitful things;—
One good-sized diamond in a pin,—
      Some, *not so large*, in rings,—
A ruby, and a pearl, or so,
Will do for me;—I laugh at show.

My dame should dress in cheap attire;
  (Good, heavy silks are never dear;)—
I own perhaps I *might* desire
      Some shawls of true cashmere,—
Some narrowy crapes of China silk,
Like wrinkled skins on scalded milk.

I would not have the horse I drive
  So fast that folks must stop and stare;
An easy gait—two, forty-five—
      Suits me; I do not care;—
Perhaps, for just a *single spurt*,
Some seconds less would do no hurt.

Of pictures, I should like to own
  Titians and Raphaels three or four,—
I love so much their style and tone,—
      One Turner, and no more
(A landscape,—foreground golden dirt;
The sunshine painted with a squirt).

Of books but few,—some fifty score
  For daily use, and bound for wear;
The rest upon an upper floor;—
      Some *little* luxury *there*
Of red morocco's gilded gleam,
And vellum rich as country cream.

Busts, cameos, gems,—such things as these,
  Which others often show for pride,
I value for their power to please,
      And selfish churls deride;—
One Stradivarius, I confess,
Two Meerschaums, I would fain possess.

Wealth's wasteful tricks I will not learn
 Nor ape the glittering upstart fool;—
Shall not carved tables serve my turn,
  But *all* must be of buhl?
Give grasping pomp its double share,—
I ask but *one* recumbent chair.

Thus humble let me live and die,
 Nor long for Midas' golden touch;
If heaven more generous gifts deny,
  I shall not miss them *much*,—
Too grateful for the blessing lent
Of simple tastes and mind content!

OLIVER WENDELL HOLMES

One-and-Twenty

A short song of congratulation to Sir John Lade

Long-expected one-and-twenty,
 Lingering year, at length is flown:
Pride and pleasure, pomp and plenty,
 Great Sir John, are now your own.

Loosened from the minor's tether,
 Free to mortgage or to sell,
Wild as wind and light as feather,
 Bid the sons of thrift farewell.

Call the Betsies, Kates, and Jennies,
 All the names that banish care;
Lavish of your grandsire's guineas,
 Show the spirit of an heir.

All that prey on vice and folly
 Joy to see their quarry fly:
There the gamester, light and jolly,
 There the lender, grave and sly.

Wealth, my lad, was made to wander,
  Let it wander as it will;
Call the jockey, call the pander,
  Bid them come and take their fill.

When the bonny blade carouses,
  Pockets full, and spirits high—
What are acres? What are houses?
  Only dirt, or wet or dry.

Should the guardian friend or mother
  Tell the woes of wilful waste,
Scorn their counsel, scorn their pother;—
  You can hang or drown at last!

                              SAMUEL JOHNSON

The Curse

*(To a sister of an enemy of the author's, who disapproved of
'The Playboy')*

Lord, confound this surly sister,
Blight her brow with blotch and blister,
Cramp her larynx, lung and liver,
In her guts a galling give her.
Let her live to earn her dinners
In Mountjoy with seedy sinners:
Lord, this judgement quickly bring,
And I'm your servant, J. M. Synge.

                              J. M. SYNGE

214

'Lunching one day with Morgan'

Lunching one day with Morgan
I was weary and ill at ease,
For he started quoting 'Sparkenbroke'
Before we had reached the cheese;
I knew not what he was saying
(And was past caring then),
So I struck him on the schnozzle
With the Corton, 1910.

NICOLAS BENTLEY

Daily Trials

(By a dyspeptic)

Prestissimo

'Lunch, Sir? Yes, 'er. Pickled salmon,
Lobster, kidneys, greens, and——' 'Gammon!
Have you got no wholesome meat, Sir?
Flesh or fowl that one can eat, Sir?'
'Eat, Sir? Yes, 'er. Heaven bless yer!
Pork, Sir.' 'Pork, Sir, I detest, Sir.'
'Oysters?' 'Are to me unblest, Sir.'
'Duck, Sir?' 'No, Sir; gutter-roker—
Sooner eat the kitchen poker.'
'Fish, Sir?' 'Pish, Sir!' 'Bones, Sir?' 'Devil!'
'Sausage?' 'I shall be uncivil!
Hath a puppy charms for Briton?'

Can the soul rejoice in kitten?'
'Shrimps, Sir? Prawns, Sir? Crawfish? Winkle?
Scallops ready in a twinkle?
Wilks and cockles? Crabs to follow?'
'Heavens! *nothing* I can swallow!'
'Swallow? Yes, 'er; on the dresser
Dishes stand, from one to twenty.'
'Cuss you, Waiter! bring a tater—
I shall starve in midst of plenty!'

H. CHOLMONDELEY PENNELL

Epitaph

Malcolm Lowry
Late of the Bowery
His prose was flowery
And often glowery
He lived, nightly, and drank, daily,
And died playing the ukulele.

MALCOLM LOWRY

Molly Bloom

(To the tune of 'Molly Brannigan')

Man dear, did you never hear of buxom Molly Bloom at all
As plump an Irish beauty, sir, as Annie Levy Blumenthal,
If she sat in the vice-regal box Tim Healy'd have no room at all,
　　But curl up in a corner at a glance from her eye.
The tale of her ups and downs would aisy fill a handybook
That would cover the whole world across from Gib right on to
　　Sandy Hook,
But now that tale is told, ahone, I've lost my daring dandy look
　　Since Molly Bloom has gone and left me here for to die.

Man dear, I remember when my roving time was troubling me
We picnicked fine in storm or shine in France and Spain and
    Hungary,
And she said I'd be her first and last while the wine I poured went
    bubbling free.
    Now every male she meets with has a finger in her pie.
Man dear, I remember how with all the heart and brain of me
I arrayed her for the bridal, but, oh, she proved the bane of me,
With more puppies sniffing round her than the wooers of
    Penelope
    She's left me on the doorstep like a dog for to die.

My left eye is awash and his neighbour full of water, man,
I cannot see the lass I limned for Ireland's gamest daughter, man,
When I hear her lovers tumbling in their thousands for to court
    her, man,
    If I were sure I'd not be seen I'd sit down and cry.
May you live, may you love like this gaily spinning earth of ours,
And every morn a gallous sun awake you to fresh wealth of gold,
But if I cling like a child to the clouds that are your petticoats,
    O Molly, handsome Molly, sure you won't let me die?

JAMES JOYCE

Ballad of the Bread Man

Mary stood in the kitchen
    Baking a loaf of bread.
An angel flew in through the window.
    'We've a job for you,' he said.

'God in his big gold heaven,
    Sitting in his big blue chair,
Wanted a mother for his little son.
    Suddenly saw you there.'

Mary shook and trembled,
    'It isn't true what you say.'
'Don't say that,' said the angel.
    'The baby's on its way.'

Joseph was in the workshop
  Planing a piece of wood.
'The old man's past it,' the neighbours said.
  'That girl's been up to no good.'

'And who was that elegant fellow',
  They said, 'in the shiny gear?'
The things they said about Gabriel
  Were hardly fit to hear.

Mary never answered,
  Mary never replied.
She kept the information,
  Like the baby, safe inside.

It was election winter.
  They went to vote in town.
When Mary found her time had come
  The hotels let her down.

The baby was born in an annexe
  Next to the local pub.
At midnight, a delegation
  Turned up from the Farmers' Club.

They talked about an explosion
  That made a hole in the sky,
Said they'd been sent to the Lamb & Flag
  To see God come down from on high.

A few days later a bishop
  And a five-star general were seen
With the head of an African country
  In a bullet-proof limousine.

'We've come', they said, 'with tokens
  For the little boy to choose.'
Told the tale about war and peace
  In the television news.

After them came the soldiers
　　With rifle and bomb and gun,
Looking for enemies of the state.
　　The family had packed and gone.

When they got back to the village
　　The neighbours said, to a man,
'That boy will never be one of us,
　　Though he does what he blessed well can.'

He went round to all the people
　　A paper crown on his head.
Here is some bread from my father.
　　Take, eat, he said.

Nobody seemed very hungry.
　　Nobody seemed to care.
Nobody saw the god in himself
　　Quietly standing there.

He finished up in the papers.
　　He came to a very bad end.
He was charged with bringing the living to life.
　　No man was that prisoner's friend.

There's only one kind of punishment
　　To fit that kind of a crime.
They rigged a trial and shot him dead.
　　They were only just in time.

They lifted the young man by the leg,
　　They lifted him by the arm,
They locked him in a cathedral
　　In case he came to harm.

They stored him safe as water
　　Under seven rocks.
One Sunday morning he burst out
　　Like a jack-in-the-box.

Through the town he went walking.
He showed them the holes in his head.
Now do you want any loaves? he cried.
'Not today,' they said.

CHARLES CAUSELEY

Sweetness and Light

Maud, a most ingenious lass,
Made meringues of powdered glass;
Served them on a plastic plate
At St Botolph's Garden Fete.
While the Parson talked of tithing,
Half the Parish lay there writhing.
Said the Dean 'Here's half a nicker.
Slip the last one to the Vicar.'

URSULA WADEY

The Traveller's Curse after Misdirection

(From the Welsh)

May they wander stage by stage
Of the same vain pilgrimage,
Stumbling on, age after age,
Night and day, mile after mile,
At each and every step, a stile;
At each and every stile, withal,
May they catch their feet and fall;
At each and every fall they take,
May a bone within them break,
And may the bones that break within
Not be, for variation's sake,
Now rib, now thigh, now arm, now shin,
But always, without fail, THE NECK.

ROBERT GRAVES

220

Old Bridget Complains to the Lord

Merciful hour! God mend the pig,
He'd lead the Archangel himself a jig.
Eight chickens he's killed, and this makes nine,
And ate my old nightshift off o' the line,
And the brim of Darius's billycock hat.
Go on, ye brute! Go on out of that!

That animal does whatever he plazes,
He'll be staid by no one. O holy Jasus,
'Twas yourself that put the divil in swine,
So it's not for the likes of me to repine.
Sure we all has our hardship and must go through it—
But, Jasus dear, oh, for why did Ye do it?

L. A. G. STRONG

The Atheist and the Acorn

Methinks this world is oddly made,
  And everything's amiss,
A dull presuming atheist said,
As stretched, he lay beneath a shade,
  And instanced in this:

Behold, quoth he, that mighty thing,
  A pumpkin, large and round,
Is held but by a little string,
Which upwards cannot make it spring,
  Or bear it from the ground.

Whilst on this oak a fruit so small,
  So disproportioned, grows,
That, who with sense surveys this All,
This universal, casual ball,
  Its ill contrivance knows.

My better judgment would have hung
    That weight upon a tree,
And left this mast, thus slightly strung,
'Mongst things which on the surface sprung,
    And small and feeble be.

No more the caviller could say,
    Nor further faults descry,
For as he upward, gazing lay,
An acorn, loosened from the stay,
    Fell down upon his eye.

Th' offended part with tears ran o'er,
    As punished for the sun.
Fool! had that bough a pumpkin bore,
Thy whimsies must have worked no more,
    Nor skull had kept them in.

                        LADY WINCHILSEA

Peekaboo, I Almost See You

Middle-aged life is merry, and I love to lead it,
But there comes a day when your eyes are all right but your arm
    isn't long enough to hold the telephone book where you can
    read it,
And your friends get jocular, so you go to the oculist,
And of all your friends he is the joculist,
So over his facetiousness let us skim,
Only noting that he has been waiting for you ever since you said
    Good evening to his grandfather clock under the impression
    that it was him,
And you look at his chart and it says SHRDLU QWERTYOP, and
    you say Well, why SHRDNTLU QWERTYOP? and he says
    one set of glasses won't do.
You need two,
One for reading Erle Stanley Gardner's Perry Mason and Keats's
    'Endymion' with,
And the other for walking around without saying Hello to strange
    wymion with.

222

So you spend your time taking off your seeing glasses to put on your
 reading glasses, and then remembering that your reading
 glasses are upstairs or in the car,
And then you can't find your seeing glasses again because without
 them on you can't see where they are.
Enough of such mishaps, they would try the patience of an ox,
I prefer to forget both pairs of glasses and pass my declining years
 saluting strange women and grandfather clocks.

OGDEN NASH

The Private Dining Room

Miss Rafferty wore taffeta,
Miss Cavendish wore lavender.
We ate pickerel and mackerel
And other lavish provender.
Miss Cavendish was Lalage,
Miss Rafferty was Barbara.
We gobbled pickled mackerel
And broke the candelabara,
Miss Cavendish in lavender,
In taffeta, Miss Rafferty,
The girls in taffeta lavender,
And we, of course, in mufti.

Miss Rafferty wore taffeta,
The taffeta was lavender,
Was lavend, lavender, lavenderest,
As the wine improved the provender.
Miss Cavendish wore lavender,
The lavender was taffeta.
We boggled mackled pickerel,
And bumpers did we quaffeta.
And Lalage wore lavender,
And lavender wore Barbara,
Rafferta taffeta Cavender lavender
Barbara abracadabra.

Miss Rafferty in taffeta
Grew definitely raffisher.
Miss Cavendish in lavender
Grew less and less stand-offisher.
With Lalage and Barbara
We grew a little pickereled,
We ordered Mumm and Roederer
Because the bubbles tickereled.
But lavender and taffeta
Were gone when we were soberer.
I haven't thought for thirty years
Of Lalage and Barbara.

OGDEN NASH

Miss Twye

Miss Twye was soaping her breasts in her bath
When she heard behind her a meaning laugh
And to her amazement she discovered
A wicked man in her bathroom cupboard.

GAVIN EWART

Blackheath

Mister Jones is very old—
Eighty-seven, I've been told—
And he has bags and bags of Gold
    In Bar——clay's——Bank.
His life is steady as a clock,
His principles are firm as rock;
He comes of Nonconformist stock,
    Of Wealth—and—Rank.
    His Father was a Quaker;
    His mother, Lady Ethel,
    Preferred the Little Bethel
        Her Tablet now adorns;

And on a bright May morning, still,
When blooms the gorse on Shooter's Hill,
   He toddles down to Greenwich
   To praise the Lord his Maker
   With Gammon and with Spinach,
     With Crumpets and with Prawns.

         W. BRIDGES-ADAMS

For a' That and a' That

More luck to honest poverty,
   It claims respect, and a' that;
But honest wealth's a better thing,
   We dare be rich for a' that.
     For a' that, and a' that,
      And spooney cant and a' that,
     A man may have a ten-pun note,
      And be a brick for a' that.

What though on soup and fish we dine,
   Wear evening togs and a' that,
A man may like good meat and wine,
   Nor be a knave for a' that.
     For a' that, and a' that,
      Their fustian talk and a' that,
     A gentleman, however clean,
      May have a heart for a' that.

You see yon prater called a Beales,
   Who bawls and brays and a' that,
Tho' hundreds cheer his blatant bosh,
   He's but a goose for a' that.
     For a' that, and a' that,
      His Bubblyjocks, and a' that,
     A man with twenty grains of sense,
      He looks and laughs at a' that.

225

A prince can make a belted knight,
   A marquis, duke, and a' that,
And if the title's earned, all right,
   Old England's fond of a' that.
     For a' that, and a' that,
       Beales' balderdash, and a' that,
     A name that tells of service done
     Is worth the wear, for a' that.

Then let us pray that come it may
   And come it will for a' that,
That common sense may take the place
   Of common cant and a' that.
     For a' that, and a' that,
       Who cackles trash and a' that,
     Or be he lord, or be he low,
     The man's an ass for a' that.

SHIRLEY BROOKS

Journalism

Mr Ernest Newman
Said 'Next week, Schumann.'
But when next week came
It was Wagner just the same.

L. E. JONES

Mr Ody

Mr Ody met a body
Hanging from a tree;
And what was worse
He met a hearse
As black as black could be.

Mr Ody said 'By God, he
Ought to have a ride.'
Said the driver 'I'd oblige yer,
But we're full inside.'

E. NESBIT

Mrs Simpkins

Mrs Simpkins never had very much to do
So it occurred to her one day that the Trinity wasn't true
Or at least but a garbled version of the truth
And that things had moved very far since the days of her youth.
So she became a spiritualist and at her very first party
Just to give her a feeling of confidence the spirit spoke up
hearty:
'Since I crossed over dear friends' it said 'I'm no different to what I
was before
Death's not a separation or alteration or parting it's just a
one-handled door
We spirits can come back to you if your seance is orthodox
But you can't come over to us till your body's shut in a box
And this is the great thought I want to leave with you today
You've heard it before but in case you forgot death isn't a
passing away
It's just a carrying on with friends relations and brightness
Only you don't have to bother with sickness and there's no
financial tightness.'
Mrs Simpkins went home and told her husband he was a weak
pated fellow
And when he heard the news he turned a daffodil shade of
yellow
'What do you mean, Maria?' he cried, 'it can't be true there's
no rest
From one's uncles and brothers and sisters nor even the wife
of one's breast?'
'It's the truth,' Mrs Simpkins affirmed, 'there is no separation
There's a great reunion coming for which this life's but a
preparation.'

This worked him to such a pitch that he shot himself through
                                    the head
And now she has to polish the floors of Westminster County
                                 Hall for her daily bread.

STEVIE SMITH

The Bards

My aged friend, Miss Wilkinson,
Whose mother was a Lambe,
Saw Wordsworth once, and Coleridge too,
One morning in her pram.*

Bird-like the bards stooped over her—
Like fledgling in a nest;
And Wordsworth said, 'Thou harmless babe!'
And Coleridge was impressed.

The pretty thing gazed up and smiled,
And softly murmured, 'Coo!'
William was then aged sixty-four
And Samuel sixty-two.

* This was a three-wheeled vehicle
  Of iron and of wood;
  It had a leather apron
  But it hadn't any hood.

WALTER DE LA MARE

First Fig

My candle burns at both ends;
  It will not last the night;
But ah, my foes, and oh, my friends—
  It gives a lovely light!

EDNA ST VINCENT MILLAY

A Suggestion

*(Addressed to the lady or gentleman who had abstracted two
pictures from the Royal Academy)*

My friend, why did you hold your hand,
  Why falter, why desist,
When there are treasures in the land
  That never would be missed?
Next time you plunder the RA,
  Its precincts do not quit
Till you have made, as plumbers say,
  A thorough job of it.
Take ev'ry so-called work of art
And (with a nation's thanks) depart!

Remove each Royal Portrait, do,
  Each Presentation Bust,
And all those Problem Pictures, too,
  Which have to be discussed.
Take ev'ry daub that's labelled 'Spring'
  Or 'Chelsea in a Fog',
Or 'Home again!' or 'Baby's Swing',
  Or 'Mrs A. and Dog'.
Take 'Hanging up the Mistletoe!'
And (with the public's blessing) go!

Then prosecute your search elsewhere,
  If fame you wish to win;
Take Shakespeare's bust from Leicester Square
  And Cleopatra's Pin.
Take sculptured Statesmen, hand to breast,
  Who on our pavements smile,
And half the statues that congest
  The Abbey's crowded aisle,
And, last of all, whate'er befall,
Don't fail to take the Albert Hall!

ANON

To Cosmo Cantuar: on the occasion of his broadcast concerning a Royal abdication

My lord Archbishop, what a scold you are!
And when your man is down how bold you are!
Of charity how oddly scant you are!
How Lang O Lord, how full of Cantuar!

GERALD BULLETT

Epigram

My Lord complains that Pope, stark mad with gardens,
Has cut three trees, the value of three farthings.
'But he's my neighbour,' cries the peer polite:
'And if he visit me, I'll waive the right.'
What! on compulsion, and against my will,
A lord's acquaintance? Let him file his bill!

ALEXANDER POPE

My Muse

My muse and I, ere youth and spirits fled,
Sat up together many a night, no doubt:
But now I've sent the poor old lass to bed,
Simply because my fire is going out.

GEORGE COLMAN, THE YOUNGER

A New Song of New Similes

My passion is as mustard strong:
  I sit all sober sad;
Drunk as a piper all day long,
  Or like a March hare mad.

Round as a hoop the bumpers flow;
  I drink, yet can't forget her;
For though as drunk as David's sow,
  I love her still the better.

Pert as a pear-monger I'd be,
  If Molly were but kind;
Cool as a cucumber could see
  The rest of womankind.

Like a stuck pig I gaping stare,
  And eye her o'er and o'er;
Lean as a rake with sighs and care,
  Sleek as mouse before.

Plump as a partridge was I known,
  And soft as silk my skin,
My cheeks as fat as butter grown;
  But as a groat now thin!

I melancholy as a cat,
  Am kept awake to weep;
But she, insensible of that,
  Sound as a top can sleep.

Hard is her heart as flint or stone,
  She laughs to see me pale,
And merry as a grig is grown,
  And brisk as bottled ale.

The God of Love at her approach
　　Is busy as a bee.
Hearts sound as any bell or roach,
　　Are smit and sigh like me.

Ah me! as thick as hops or hail,
　　The fine men crowd about her;
But soon as dead as a door-nail
　　Shall I be if without her.

Straight as my leg her shape appears;
　　O were we joined together!
My heart would be scot-free from cares,
　　And lighter than a feather.

As fine as five-pence is her mien,
　　No drum was ever tighter;
Her glance is as the razor keen,
　　And not the sun is brighter.

As soft as pap her kisses are,
　　Methinks I taste them yet;
Brown as a berry is her hair,
　　Her eyes as black as jet:

As smooth as glass, as white as curds,
　　Her pretty hand invites;
Sharp as a needle are her words,
　　Her wit like pepper, bites:

Brisk as a body-louse she trips,
　　Clean as a penny drest;
Sweet as a rose her breath and lips,
　　Round as the globe her breast.

Full as an egg was I with glee;
　　And happy as a king.
Good L——d! how all men envied me!
　　She loved like any thing.

But false as hell, she, like the wind,
    Changed, as her sex must do;
Though seeming as the turtle kind,
    And like the gospel true.

If I and Molly could agree,
    Let who would take Peru!
Great as an emp'eror should be,
    And richer than a Jew;

Till you grow tender as a chick
    I'm dull as any post;
Let us like burs together stick,
    And warm as any toast.

You'll know me truer than a die,
    And wish me better sped;
Flat as a flounder when I lie,
    And as a herring dead.

Sure as a gun, she'll drop a tear
    And sigh perhaps and wish,
When I am rotten as a pear,
    And mute as any fish.

JOHN GAY

To Minerva

From the Greek

My temples throb, my pulses boil,
    I'm sick of song, and ode, and ballad—
So Thyrsis, take the midnight oil,
    And pour it on a lobster salad.

My brain is dull, my sight is foul,
  I cannot write a verse, or read,—
Then Pallas take away thine owl,
  And let us have a lark instead.

THOMAS HOOD

Inconsiderate Hannah

Naughty little Hannah said
She could make her Grandma whistle,
So, that night, inside her bed,
Placed some nettles and a thistle.

Though dear Grandma quite infirm is,
Heartless Hannah watched her settle,
With her poor old epidermis
Resting up against a nettle.

Suddenly she reached the thistle!
My! you should have heard her whistle!

A successful plan was Hannah's
But I cannot praise her manners.

HARRY GRAHAM

Maud

Nay, I cannot come into the garden just now,
  Though it vexes me much to refuse:
But I *must* have the next set of waltzes, I vow,
  With Lieutenant de Boots of the Blues.

I am sure you'll be heartily pleased when you hear
  That our ball has been quite a success.
As for *me*,—I've been looking a monster, my dear,
  In that old-fashioned guy of a dress.

234

You had better at once hurry home, dear, to bed;
  It is getting so dreadfully late.
You may catch the bronchitis or cold in the head
  If you linger so long at our gate.

Don't be obstinate, Alfy; come, take my advice—
  For I know you're in want of repose:
Take a basin of gruel (you'll find it *so* nice),
  And remember to tallow your nose.

No, I tell you I can't and I shan't get away,
  For De Boots has implored me to sing.
As to *you*—if you like it, of course you can stay,
  You were always an obstinate thing.

If you feel it a pleasure to talk to the flowers
  About 'babble and revel and wine',
When you might have been snoring for two or three hours,
  Why, it's not the least business of mine.

HENRY S. LEIGH

Ned

Ned was my uncle's handy man,
  Old stubby Ned Magee.
He wheeled me out in a bath chair
  The time I hurt my knee.

He waited till I was tucked in
  By Nora, my tall cousin,
And ran me through the Dublin streets
  Nineteen to the dozen.

Head down he scuttled on the kerb
  As hard as he could go,
Till we ran over at a turn
  A colonel's gouty toe.

'Where are you going, damn your eyes!'
  Curses came thick and fast:
'The hill o' Howth, sir—hill o' Howth,'
  Said Ned, and scuttled past.

*   *   *   *   *   *   *

And many a happy fishing day
  I had by old Ned's side,
And Dublin seemed a lonely place
  The Thursday that he died.

L. A. G. STRONG

The Knife-grinder

A dialogue in Sophics

Friend of humanity
'Needy knife-grinder! whither are you going?
Rough is the road—your wheel is out of order—
Bleak blows the blast; your hat has got a hole in't,
      So have your breeches!

'Weary knife-grinder! little think the proud ones,
Who in their coaches roll along the turnpike
Road, what hard work 'tis crying all day, "Knives and
      Scissors to grind, O!"

'Tell me, knife-grinder, how you came to grind knives?
Did some rich man tyrannically use you?
Was it the squire? or parson of the parish?
      Or the attorney?

'Was it the squire for killing of his game, or
Covetous parson for his tithes distraining?
Or roguish lawyer made you lose your little
      All in a lawsuit?

236

'(Have you not read the "Rights of Man", by Tom Paine?)
Drops of compassion tremble on my eyelids,
Ready to fall as soon as you have told your
            Pitiful story.'

Knife-grinder
'Story! God bless you! I have none to tell, sir,
Only last night, a drinking at the Chequers,
This poor old hat and breeches, as you see, were
            Torn in a scuffle.

'Constables came up for to take me into
Custody; they took me before the justice;
Justice Oldmixon put me in the parish-
            Stocks for a vagrant.

'I should be glad to drink your honour's health in
A pot of beer, if you will give me sixpence;
But for my part, I never love to meddle
            With politics, sir.'

Friend of humanity
'*I* give thee sixpence! I will see thee damned first—
Wretch! whom no sense of wrongs can rouse to vengeance—
Sordid, unfeeling, reprobate, degraded,
            Spiritless outcast!

(*Kicks the knife-grinder, overturns his wheel, and exit in a transport of
republican enthusiasm and universal philanthropy*)

GEORGE CANNING and J. H. FRERE

To a Cat

Nelly, methinks, 'twixt thee and me,
There is a kind of sympathy;
And could we interchange our nature—
If I were cat, thou human creature,—
I should, like thee, be no great mouser,
And thou, like me, no great composer;

237

For, like thy plaintive mews, my muse,
With villainous whine doth fate abuse,
Because it hath not made me sleek
As golden down on Cupid's cheek;
And yet thou canst upon the rug lie,
Stretched out like snail, or curled up snugly,
As if thou wert not lean or ugly;
And I, who in poetic flights
Sometimes complain of sleepless nights,
Regardless of the sun in heaven,
Am apt to dose till past eleven,—
The world would just the same go round
If I were hanged and thou wert drowned;
There is one difference, 'tis true,—
Thou dost not know it, and I do.

HARTLEY COLERIDGE

The Hen

No bird can sing so sweetly
          As the Hen;
No bird can walk so neatly,
          And again,
    Apart from being beautiful,
    I know no bird so dutiful,
For it lays an egg discreetly—
          Now and then.

How nice, when dawn is bringing
          In the day,
To wake and hear it singing
          O'er its *lay*.
    Ah yes! how good the Hen is,
    So save up all your pennies,
And buy one (one with trousers)—
          It will pay.

JOHN JOY BELL

After Reading the Reviews of 'Finnegans Wake'

Nothing has been quite the same
Since I heard your liquid name,
Since it cast a magic spell,
Anna Livia Plurabelle.

Maid or river, bird or beast,
Doesn't matter in the least;
Quite enough that tongue may tell
Anna Livia Plurabelle.

What you've done, you'll never guess,
To my stream of consciousness!
Hang the meaning! What the hell!
Anna Livia Plurabelle.

MELVILLE CANE

A Song About Wordsworth

Now ole man Wordsworth, so they say,
'E loved to roam the 'ills,
Wiv 'is butterfly net an' 'is botany book,
An' a sixpenny packet o' Wills.
An' when 'e come 'ome in the twilight,
You'd 'ear 'is missus cry:
'Now Willie, me lad, where the 'ell 'ave you bin?'
And Willie 'e'd reply:

'I've been looking for daisies;
   A daisy drives me wild,
An' whenever I see a primrose
   I giggle just like a child.'
Then 'is wife says, 'Chuck yer kiddin',
   I can't swallow that stuff—
The only daisy that tickles you
   Is a bit o' mountain fluff.'

239

One night 'e come 'ome extra late
Wiv 'is eyes all glowin' bright,
An' 'is wife says, 'Where you bin to, mate,
T' come 'ome this time o' night?'
An' Will 'e answers 'er promptly,
'I'm nearly orf me 'ead,
For I've found another new kind o' bird'—
But 'is missus ups and said:

'You an' yer bloomin' daisies,
    An' yer different kind o' bird,
Is about the fishiest story
    Wot ever I 'ave 'eard.
'Op off, then, back to yer 'ill-tops
    An' yer innocent nature-stuff—
An' I'll warrant the bird that sings to you
    Is a bit o' mountain fluff.'

J. B. MORTON

Ballad of a Recurring Anomaly in Berkeley Square

O, Berkeley Square is brown and green,
    With its ancient bricks and grass,
There's never a lad can tell how old
    'Twill be come Candlemas.

Its hoary pride holds even now
    Democracy at bay,
And revels in gaunt memories
    Of George the Third his day.

O, good to see on either side
    Of some great Noble's porch
An iron-wrought extinguisher
    For the running footman's torch,

And good to see that when she fares
        Forth to some rout or ball
His Lady has a stepping-stone
        To mount her coach withal!

Stands that great landmark, Lansdowne House—
        O, stands it where it did?
Yea, as irrefragably as
        Cheops his pyramid.

And round the Square's three other sides
        Old Tories and old Whigs
Splendidly, crabbedly defy
        Time and his whirligigs.

Yet, ever since my childhood's hour
        (And that is now remote)
I've found in this harmonious Square
        One slightly jarring note.

I think it was in 'eighty-three,
        Or praps a trifle later,
That Mr Bancroft came here from
        The Haymarket Theayter.

And with him his good lady—whose
        Goodness, I grieve to state,
Was commonly regarded as
        A thing of recent date.

They came, these two. The grim façades
        Seemed to frown black with thunder
Olympian (and I am bound
        To say I didn't wonder).

But, as time passed, this frown relaxed,
        By reason that this pair
Were so pathetically keen
        To live up to this Square.

Bancroft himself tried hard to look
　　Not like a bold bad mime,
But like a fine old English Gentleman—
　　One of the Olden Time.

And not less hard his lady strove
　　To compass the effect
Of a firmly-based Victorian dame—
　　One of the straitest sect.

Gallant Val Baker she lived down,
　　And down Alf Edinborough.
Mother and wife, she had but one
　　Word for her motto: Thorough.

And yet, however earnestly
　　The Bancroft couple strove,
Always I wished them somewhere else—
　　Somewhere in Westbourne Grove.

It seemed to my old-fashioned sense
　　That they, for all their care,
Misfitted the amenities
　　Of Berkeley's holy Square.

The years rolled by. From out his home
　　Bancroft, in chaste apparel,
Went reading to the Provinces
　　Dickens's Christmas Carol.

It mastered him, that simple tale,
　　It emptied him of pride,
It set him longing for some in-
　　conspicuous fireside—

A small hearth in an humble cot,
　　Hid far from Mammon's eye . . .
Sir Squire and Lady Bancroft moved
　　Into the Albany.

'Now Heaven be praised!' said I. 'Henceforth'—
    But that is all I said.
Lo, Seymour Hickses had rushed in
    Where Bancrofts ceased to tread.

Perspiring Seymour suddenly
    Had darted on the scene,
With that sweet old English rosebud,
    The winsome Ellaline.

I said, 'In this Square's atmosphere
    You're both of you all wrong!'
'Oh, surely not!' said Ellaline;
    Said Seymour, 'Go along!'

For a brief, brief while they revelled here,
    Cutting a great, great dash;
Then, in the street called Portugal,
    I heard a deaf-ning crash:

Hicks had gone broke. He swam away
    In floods of perspiration,
Which must have added greatly to
    That other liquidation.

'Now Heaven be praised!' said I. 'Henceforth'—
    But the words died on my lips . . .
Behold, two scorpions came to take
    The place of those two whips.

A svelte young person, whose good name
    Was wholly without voucher,
Came languishing upon the arm
    Of Mr Rarthur Bourchier.

Rarthur, it seems, had recently
    Writ in his mad agenda:
'Commodious Mansion—Berkeley Square—
    Miss Bellew—Guilty Splenda!'

So here they were—yea, and still are.
    Throughout the stricken Square
The grass lies withered, and the trees
    Stand blasted, writhen, bare.

You think that I exaggerate?
    I daresay that I do.
Had you loved this Square as much as I
    Have loved it, so would you.

No!—do not try to comfort me!
    Rarthur will hook it soon?
Yes, yes, his gun is even now
    Aimed straight up at the moon.

But after that,—what then, what next?
    Something, I feel, still worse,
Will settle down upon the Square,
    To carry on the curse.

I feel that one of these august
    Houses (I'm not sure which)
Is destined to contain the vast
    Harem of Little Tich.

MAX BEERBOHM

Satire on the Heads of Houses

O Cambridge, attend
To the satire I've penned
On the heads of thy Houses,
Thou seat of the Muses!

DORSET COUNTY LIBRARY

Know the Master of Jesus
Does hugely displease us;
The Master of Maudlin
In the same dirt is dawdling;
The Master of Sidney
Is of the same kidney;
The Master of Trinity
To him bears affinity;
As the Master of Keys
Is as like as two peas,
So the Master of Queen's
Is as like as two beans;
The Master of King's
Copies them in all things;
The Master of Catherine
Takes them all for his pattern;
The Master of Clare
Hits them all to a hair;
The Master of Christ
By the rest is enticed;
But the Master of Emmanuel
Follows them like a spaniel;
The Master of Benet
Is of the like tenet;
The Master of Pembroke
Has from them his system took;
The Master of Peter's
Has all the same features;
The Master of St John's
Like the rest of the dons.

PS As to Trinity Hall
　　We say nothing at all.

THOMAS GRAY

245

Salad

(Swinburne)

O cool in the summer is salad,
And warm in the winter is love;
And a poet shall sing you a ballad
Delicious thereon and thereof.
A singer am I, if no sinner,
My muse has a marvellous wing,
And I willingly worship at Dinner
The Sirens of the Spring.

Take endive—like love it is bitter,
Take beet—for like love it is red:
Crisp leaf of the lettuce shall glitter,
And cress from the rivulet's bed:
Anchovies, foam-born, like the lady
Whose beauty has maddened this bard;
And olives, from groves that are shady,
And eggs—boil 'em hard.

MORTIMER COLLINS

Basingstoke

Of Basingstoke in Hampshire
The claims to fame are small:—
A derelict canal
And a cream and green Town Hall.

At each weekend the 'locals'
Line the Market Square,
And as the traffic passes,
They stand and stand and stare.

LESLIE THOMAS

To Mrs Thrale on Her Thirty-fifth Birthday

Oft in danger yet alive
We are come to thirty-five;
Long may better years arrive,
Better years than thirty-five;
Could philosophers contrive
Life to stop at thirty-five,
Time his hours should never drive
O'er the bounds of thirty-five:
High to soar and deep to dive
Nature gives at thirty-five;
Ladies—stock and tend your hive,
Trifle not at thirty-five:
For howe'er we boast and strive,
Life declines from thirty-five;
He that ever hopes to thrive
Must begin by thirty-five:
And those who wisely wish to wive,
Must look on Thrale at thirty-five.

SAMUEL JOHNSON

Abraham, 'The Laurels', Ur

*(An archæologist has stated that quite possible Abraham lived in Ur in
a jolly house with practically all the modern conveniences)*

Oh, Abraham lived in a maisonette,
    As the learned gents aver,
With a super-Hittite gramophone,
And a novel to read when left alone,
And a tenpenny bottle of chemical Beaune,
    At the Laurels, Smith Street, Ur.

He lay in his bath, and he listened-in
    As happy as could be,
With the hot pipes on whenever he chose,
And the telephone shoved right under his nose
To ring up his dear little Irish rose,
    For a jolly old man was he.

J. B. MORTON

O Have You Caught the Tiger

O have you caught the tiger?
  And can you hold him tight?
And what immortal hand or eye
Could frame his fearful symmetry?
  And does he try to bite?

Yes, I have caught the tiger,
  And he was hard to catch.
O tiger, tiger, do not try
To put your tail into my eye,
  And do not bite and scratch.

Yes, I have caught the tiger.
  O tiger, do not bray!
And what immortal hand or eye
Could frame his fearful symmetry
  I should not like to say.

And may I see the tiger?
  I should indeed delight
To see so large an animal
Without a voyage to Bengal.
  And mind you hold him tight.

Yes, you may see the tiger;
  It will amuse you much.
The tiger is, as you will find,
A creature of the feline kind.
  And mind you do not touch.

And do you feed the tiger,
  And do you keep him clean?
He has a less contented look
Than in the Natural History book,
  And seems a trifle lean.

Oh yes, I feed the tiger,
   And soon he will be plump;
I give him groundsel fresh and sweet,
And much canary-seed to eat,
   And wash him at the pump.

It seems to me the tiger
   Has not been lately fed,
Not for a day or two at least;
And that is why the noble beast
   Has bitten off your head.

A. E. HOUSMAN

Translation of the Nurse's Dole in the Medea of Euripides

Oh how I wish that an embargo
Had kept in port the good ship Argo!
Who, still unlaunched from Grecian docks,
Had never passed the Azure rocks;
But now I fear her trip will be a
Damned business for my Miss Medea,
   &c. &c.

LORD BYRON

Billy M'Caw: the Remarkable Parrot

Oh, how well I remember the old Bull and Bush,
   Where we used to go down of a Sattaday night—
Where, when anythink happened, it come with a rush,
   For the boss, Mr Clark, he was very polite;
And what with the Station it being so near,
And what with the water got into the beer
   (There was two kinds of beer, the thick and the clear)
A very nice House it was. Oh dear!

I'll never forget it. From basement to garret
A very nice House. Ah, but it was the parret—
The parret, the parret named Billy M'Caw,
   That brought all those folk to the bar.
   Ah! he was the Life of the bar.
Of a Sattaday night, we was all feeling bright,
And Lily La Rose—the Barmaid that was—
She'd say:'Billy!
           Billy M'Caw!
Come give us a dance on the bar!'
   And Billy would dance on the bar.

Lily, she was a girl what had brains in her head;
She wouldn't have nothink, no not that much said.
If it come to an argument, or a dispute,
She'd settle it offhand with the toe of her boot
   Or as likely as not put her fist through your eye.
But when we was thirsty, and just a bit sad,
Or when we was happy, and just a bit dry,
She would rap on the bar with the corkscrew she had
And say: 'Billy!
           Billy M'Caw!
Come give us a tune on your pastoral flute!'
   And Billy'd strike up on his pastoral flute.

And then we'd feel balmy, in each eye a tear,
And emotion would make us all order more beer—
For the way that Bird played, with his Robin Adairs,
And his All in the Downs, and his Wapping Old Stairs,
Would bring tears to the eyes of a donkey, it would.
There was no use of saying that Bird wasn't good.
And when we was feeling exceedingly tearful,
Then Lily would say: 'Now, let's have something cheerful!
Billy!
           Billy M'Caw!
Come give us a tune on your moley guitar!'
   And Billy'd strike up on his moley guitar.

Oh, how well I remember the old Bull and Bush
   Where the folk came from near and from far.
A very nice House. From basement to garret
A very nice House. Ah but it was the parret,
   The parret, the parret named Billy M'Caw,
Who brought all those folk to the bar.
   Ah, he was the Life of the bar.

T. S. ELIOT

A Nursery Legend

Oh! listen, little children, to a proper little song
Of a naughty little urchin who was always doing wrong:
He disobeyed his mammy, and he disobeyed his dad,
And he disobeyed his uncle, which was very near as bad.
He wouldn't learn to cypher, and he wouldn't learn to write,
But he *would* tear up his copy-books to fabricate a kite;
And he used his slate and pencil in so barbarous a way,
That the grinders of his governess got looser ev'ry day.

At last he grew so obstinate that no one could contrive
To cure him of a theory that two and two made five;
And, when they taught him how to spell, he showed his wicked
    whims
By mutilating Pinnock and mislaying Watts's Hymns.
Instead of all such pretty books (which *must* improve the mind,)
He cultivated volumes of a most improper kind;
Directories and almanacks he studied on the sly,
And gloated over Bradshaw's Guide when nobody was by.

From such a course of reading you can easily divine
The condition of his morals at the age of eight or nine.
His tone of conversation kept becoming worse and worse,
Till it scandalized his governess and horrified his nurse.
He quoted bits of Bradshaw that were quite unfit to hear,
And recited from the Almanack, no matter who was near:
He talked of Reigate Junction and of trains both up and down,
And referred to men who called themselves Jones, Robinson, and
    Brown.

251

But when this naughty boy grew up he found the proverb true,
That Fate one day makes people pay for all the wrong they do.
He was cheated out of money by a man whose name was Brown,
And got crippled in a railway smash while coming up to town.
So, little boys and little girls, take warning while you can,
And profit by the history of this unhappy man.
Read Dr Watts and Pinnock, dears; and when you learn to spell,
Shun Railway Guides, Directories, and Almanacks as well!

H. D. TRAILL

Hildebrand

who was frightened by a passing motor, and was brought to reason

'Oh Murder! What was that, Papa!'
'My child, it was a Motor-Car,
A Most Ingenious Toy!
Designed to Captivate and Charm
Much rather than to rouse Alarm
In any English Boy.

'What would your Great Grandfather who
Was Aide-de-Camp to General Brue,
And lost a leg at Waterloo,
And Quatre-Bras and Ligny too!
And died at Trafalgar!—
What would he have remarked to hear
His Young Descendant shriek with fear,
Because he happened to be near
    A Harmless Motor-Car!
But do not fret about it! Come!
We'll off to Town and purchase some!'

HILAIRE BELLOC

The Schoolmaster Abroad

(The steam-yacht Argonaut *was chartered from Messrs Perowne &*
Lunn by a body of public school masters for the purposes of an
educative visit to the Levant)

O 'Isles' (as Byron said) 'of Greece!'
　　For which the firm of Homer sang,
Especially that little piece
　　Interpreted by Mr Lang;
Where the unblushing Sappho wrote
The hymns we hardly like to quote;—

I cannot share his grave regret
　　Who found your fame had been and gone;
There seems to be a future yet
　　For Tenedos and Marathon;
Fresh glory gilds their deathless sun,
And this is due to Dr Lunn!

What though your harpers twang no more?
　　What though your various lyres are dumb?
See where by Cirrha's sacred shore,
　　Bold Argonauts, the Ushers come!
All bring their maps and some their wives,
And at the vision Greece revives!

The Delphic oracles are off,
　　But still the site is always there;
The fumes that made the Pythian cough
　　Still permeate the conscious air;
Parnassus, of the arduous 'grade',
May still be climbed, with local aid.

Lunching upon the self-same rock
　　Whence Xerxes viewed the wine-red frith,
They realize with vivid shock
　　The teachings of 'the smaller Smith';
With bated breath they murmur—'This
Is actually Salamis!'

They visit where Penelope
   Nightly unwove the work of day,
Staving her suitors off till he,
   Ulysses, let the long-bow play,
And on his brave grass-widow's breast
Forgot Calypso and the rest.

In Crete, where Theseus first embraced
   His Ariadne, they explore
(Just now authentically traced)
   The footprints of the Minotaur;
And follow, to the maze's source,
The thread of some profound discourse.

That isle where Leto, sick with fright,
   So scandalized her mortal kin,
Where young Apollo, lord of light,
   Commenced his progress as a twin—
Fair Delos, they shall get to know,
And Paros, where the marbles grow.

Not theirs the course of crude delight
   On which the common tourist wends;
From faith they move, by way of sight,
   To knowledge meant for noble ends;
'Twill be among their purest joys
To work it off upon the boys.

One hears the travelled teacher call
   Upon the Upper Fifth to note
(Touching the Spartan counter-wall)
   How great the lore of Mr Grote;
And tell them, 'His are just the views
I formed myself—at Syracuse!'

When Jones is at a loss to show
   Where certain islands ought to be,
How well to whack him hard and low
   And say, 'The pain is worse for me,
To whom the Cyclades are quite
Familiar, like the Isle of Wight.'

And then the lecture after prep.!
  The Magic Lantern's lurid slide!
The speaker pictured on the step
  Of some old shrine, with no inside;
Or groping on his reverent knees
For Eleusinian mysteries!

Hellas defunct? O say not so,
  While Public School-boys faint to hear
The tales of antique love or woe,
  Brought home and rendered strangely clear
With instantaneous Kodak-shots
Secured by Ushers on the spots!

OWEN SEAMAN

A Valentine for James Joyce, Schoolboy,

in the name of the girl who lived opposite his house in Bray . . .

O Jimmie Joyce you are my darling
You are my looking glass from night till morning
I'd rather have you without one farthing
Than Harry Newall* and his ass and garden.

EILEEN VANCE

* *an old cripple.*

Bonnie Jeanie

(Air: 'The Eighty-three Men of Moidart')

O ken ye Wullie Broon, Jeanie,
  O ken ye Brulzie Glen,
Wi' the haslock on the brig, Jeanie,
  A' bu' ca' fu' big ben?

255

Whaur's the loof noo, Jeanie,
    Whaur's the bannock, jo?
My luv's a bleerit caulsie, Jeanie,
    An' the gutcher's doit sae low.

Snaw-white was her hairt, Jeanie,
    Waulkin' doon the warl,
The midden-creel's a' bracht, Jeanie,
    The loof's anint the sparl.

Sair rins the Tees noo, Jeanie,
    Deevin' through the glaes,
But a mon's mon's a mon, Jeanie,
    Wi'oot a guidman's claes.

Sair rins the Tweed hoocht, Jeanie,
    Blithe towmond, bonnie skirl,
The Snowther's blate the criffe, Jeanie,
    Wi' birkie frae the sirl.

O ken ye Wullie Broon, Jeanie,
    Whaur's the limmer noo,
Flicht stricht the bricht licht fa's, Jeanie,
    An' mony mair tae you.

Glossary

Bannock: a small ban, white in colour.
Jo: short for O.
Gutcher: a ramrod used in curing whitebait.
Warl: decayed treacle.
Loof: a cabman's collar in a teapot.
Sparl: a method of boiling glue in Lanark.
Deevin': a goyling sound, like the hoof le of a fracht.
Towmond: the edge of an egg in midwinter.
Snowther: a frozen handcuff.
Sirl: a glimpse of red flannel on a bridge.

J. B. MORTON

Founder's Feast

Old as a toothless Regius Professor
Ebbed the Madeira wine. Loquacious graduates
Sipped it with sublimation. They'd been drinking
The health of . . . was it Edward the Confessor?
A solemn banquet glowed in every cheek,
While nicotinean fumes befogged the roof
And the carved gallery where prim choristers
Sang like Pre-Raphaelite angels through the reek.

Gowns, rose and scarlet in flamingo ranks,
Adorned the dais that shone with ancient silver;
And guests of honour gazed far down the Hall
With precognition of returning thanks.
There beamed the urbanest Law-lord on the Bench,
Debating with the Provost (ceremonious
In flushed degrees of vintage scholarship),
The politics of Plato,—and the French.

But on the Provost's left, in gold and blue,
Sat . . . O my God! . . . great Major-General Bluff . . .
Enough enough enough enough enough!

SIEGFRIED SASSOON

Merry Old Souls

Old Ben Franklin was a merry old soul,
He walked up Market Street munching a roll,
And a girl laughed loud, and her laughter was so ranklin'
That old Ben Franklin made her Mrs Ben Franklin.

Old Julius Caesar was a merry old soul,
To be a Roman emperor was all his goal;
But he put away the crown; he was such an old teaser
That the mob put the finger on Gaius Julius Caesar.

Old Isaac Newton was a merry old soul,
He invented gravitation when out for a stroll,
And no one up to now has succeeded in refutin'
The good old hypothesis of old Isaac Newton.

Old Savonarola was a merry old soul,
He held all of Florence under rigid control;
The people didn't like it, and doped his Coca-Cola,
And then they heated Florence with old Savonarola.

Rabelais also was a merry old soul;
Many of his writings are very, very droll;
Censors in the customhouse treat him rather shabbily
By cutting out the better bits of Master Francis Rabelais.

MORRIS BISHOP

Lord Gorbals

Once, as old Lord Gorbals motored
    Round his moors near John o' Groats
He collided with a goatherd
    And a herd of forty goats.
By the time his car got through
They were all defunct but two.

Roughly he addressed the goatherd:
    'Dash my whiskers and my corns!
Can't you teach your goats, you dotard,
    That they ought to sound their horns?
Look, my AA badge is bent!
I've a mind to raise your rent!'

HARRY GRAHAM

Grace During Meat

(Calais, Palm Sunday, 1938)

On china blue my lobster red
    Precedes my cutlet brown,
With which my salad green is sped
    By yellow Chablis down.

Lord, if good living be no sin,
    But innocent delight,
O polarize these hues within
    To one eupeptic white!

STEPHEN GASELEE

A Reasonable Affliction

On his death-bed poor Lubin lies;
    His spouse is in despair:
With frequent sobs, and mutual cries,
    They both express their care.

A different cause, says Parson Sly,
    The same effect may give:
Poor Lubin fears, that he shall die;
    His wife, that he may live.

MATTHEW PRIOR

Lines on an Envelope Addressed to Clive Bell Esq

O stalwart SUSSEX postman, who is
Delivering the post from LEWES,
Cycle apace to CHARLESTON, FIRLE,
While knitting at your plain and purl,
Deliver there to good CLIVE BELL
(You know the man, you know him well,
He plays the virginals and spinet),
This note—there's almost nothing in it.

T. S. ELIOT

Fragment of a Greek Tragedy

ALCMAEON, CHORUS

Chorus: O suitably-attired-in-leather-boots
Head of a traveller, wherefore seeking whom
Whence by what way how purposed art thou come
To this well-nightingaled vicinity?
My object in enquiring is to know,
But if you happen to be deaf and dumb
And do not understand a word I say,
Then wave your hand, to signify as much.
Alcmaeon: I journeyed hither a Bœotian road.
Chorus: Sailing on horseback, or with feet for oars?
Alcmaeon: Plying with speed my partnership of legs.
Chorus: Beneath a shining or a rainy Zeus?
Alcmaeon: Mud's sister, not himself, adorns my shoes.
Chorus: To learn your name would not displease me much.
Alcmaeon: Not all that men desire do they obtain.
Chorus: Might I then hear at what your presence shoots?
Alcmaeon: A shepherd's questioned mouth informed me that—
Chorus: What? for I know not yet what you will say—
Alcmaeon: Nor will you ever, if you interrupt.
Chorus: Proceed, and I will hold my speechless tongue.

Alcmaeon:	—This house was Eriphyla's, no one's else.
Chorus:	Nor did he shame his throat with hateful lies.
Alcmaeon:	May I then enter, passing through the door?
Chorus:	Go, chase into the house a lucky foot,
	And, O my son, be, on the one hand, good,
	And do not, on the other hand, be bad;
	For that is very much the safest plan.
Alcmaeon:	I go into the house with heels and speed.

Chorus: In speculation   *Strophe*
I would not willingly acquire a name
    For ill-digested thought;
    But after pondering much
To this conclusion I at last have come:
    Life is uncertain.
    This truth I have written deep
    In my reflective midriff
    On tablets not of wax,
Nor with a pen did I inscribe it there,
For many reasons: *Life, I say, is not*
    A stranger to uncertainty.
Not from the flight of omen-yelling fowls
    This fact did I discover.
Nor did the Delphic tripod bark it out,
    Nor yet Dodona.
Its native ingenuity sufficed
    My self-taught diaphragm.

    Why should I mention   *Antistrophe*
The Inachean daughter, loved of Zeus?
    Her whom of old the gods,
    More provident than kind,
Provided with four hoofs, two horns, one tail,
    A gift not asked for,
    And sent her forth to learn
    The unfamiliar science
    Of how to chew the cud.
She therefore, all about the Argive fields,
Went cropping pale green grass and nettle-tops,
    Nor did they disagree with her.
But yet, howe'er nutritious, such repasts
    I do not hanker after:

Never may Cypris for her seat select
    My dappled liver!
Why should I mention Io! Why indeed?
    I have no notion why.

But now does my boding heart,   *Epode*
Unhired, unaccompanied, sing
A strain not meet for the dance.
Yea even the palace appears
To my yoke of circular eyes
(The right, nor omit I the left)
Like a slaughterhouse, so to speak,
Garnished with woolly deaths
And many shipwrecks of cows.
I therefore in a Cissian strain lament;
    And to the rapid,
Loud, linen-tattering thumps upon my chest
    Resounds in concert
The battering of my unlucky head.

ERIPHYLA (*within*). O, I am smitten with a hatchet's jaw;
    And that in deed and not in word alone.
Chorus: I thought I heard a sound within the house
    Unlike the voice of one that jumps for joy.
Eriphyla: He splits my skull, not in a friendly way,
    One more: he purposes to kill me dead.
Chorus: I would not be reputed rash, but yet
    I doubt if all be gay within the house.
Eriphyla: O! O! another stroke! that makes the third.
    He stabs me to the heart against my wish.
Chorus: If that be so, thy state of health is poor;
    But thine arithmetic is quite correct.

A. E. HOUSMAN

To the Brothers Fay, after he had collapsed, drunk, in a passageway of their theatre . . .

O, there are two brothers, the Fays,
Who are excellent players of plays,
    And, needless to mention, all
    Most unconventional,
Filling the world with amaze.

But I angered those brothers, the Fays,
Whose ways are conventional ways,
    For I lay in my urine
    While ladies so pure in
White petticoats ravished my gaze.

JAMES JOYCE

Our Budgie

Our budgie lives in a cage of wire
Equipped to please his each desire,
He has a little ladder to climb
And he's up and down it all the time.
And a little mirror in which he peeps
As he utters his self-admiring cheeps,
And two little pink plastic budgie mates
Whom he sometimes loves and sometimes hates.
And a little bell all made of tin
On which he makes a merry din.
Though sometimes, when things aren't going well,
He hides his head inside the bell.

His feathers are a brilliant green
And take most of his time to preen,
His speech is limited and blurred
But he doesn't do badly, for a bird.
And though he can but poorly talk
If you ignore him he'll squawk and squawk
And fly into a fearful rage
And rattle the bars of his pretty cage,
But he won't get out, he'll never try it,
And a cloth on the cage will keep him quiet.

This futile bird, it seems to me,
Would make a perfect Welsh MP.

PS to the above
    Despite his repertoire of tricks
    Poor budgie died in 1966.

HARRI WEBB

Doggerel by a Senior Citizen
(for Robert Lederer)

Our earth in 1969
Is not the planet I call mine,
The world, I mean, that gives me strength
To hold off chaos at arm's length.

My Eden landscapes and their climes
Are constructs from Edwardian times,
When bathrooms took up lots of space,
And, before eating, one said Grace.

The automobile, the aeroplane,
Are useful gadgets, but profane:
The enginry of which I dream
Is moved by water or by steam.

Reason requires that I approve
The light-bulb which I cannot love:
To me more reverence-commanding
A fish-tail burner on the landing.

My family ghosts I fought and routed,
Their values, though, I never doubted:
I thought their Protestant Work-Ethic
Both practical and sympathetic.

When couples played or sang duets,
It was immoral to have debts:
I shall continue till I die
To pay in cash for what I buy.

The Book of Common Prayer we knew
Was that of 1662:
Though with-it sermons may be well,
Liturgical reforms are hell.

Sex was, of course—it always is—
The most enticing of mysteries,
But news-stands did not yet supply
Manichaean pornography.

Then Speech was mannerly, an Art,
Like learning not to belch or fart:
I cannot settle which is worse,
The Anti-Novel or Free Verse.

Nor are those Ph.D's my kith,
Who dig the symbol and the myth:
I count myself a man of letters
Who writes, or hopes to, for his betters.

Dare any call Permissiveness
An educational success?
Saner those classrooms which I sat in,
Compelled to study Greek and Latin.

Though I suspect the term is crap,
If there *is* a Generation Gap,
Who is to blame? Those, old or young,
Who will not learn their Mother-Tongue.

But Love, at least, is not a state
Either *en vogue* or out-of-date,
And I've true friends, I will allow,
To talk and eat with here and now.

Me alienated? Bosh! It's just
As a sworn citizen who must
Skirmish with it that I feel
Most at home with what is Real.

W. H. AUDEN

Commercial Candour

(On the outside of a sensational novel is printed the statement: 'The back of the cover will tell you the plot')

Our fathers to creed and tradition were tied,
They opened a book to see what was inside,
And of various methods they deemed not the worst
Was to find the first chapter and look at it first.
And so from the first to the second they passed,
Till in servile routine they arrived at the last.
But a literate age, unbenighted by creed,
Can find on two boards all it wishes to read;
For the front of the cover shows somebody shot
And the back of the cover will tell you the plot.

Between, that the book may be handily padded,
Some pages of mere printed matter are added,
Expanding the theme, which in case of great need
The curious reader might very well read
With the zest that is lent to a game worth the winning,
By knowing the end when you start the beginning;
While our barbarous sires, who would read every word
With a morbid desire to find out what occurred
Went dearily drudging through Dickens and Scott.
But the back of the cover will tell you the plot.

The wild village folk in earth's earliest prime
Could often sit still for an hour at a time
And hear a blind beggar, nor did the tale pall
Because Hector must fight before Hector could fall:
Nor was Scheherazade required, at the worst,
To tell her tales backwards and finish them first;
And the minstrels who sang about battle and banners
Found the rude camp-fire crowd had some notion of manners.
Till Forster (who pelted the people like crooks.
The Irish with buckshot, the English with books),
Established the great educational scheme
Of compulsory schooling, that glorious theme.
Some learnt how to read, and the others forgot,
And the back of the cover will tell you the plot.

O Genius of Business! O marvellous brain,
Come in place of the priests and the warriors to reign!
O Will to Get On that makes everything go—
O Hustle! O Pep! O Publicity! O!
Shall I spend three-and-sixpence to purchase the book,
Which we all can pick up on the bookstall and look?
Well, it may appear strange, but I think I shall not,
For the back of the cover will tell you the plot.

G. K. CHESTERTON

Cavalcade for the General

*To be sung with appropriate (yet not improper) gestures by one of Mr
Cochran's Old Ladies*

Our Mr Coward's such a nice young man (such a
    nice young man is he).
It must be remorse for being so coarse in the days when
    love was free;
when private lives and other men's wives were a riot
    of dope and gin.
Ah, vice on the stage was all the rage when Coward
    and sin came in.

But now Mr Coward is much too nice (such a nice
    young man is he)
to shatter and vex our ideals of sex with themes of
    adultery.
Now he mirrors the age on a larger stage and his
    people are loyal and true,
and when they sing, it's 'God Save the King' or
    'Three Cheers for the Red, White, and Blue'.

What a change to go to a nice, clean show (such a nice
    clean show, my dears),
and to see the vast and impersonal cast march past to
    deafening cheers.
It's not quite art or terribly smart, but dowagers weep
    in the stalls.
and I really can't see why the man next to me re-
    peatedly said it was balls!

CHRISTOPHER SALTMARSHE

Our Village—by a Villager

'Sweet Auburn, loveliest village of the plain'—*Goldsmith*

Our village, that's to say not Miss Mitford's village, but our village
    of Bullock Smithy,

Is come into by an avenue of trees, three oak pollards, two elders,
and a withy;
And in the middle, there's a green of about not exceeding an
acre and a half;
It's common to all, and fed off by nineteen cows, six ponies, three
horses, five asses, two foals, seven pigs, and a calf!
Besides a pond in the middle, as is held by a similar sort of
common law lease,
And contains twenty ducks, six drakes, three ganders, two dead
dogs, four drowned kittens, and twelve geese.
Of course the green's cropt very close, and does famous for
bowling when the little village boys play at cricket;
Only some horse, or pig, or cow, or great jackass, is sure to come
and stand right before the wicket.
There's fifty-five private houses, let alone barns and workshops,
and pigstyes, and poultry huts, and such-like sheds;
With plenty of public-houses—two Foxes, one Green Man, three
Bunch of Grapes, one Crown and six King's Heads.
The Green Man is reckoned the best, as the only one that for love
or money can raise
A postilion, a blue jacket, two deplorable lame white horses, and
a ramshackled 'neat postchaise'.
There's one parish church for all the people, whatsoever may be
their ranks in life or their degrees,
Except one very damp, small, dark, freezing cold, little
Methodist chapel of ease;
And close by the churchyard there's a stonemason's yard, that
when the time is seasonable
Will furnish with afflictions sore and marble urns and cherubims
very low and reasonable.
There's a cage, comfortable enough; I've been in it with old Jack
Jeffrey and Tom Pike;
For the Green Man next door will send you in ale, gin or any-
thing else you like.
I can't speak of the stocks, as nothing remains of them but the
upright post;
But the pound is kept in repairs for the sake of Cob's horse, as is
always there almost.
There's a smithy of course, where that queer sort of a chap in his
way, Old Joe Bradley,

Perpetually hammers and stammers, for he stutters and shoes
    horses very badly.
There's a shop of all sorts, that sells everything, kept by the widow
    of Mr Task;
But when you go there it's ten to one she's out of every thing you
    ask.
You'll know her house by the swarm of boys, like flies, about the
    old sugary cask:
There are six empty houses, and not so well papered inside as out,
For billstickers won't beware, but sticks notices of sales and
    election placards all about.
That's the Doctor's with a green door, where the garden pots in
    the windows is seen;
A weakly monthly rose that don't blow, and a dead geranium, and
    a tea-plant with five black leaves and one green.
As for hollyoaks at the cottage doors, and honeysuckles and
    jasmines, you may go and whistle;
But the Tailor's front garden grows two cabbages, a dock, a
    ha'porth of pennyroyal, two dandelions, and a thistle.
There are three small orchards—Mr Busby's the schoolmaster's
    is the chief—
With two pear-trees that don't bear; one plum and an apple, that
    every year is stripped by a thief.
There's another small day-school too, kept by the respectable Mrs
    Gaby.
A select establishment, for six little boys and one big, and four
    little girls and a baby;
There's a rectory, with pointed gables and strange odd chimneys
    that never smokes,
For the rector don't live on his living like other Christian sort of
    folks;
There's a barber's, once a week well filled with rough black-
    bearded, shock-headed churls,
And a window with two feminine men's heads, and two masculine
    ladies in false curls;
There's a butcher's, and a carpenter's, and a plumber's, and a
    small greengrocer's, and a baker,
But he won't bake on a Sunday, and there's a sexton that's a
    coal-merchant besides, and an undertaker;
And a toy-shop, but not a whole one, for a village can't compare
    with the London shops;

One window sells drums, dolls, kites, carts, bats, Clout's balls,
   and the other sells malt and hops.
And Mrs Brown, in domestic economy not to be a bit behind her
   betters,
Lets her house to a milliner, a watchmaker, a rat-catcher, a
   cobbler, lives in it herself, and it's the post-office for letters.
Now I've gone through all the village—ay, from end to end, save
   and except one more house,
But I haven't come to that—and I hope I never shall—and that's
   the Village Poor House!

THOMAS HOOD

Time Gentlemen, Time

O would not Life be charming
   Could we get rid of clocks,
The still ones and alarming
   That break on sleep with shocks,

Then it would be respected
   And worthier far of Man
Than when by springs directed
   From gold or a tin can.

Why should Man's life be reckoned
   By anything so queer
As that which splits the second
   But cannot tell the year?

If we got rid of watches
   The trains would cease to run,
We could not fight a battleship
   Or aim a battle gun,

Nor tune the little engines
   Which fill the towns with fumes
And send men with a vengeance
   (Quite rightly) to their tombs.

271

If we got rid of watches
  And wanted to approach
The pallid peopled cities
  We'd have to hire a coach

And guard, who, to arouse us,
  So hardy in the morn,
Outside the licensed houses
  Would blow a long bright horn.

Our stars know naught of watches,
  There's not a wind that wists
Of mischief that Time hatches
  When handcuffed to our wrists.

No wonder stars are winking,
  No wonder heaven mocks
At men who cease from drinking
  Good booze because of clocks!

'Twould make a devil chortle
  To see how all the clean
Free souls God made immortal
  Must march to a machine.

It makes me wonder whether
  In this grim pantomime
Did fiend or man first blether:
  'Time, Gentlemen, Time!'

We must throw out the timing
  That turns men into gnomes,
Of piece-work and of miming
  That fills the mental homes.

We must get rid of errors,
  And tallies and time checks,
And all the slavish terrors
  That turn men into wrecks.

They have not squared the circle,
  They have not cubed the sphere,
Their calendars all work ill
  Corrected by 'leap' year.

But we should all be leaping
  As high as hollyhocks
Did we desist from keeping
  Our trysts with slaves of clocks.

How should we tell the seconds?
  The time a blackbird takes,
To screech across a laneway,
  And dive into the brakes.

How should we tell the minutes?
  The time it takes to swipe
A lonely pint of Guinness,
  Or load a friendly pipe.

O make the heart Time's measure
  Because, the more it beats,
The more Life fills with pleasure
  With songs or sturdy feats;

Our clocks our lives are cheating
  They go, and ground we give;
The higher the heart's beating,
  The higher then we live.

OLIVER ST JOHN GOGARTY

Fragment from the Elizabethans

Paracelcus (*entering hurriedly*)

I am become a frightful Bloody murtherer,
Meeting my grandam in the buttery hatch,
I hackt, forsooth, and hewed her jauntilie,
And cast her reeking fragments on the air.

(*Exit, pursued by a Cow*)

W. BRIDGES-ADAMS

Food

'Pêche Melba,
And then—Elba!'
This saying of Napoleon's, though characteristic,
Was anachronistic.

L. E. JONES

How to Get On in Society

Phone for the fish knives Norman,
    As cook is a little unnerved;
Your kiddies have crumpled the serviettes
    And I must have things daintily served.

Are the requisites all in the toilet?
    The frills round the cutlets can wait
Till the girl has replenished the cruets
    And switched on the logs in the grate.

It's ever so close in the lounge dear,
    But the vestibule's comfy for tea,
And Howard is out riding on horseback
    So do come and take some with me.

274

Now here is a fork for your pastries
    And do use the couch for your feet;
I know what I wanted to ask you—
    Is trifle sufficient for sweet?

Milk and then just as it comes dear?
    I'm afraid the preserve's full of stones.
Beg pardon, I'm soiling the doileys
    With afternoon tea-cake and scones.

JOHN BETJEMAN

The preceding verses appeared in the competition section of the magazine *Time and Tide* in 1951. The poet pointed out that the lines contained thirty-four 'of what some people might call Social Errors'. He invited competitors to compose a further stanza in the same metre. Of the verses received, Betjeman judged the following five stanzas – signed 'Mopev' – to be 'better than my own' . . .

Would you care for a smoke or a sherry?
    The cocktail cabinet's there.
No, the savoury spread and the vitamin bread's
    In the cubby hole under the stair.

Has Uncle gone out on his cycle?
    He left making terrible sounds,
Saying 'Just what the medico ordered'.
    I'm afraid he'll get lost in the grounds.

We've several new gnomes in the rockery
    And his eyesight's not dreadfully strong.
Bring the flash from my handbag. Good gracious,
    He's had a mishap! Hark, the gong.

Just leave your bootees in the hallway
    Till the cloakroom is free, there's a pet.
My friend left his mac in the dining recess
    And ruined our condiment set!

Yes, this costume was made for my Auntie.
　　She said I must have a new gown.
I wear any old bags in the country,
　　But one has to be soignée in town.

MOPEV

But since the competition called for one stanza only Betjeman gave first prize to HMB because her verse made the best ending to his own poem . . .

Your pochette's on the pouffe by the cake-stand
　　Beneath your fur-fabric coatee.
Now, before we remove to the study
　　Let me pass you these chocs from Paris.

HMB

Betjeman quotes two more of HMB's verses . . .

I was out in the grounds in my costume
　　When this photo was snapped by Colleen;
That's her gentleman friend in the homburg—
　　His picture was once in *The Queen*.

Should you need a shampoo or a hair-do
　　You have only to push on the bell;
My personal maid comes from Monte
　　And does a Marcel very well.

HMB

Second prize was shared by W. M. and J. A. Gere . . .

My daughter's in Town for the week-end,
  She's engaged to a charming Guardee,
He sent me some perfume for Xmas,
  Allow me to sweeten your tea!

W. M.

Just one wee portion of gateau?
  I made it with my own fair hand,
And—though I says it as shouldn't—
  My menfolk have voted it grand.

J. A. GERE

And honourable mention was accorded to the following . . .

Put the tea-cosy back on the pot, dear;
  Where the sugar tongs are I don't know.
Auntie's promised to drop us a line here
  If she pops up to town for a show.

Last time Auntie stayed here in August
  The commotion I'll never forget,
She would wash her smalls in her bedroom
  And made the new quilt sopping wet.

KAREN LANCASTER

Late dinner—DJ—at half-seven,
  (There are gaspers and lights in the box),
Meanwhile, squattez-vous with the mags, dear,
  And a glass of port-wine and some chocs.

C. S. W.

If your journey from Town was fatiguing,
  Let me close the door gently, and then
Before you commence to assist me
  You can have a nice nap in the den.

COLONEL FERGUSSON

Ease the chesterfield nearer the radio—
  (Dainty cretonnes are such an expense!)
Now! Mum's chocs won't adhere to your dentures,
  Cheeriho, till the programmes commence.

F. J. A. CRUSO

The WC's locked from the inside:
  Just beat on the door, there's a dear.
Ask Father to slide out the papers
  And tell him the bathroom is clear.

RANI SINHA

Wordsworth

Permit me to remark
With the faintest touch of malice
That the straws in Wordsworth's hair
Would have thatched the Crystal Palace.

J. B. MORTON

Literary Party, 1949

Pipe-puffing PRIESTLEY pawkily began
In Doric speech to praise the Common Man,
Till OSBERT, looking drearier and drearier,
Broke in: 'I'm never rude to an inferior;
But, speaking as an artist, whole, unique'—
(Here MORGAN looked as if about to speak,
But only sneezed). 'Or shall we', murmured WAUGH,
'Try to say things we never said before?'
Glumly consenting, all in silence sat
Till E. M. FORSTER, smiling, fetched his hat.

L. E. JONES

Orchestra Notes

Pity the wretched harp-player!
Lord, he must suffer a pang or two,
Sitting up there
For the whole of a symphony,
Plucking no more than a twang or two.

Pity the hapless drummer!
What man's lot could be glummer?
Tense with concern,
Waiting his turn
To release his appropriate bang or two.

And the scrupulous wielder of cymbals,
On pins and needles and thimbles!
Marking each beat
For the moment discreet
To crash his climacteric zing or two.
(*He* surely could tell us a thing or two.)

But what, if anyone misses?
Who gets the hisses, the odium?
Would anyone choose
To step into the shoes
Of the guy on the brink of the podium?

MELVILLE CANE

The Poets at Tea

I – MACAULAY

Pour, varlet, pour the water,
  The water steaming hot!
A spoonful for each man of us,
  Another for the pot!
We shall not drink from amber,
  No Capuan slave shall mix
For us the snows of Athos
  With port at thirty-six;
Whiter than snow the crystals
  Grown sweet 'neath tropic fires,
More rich the herb of China's field,
The pasture-lands more fragrance yield;
For ever let Britannia wield
  The teapot of her sires!

II – TENNYSON

I think that I am drawing to an end:
For on a sudden came a gasp for breath,
And stretching of the hands, and blinded eyes,
And a great darkness falling on my soul.
O Hallelujah! . . . Kindly pass the milk.

III – SWINBURNE

As the sin that was sweet in the sinning
   Is foul in the ending thereof,
As the heat of the summer's beginning
   Is past in the winter of love:
O purity, painful and pleading!
   O coldness, ineffably gray!
O hear us, our handmaid unheeding,
   And take it away!

IV – COWPER

The cosy fire is bright and gay,
The merry kettle boils away
         And hums a cheerful song.
I sing the saucer and the cup;
Pray, Mary, fill the teapot up,
         And do not make it strong.

V – BROWNING

Tst! Bah! We take as another case—
   Pass the pills on the window-sill;
      notice the capsule
(A sick man's fancy, no doubt, but I place
   Reliance on trade-marks, Sir)—so perhaps you'll
Excuse the digression—this cup which I hold
   Light-poised—Bah, it's spilt in the bed!—well,
      let's on go—
Hold Bohea and sugar, Sir; if you were told
   The sugar was salt, would the Bohea be Congo?

VI – WORDSWORTH

'Come, little cottage girl, you seem
   To want my cup of tea;
And will you take a little cream?
   Now tell the truth to me.'

She had a rustic, woodland grin,
   Her cheek was soft as silk,
And she replied, 'Sir, please put in
   A little drop of milk.'

281

'Why, what put milk into your head?
  'Tis cream my cows supply';
And five times to the child I said,
  'Why, pig-head, tell me, why?'

'You call me pig-head,' she replied;
  'My proper name is Ruth.
I call that milk'—she blushed with pride—
  'You bade me speak the truth.'

VII – POE

Here's a mellow cup of tea—golden tea!
What a world of rapturous thought its fragrance brings to me!
        Oh, from out the silver cells
        How it wells!
        How it smells!
Keeping tune, tune, tune, tune
To the tintinnabulation of the spoon.
And the kettle on the fire
Boils its spout off with desire,
With a desperate desire
And a crystalline endeavour
Now, now to sit, or never,
On the top of the pale-faced moon,
But he always came home to tea, tea, tea, tea, tea,
        Tea to the n—th.

VIII – ROSSETTI

The lilies lie in my lady's bower
(O weary mother, drive the cows to roost),
They faintly droop for a little hour;
My lady's head droops like a flower.

She took the porcelain in her hand
(O weary mother, drive the cows to roost);
She poured; I drank at her command;
Drank deep, and now—you understand!
(O weary mother, drive the cows to roost.)

282

IX – BURNS

Weel, gin ye speir, I'm no inclined,
Whusky or tay—to state my mind
    For ane or ither;
For, gin I tak the first, I'm fou,
And gin the next, I'm dull as you,
    Mix a' thegither.

X – WALT WHITMAN

One cup for my self-hood,
Many for you. *Allons, camerados*, we will drink
       together
O hand-in-hand! That tea-spoon, please, when you've
    done with it.
What butter-colour'd hair you've got. I don't
    want to be personal.
All right, then, you needn't—you're a stale—
    cadaver.
Eighteen-pence if the bottles are returned,
Allons, from all bat-eyed formules.

BARRY PAIN

Hamlet

Prince Hamlet thought Uncle a traitor
For having it off with his Mater:
    Revenge Dad or not?
    That's the gist of the plot,
And he did, nine soliloquies later . . .

STANLEY J. SHARPLESS

Don's Holiday

Professor Robinson each summer beats
The fishing record of the world—such feats
As one would hardly credit from a lesser
Person than a history professor.

GEORGE ROSTREVOR HAMILTON

Queen Victoria

Queen Victoria's
statue is
the work of her
daughter Beatrice.
The shape's all wrong
and the crown doesn't fit,
but—bless her old heart!—
she was proud of it.

HUMBERT WOLFE

The Dog and the Thief

Quoth the thief to the dog; 'let me into your door,
  And I'll give you these delicate bits':
Quoth the dog, 'I should then be more villain than you're,
  And besides must be out of my wits:

'Your delicate bits will not serve me a meal,
  But my master each day gives me bread;
You'll fly when you get what you come here to steal,
  And I must be hanged in your stead.'

The stockjobber thus, from Change Alley goes down,
  And tips you the freeman a wink;
'Let me have but your vote to serve for the town,
  And here is a guinea to drink.'

Said the freeman, 'your guinea tonight would be spent,
  Your offers of bribery cease;
I'll vote for my landlord to whom I pay rent,
  Or else I may forfeit my lease.'

From London they come, silly people to chouse,*
  Their lands and their faces unknown;
Who'd vote a rogue into the parliament-house,
  That would turn a man out of his own?

JONATHAN SWIFT

* *chouse = cheat*

Infant Innocence

Reader, behold! this monster wild
Has gobbled up the infant child.
The infant child is not aware
It has been eaten by the bear.

A. E. HOUSMAN

Lines to a Don

Remote and ineffectual Don
That dared attack my Chesterton,
With that poor weapon, half-impelled,
Unlearnt, unsteady, hardly held,
Unworthy for a tilt with men—
Your quavering and corroded pen;

Don poor at Bed and worse at Table,
Don pinched, Don starved, Don miserable;
Don stuttering, Don with roving eyes,
Don nervous, Don of crudities;
Don clerical, Don ordinary,
Don self-absorbed and solitary;
Don here-and-there, Don epileptic;
Don puffed and empty, Don dyspeptic;
Don middle-class, Don sycophantic,
Don dull, Don brutish, Don pedantic;
Don hypocritical, Don bad,
Don furtive, Don three-quarters mad;
Don (since a man must make an end),
Don that shall never be my friend.

Don different from those regal Dons!
With hearts of gold and lungs of bronze,
Who shout and bang and roar and bawl
The Absolute across the hall,
Or sail in amply billowing gown
Enormous through the Sacred Town,
Bearing from College to their homes
Deep cargoes of gigantic tomes;
Dons admirable! Dons of Might!
Uprising on my inward sight
Compact of ancient tales, and port
And sleep—and learning of a sort.
Dons English, worthy of the land;
Dons rooted; Dons that understand.
Good Dons perpetual that remain
A landmark, walling in the plain—
The horizon of my memories—
Like large and comfortable trees.

Don very much apart from these,
Thou scapegoat Don, thou Don devoted,
Don to thine own damnation quoted,
Perplexed to find thy trivial name
Reared in my verse to lasting shame.
Don dreadful, rasping Don and wearing,
Repulsive Don—Don past all bearing.
Don of the cold and doubtful breath,

Don despicable, Don of death;
Don nasty, skimpy, silent, level;
Don evil; Don that serves the devil.
Don ugly—that makes fifty lines.
There is a Canon which confines
A Rhymed Octosyllabic Curse
If written in Iambic Verse
To fifty lines. I never cut;
I far prefer to end it—but
Believe me I shall soon return.
My fires are banked, but still they burn
To write some more about the Don
That dared attack my Chesterton.

HILAIRE BELLOC

To Mr Thomas Southern
on this birthday, 1742

Resigned to live, prepared to die,
With not one sin but poetry,
This day Tom's fair account has run
(Without a blot) to eighty-one.
Kind Boyle, before his poet lays
A table, with a cloth of bays;
And Ireland, mother of sweet singers,
Presents his harp still to his fingers.
The feast, his towering genius marks
In yonder wild-goose and the larks!
The mushrooms show his wit was sudden!
And for his judgment, lo a pudden!
Roast beef, though old, proclaims him stout,
And grace, although a bard, devout.
May Tom, whom heaven sent down to raise
The price of prologues and of plays,
Be every birthday more a winner,
Digest his thirty-thousandth dinner;
Walk to his grave without reproach,
And scorn a rascal and a coach.

ALEXANDER POPE

The Three Calenders

By E. S. (I doubt if anyone would have used this title or could have written these poems but Miss Edith Sitwell)

I

Rhinoceros-glum
The tramcars come
With a quick bastinado
To shake the façado
Of the stout riverado,
And
Simpering simian viziers stare
Through the zebraed gloom in the thick furred air
Of the blue bandanaed,
Unzenanaed
Come-away-and-let's-get-a-ripe-bananaed
Strand.
Canned
Peaches are sold and peppermint drops,
But the West Ham motor-bus never stops.
Don Magnifico down in hell
Dances the shimmy-shake really well;
Te-he, tittering, sighs Mamzelle
To the bland
Titanesque, picaresque
Young clerk from the desk
Where the light creaks soft under rose-petalled trellises,
Bought it for ninepence at Simpson & Ellis's,
'Ain't the band
Sumfin' grand?'

II

The fluted plasters of the sky
Come off in long grey strips to try

And snare the clockwork birds like fish
(Fat carp with feathers). No winds swish

Our faces, peering under hats
As we walk home from Wanstead Flats;

Long lines of lamp-posts tulip-stark
Wave beards of light that flap the dark.

Mamzelle insists this is not so,
Yet were we two alone, I know,

On Wanstead Flats, unfurred by fear,
With no wood-carved policeman near,

Mamzelle would break away from me
And climb these tall posts gingerly,

And seize the tender gas-flame buds
And bite them off and chew their cuds,

As cows digest fruit-hairy Springs:
Mamzelle does most *peculiar* things.

III

When
  Dan Mephistopheles cursed at his coffee-lees
    Down in Gehenna—
    He swore they were senna
    (But the barmaid cried 'Go hon'),
  Alfred Lord Tennyson, eating cold venison
  Granting his benison, roared to each denizen,
    Rat-faced professor and don,
  That the inquisitorial Albert Memorial
  (Madam Queen Venus uplifted on horsehair
        but where was the corsair?
  Why ruling the waves of a pantomime sea)
    Was gone.
    Break, break, break;
    But free,
    And wholly audacious
    And quite contumacious
  And squirting some pomegranate juice in the eye
    Of Methuselah's ape as it fox-trots by
  On the rim of the hippopotamus sky
  Where the nightingale (stuffed) lets her singing die,
    Are we.

E. V. KNOX

Dorset

Rime Intrinsica, Fontmell Magna, Sturminster Newton and
                                Melbury Bubb,
Whist upon whist upon whist upon whist drive, in Institute,
                            Legion and Social Club.
Horny hands that hold the aces which this morning held
                                the plough—
While Tranter Reuben, T. S. Eliot, H. G. Wells and Edith
                Sitwell lie in Mellstock Churchyard now.

Lord's Day bells from Bingham's Melcome, Iwerne Minster,
                               Shroton, Plush,
Down the grass between the beeches, mellow in the evening
                                  hush.
Gloved the hands that hold the hymn-book, which this
                          morning milked the cow—
While Tranter Reuben, Mary Borden, Brian Howard and
                Harold Acton lie in Mellstock Churchyard now.

Light's abode, celestial Salem! Lamps of evening, smelling
                                  strong,
Gleaming on the pitch-pine, waiting, almost empty evensong:
From the aisles each window smiles on grave and grass and
                              yew-tree bough—
While Tranter Reuben, Gordon Selfridge, Edna Best and
               Thomas Hardy lie in Mellstock Churchyard now.

JOHN BETJEMAN

The names in the last lines of these stanzas are put in not out of malice or satire but merely for their euphony.

A Letter to Harriet Weaver, in the Style of 'The Waste Land'

Rouen is the rainiest place getting
Inside all impermeables, wetting
Damp marrow in drenched bones.
Midwinter soused us coming over Le Mans
Our inn at Niort was the Grape of Burgundy
But the winepress of the Lord thundered over that
          grape of Burgundy
And we left it in a hurgundy.
   (Hurry up, Joyce, it's time!)

I heard mosquitoes swarm in old Bordeaux
So many!
I had not thought the earth contained so many
   (Hurry up, Joyce, it's time)

Mr Anthologos, the local gardener,
Greycapped, with politeness full of cunning
Has made wine these fifty years
And told me in his southern French
Le petit vin is the surest drink to buy
For if 'tis bad
Vous ne l'avez pas payé
   (Hurry up, hurry up, now, now, now!)

But we shall have great times,
When we return to Clinic, that waste land
O Esculapios!
   (Shan't we? Shan't we? Shan't we?)

                         JAMES JOYCE

On Jessy Watson's Elopement

Run off is Jessy Watson fair—
Her eyes do sparkle, she has good hair.
But Mrs Leath you shall now be,
Now and for all Eternity.
Such merry spirits I do hate,
But now it is over, and too late—
For to retract such vows you can't,
And you must now love your gallant.
But I am sure you will repent,
And your poor heart will then relent.
Your poor, poor father will repine,
And so would I, if you were mine.
But now be good for this time past,
And let this folly be your last.

MARJORIE FLEMING (aged 8)

Bones

Said Mr Smith, 'I really cannot
  Tell you, Dr Jones—
The most peculiar pain I'm in—
  I think it's in my *bones*.'

Said Dr Jones, 'Oh, Mr Smith,
  That's nothing. Without doubt
We have a simple cure for that;
  It is to take them out.'

He laid forthwith poor Mr Smith
  Close-clamped upon the table,
And, cold as stone, took out his bones
  As fast as he was able.

And Smith said, 'Thank you, thank you, *thank* you,'
  And wished him a Good-day;
And with his parcel 'neath his arm
  He slowly moved away.

WALTER DE LA MARE

292

On His Grace the Duke of Marlborough's House
at Woodstock

See, sir, here's the grand approach;
This way is for his Grace's coach;
There lies the bridge, and here's the clock;
Observe the lion and the cock,
The spacious court, the colonnade,
And mark how wide the wall is made!
The chimney's are so well designed
They never smoke in any wind,
The gallery's contrived for walking,
The windows to retire and talk in!
The council chamber for debate,—
And all the rest are rooms of state.
Thanks, sir, cried I: 'tis very fine
But where d'ye sleep, or where d'ye dine?
I find by all you have been telling
That 'tis a house, but not a dwelling.

ALEXANDER POPE

Our Photograph

She played me false, but that's not why
I haven't quite forgiven Di,
      Although I've tried:
This curl was hers, so brown, so bright,
She gave it me one blissful night,
      And—more beside!

In photo we were grouped together;
She wore the darling hat and feather
      That I adore;
In profile by her side I sat
Reading my poetry—but that
      She'd heard before.

Why, after all, Di threw me over
I never knew, and can't discover,
      Or even guess:
Maybe Smith's lyrics, she decided,
Were sweeter than the sweetest I did—
      I acquiesce.

A week before their wedding-day
When Smith was called in haste away
      To join the Staff,
Di gave to him, with tearful mien,
Our only photograph. I've seen
      That photograph.

I've seen it in Smith's album-book!
Just think! her hat—her tender look,
      Are now that brute's!

Before she gave it, off she cut
My body, head and lyrics, but
She was obliged, the little slut,
      To leave my boots.

FREDERICK LOCKER

Sir Humphry Davy

Sir Humphry Davy
Detested gravy.
He lived in the odium
Of having discovered sodium.

E. CLERIHEW BENTLEY

Correspondence between
Mr Harrison in Newcastle
and Mr Sholto Peach Harrison
in Hull

Sholto Peach Harrison you are no son of mine
And do you think I bred you up to cross the River Tyne
And do you think I bred you up (and mother says the same)
And do you think I bred you up to live a life of shame
To live a life of shame my boy as you are thinking to
Down south in Kingston-upon-Hull a traveller in glue?
Come back my bonny boy nor break your father's heart
Come back and marry Lady Susan Smart
She has a mint in Anglo-Persian oil
And Sholto never more need think of toil.

You are an old and evil man my father
I tell you frankly Sholto had much rather
Travel in glue unrecompensed unwed
Than go to church with oily Sue and afterwards to bed.

STEVIE SMITH

from Epistle to Dr Arbuthnot

P. Shut, shut the door, good John! fatigued, I said;
Tie up the knocker, say I'm sick, I'm dead.
The Dog-star rages! nay 'tis past a doubt,
All Bedlam, or Parnassus, is let out:
Fire in each eye, and papers in each hand,
They rave, recite, and madden round the land.
  What walls can guard me, or what shades can hide?

They pierce my thickets, through my grot they glide,
By land, by water, they renew the charge,
They stop the chariot, and they board the barge.
No place is sacred, not the church is free,
Ev'n Sunday shines no sabbath-day to me:
Then from the Mint walks forth the man of rhyme,
Happy! to catch me, just at dinner-time.

  Is there a parson, much bemused in beer,
A maudlin poetess, a rhyming peer,
A clerk, foredoomed his father's soul to cross,
Who pens a stanza, when he should engross?
Is there, who, locked from ink and paper, scrawls
With desperate charcoal round his darkened walls?
All fly to Twit'nam, and in humble strain
Apply to me, to keep them mad or vain.
Arthur, whose giddy son neglects the laws,
Imputes to me and my damned works the cause:
Poor Cornus sees his frantic wife elope,
And curses wit, and poetry, and Pope.

  Friend to my life! (which did not you prolong,
The world had wanted many an idle song)
What drop or nostrum can this plague remove?
Or which must end me, a fool's wrath or love?
A dire dilemma! either way I'm sped,
If foes, they write, if friends, they read me dead.
Seized and tied down to judge, how wretched I!
Who can't be silent, and who will not lie:
To laugh, were want of goodness and of grace,
And to be grave, exceeds all power of face.
I sit with sad civility, I read
With honest anguish, and an aching head;
And drop at last, but in unwilling ears,
This saving counsel,—'Keep your piece nine years.'

  'Nine years!' cries he, who, high in Drury Lane,
Lulled by soft zephyrs through the broken pane,
Rhymes ere he wakes, and prints before term ends,
Obliged by hunger, and request of friends:
'The piece, you think, is incorrect? why take it,
I'm all submission; what you'd have it, make it.'

Three things another's modest wishes bound,
My friendship, and a prologue, and ten pound.
    Pitholeon sends to me: 'You know his grace,
I want a patron; ask him for a place.'
Pitholeon libelled me—'But here's a letter
Informs you, sir, 'twas when he knew no better.
Dare you refuse him? Curll invites to dine,
He'll write a journal, or he'll turn divine.'
Bless me! a packet. ' 'Tis a stranger sues,
A virgin tragedy, an orphan muse.'
If I dislike it, 'Furies, death and rage!'
If I approve, 'Commend it to the stage.'
There (thank my stars) my whole commission ends,
The players and I are, luckily, no friends;
Fired that the house reject him, ' 'Sdeath! I'll print it,
And shame the fools—Your interest, sir, with Lintot.'
Lintot, dull rogue! will think your price too much:
'Not, sir, if you revise it, and retouch.'
All my demurs but double his attacks;
And last he whispers, 'Do; and we go snacks.'
Glad of a quarrel, straight I clap the door:
Sir, let me see your works and you no more.

ALEXANDER POPE

The Shopwalker's Daughter

Slowly the shadows gathered,
    As the lights shone o'er the scene,
He had helped her to soup with a ladle
    From a George-the-Fourth tureen;
Pheasant had followed, then partridge,
    Lobster and Burgundy wine;
As the music played soft, he leaned forward and coughed,
    But the girl answered, knowing the sign—

I may be a shopwalker's daughter,
But my heart is a shopgirl's heart;
  You may take me to dine,
  And fête me with wine,
For that is the rich man's part.
Yet, remember, ere I leave you,
  I'm no plaything of a day;
I may be a shopwalker's daughter, sir,
  But that's not a shopgirl's way.

His burning glances redoubled
  As he plied her with champagne,
Shyly she lowered her eyelids,
  Till he winced at her disdain.
Then, thrusting his caviare from him,
  He swore to be ever true,
But all that she heard was a father's last word,
  As slowly her hand she withdrew—

  I may be a shopwalker's daughter,
  But I'm human right to the core;
    You may dazzle my eyes,
    With port and game pies,
  For that's what a rich man's for.
  But remember, ere our parting,
    I'm no chattel of a day;
  I may be a shopwalker's daughter, sir,
    But that's not a shopgirl's way.

J. B. MORTON

Free Thoughts on Several Eminent Composers

Some cry up Haydn, some Mozart,
Just as the whim bites; for my part,
I do not care a farthing candle
For either of them or for Handel.
Cannot a man live free and easy
Without admiring Pergolesé?

Or through the world with comfort go
That never heard of Doctor Blow?
So help me, heaven, I hardly have;
And yet I eat, and drink, and shave,
Like other people, if you watch it,
And know no more of stave or crotchet
Than did the primitive Peruvians;
Or those old ante-queer-diluvians
That lived in the unwashed world with Jubal,
Before that dirty blacksmith Tubal,
By stroke on anvil, or on summat,
Found out, to his great surprise, the gamut;
I care no more for Cimarosa
Than he did for Salvator Rosa,
Being no painter; and bad luck
Be mine, if I can bear that Gluck!
Old Tycho Brahe and modern Herschel
Had something in them; but who's Purcell?
The devil with his foot so cloven,
For aught I care, may take Beethoven;
And, if the bargain does not suit,
I'll throw him Weber in to boot!
There's not the splitting of a splinter
To choose 'twixt him last named and Winter.
Of Doctor Pepusch, old Queen Dido
Knew just as much, God knows, as I do.
I would not go four miles to visit
Sebastian Bach (or Batch, which is it?)
No more I would for Bononcini.
As for Novello, or Rossini,
I shall not say a word to grieve 'em,
Because they're living; so I leave 'em.

CHARLES LAMB

The Miller's Tale

Some time ago there was a rich old codger
Who lived in Oxford and who took a lodger.
The fellow was a carpenter by trade,
His lodger a poor student who had made
Some studies in the arts, but all his fancy
Turned to astrology and geomancy,
And he could deal with certain propositions
And make a forecast under some conditions
About the likelihood of drought or showers
For those who asked at favourable hours,
Or put a question how their luck would fall
In this or that, I can't describe them all.

This lad was known as Nicholas the Spark.
He was a dab at love, but kept it dark,
For he was sly, and secret and he took
Advantage of his meek and girlish look.
He rented a small chamber in the kip
All by himself without companionship.
He decked it charmingly with herbs and fruit
And he himself was sweeter than the root
Of liquorice or any fragrant herb.
His astronomic text-books were superb,
He had an astrolable to match his art
And calculating counters laid apart
On handy shelves that stood above his bed.
His press was curtained coarsely and in red;
Above there lay a gallant harp in sight
On which he played melodiously at night
With such a touch that all the chamber rang;
It was *The Virgin's Angelus* he sang,
And after that he sang *King William's Note*,
And people often blessed his merry throat.
And that was how this charming scholar spent
His time and money, which his friends had sent.

This carpenter had married a young wife
Not long before, and loved her more than life.
She was a girl of eighteen years of age.
Jealous he was and kept her in the cage,
For he was old and she was wild and young;

He thought himself quite likely to be stung.
   He might have known, were Cato on his shelf,
A man should marry someone like himself;
A man should pick an equal for his mate.
Youth and old age are often in debate.
His wits were dull, he'd fallen in the snare
And had to bear his cross as others bear.
   She was a pretty creature, fair and tender,
And had a weasel's body, softly slender.
She used to wear a girdle of striped silk,
Her apron was as white as morning milk
To deck her loins, all gusseted and pleated.
Her smock was white; embroidery repeated
Its pattern on the collar front and back,
Inside and out; it was of silk, and black.
And all the ribbons on her milky mutch
Were made to match her collar, even such.
She wore a broad silk fillet rather high,
And certainly she had a lecherous eye.
And she had plucked her eyebrows into bows,
Slenderly arched they were, and black as sloes.
And a more truly blissful sight to see
She was than blossom on a cherry-tree,
And softer than the wool upon a wether.
And by her girdle hung a purse of leather,
Tasselled in silk, with metal droplets, pearled.
If you went seeking up and down the world
The wisest man you met would have to wrench
His fancy to imagine such a wench.
She had a shining colour, gaily tinted,
And brighter than a florin newly minted,
And when she sang it was as loud and quick
As any swallow perched above a rick.
And she would skip or play some game or other
Like any kid or calf behind its mother.
Her mouth was sweet as mead or honey—say
A hoard of apples lying in the hay.
Skittish she was, and jolly as a colt,
Tall as a mast and upright as a bolt
Out of a bow. Her collaret revealed
A brooch as big as boss upon a shield.
High shoes she wore, and laced them to the top.

She was a daisy, O a lollypop
For any nobleman to take to bed
Or for an honest yeoman-chap to wed.
    Now, gentlemen, young Nicholas the Spark,
So things fell out, one day began to lark
With this young woman, and to romp about
Taking a chance, her husband being out.
Students are sly, and giving way to whim
He made a grab and caught her by the quim
And said, 'O God, I love you! Can't you see
If I don't have you it's the end of me?'
Then held her haunches hard and gave a cry
'O love-me-all-at-once or I shall die!'
    She gave a spring, just like a skittish colt
Boxed in a frame for shoeing, and with a jolt
Managed in time to wrench her head away,
And said, 'Give over, Nicholas, I say!
No, I won't kiss you! Stop it! Let me go
Or I shall scream! I'll let the neighbours know!
Where are your manners? Take away your paws!'
    Then Nicholas began to plead his cause
And spoke so fair in proffering what he could
That in the end she promised him she would,
Swearing she'd love him with a solemn promise
To be at his disposal by St Thomas,
When she could spy an opportunity.
'My husband is so full of jealousy,
Unless you watch your step and hold your breath
I know for certain it will be my death,'
She said, 'So keep it well under your hat.'
'Oh, never mind about a thing like that,'
Said he; 'A scholar doesn't have to stir
His wits so much to trick a carpenter.'
    And so they both agreed to it, and swore
To watch their chance, as I have said before.
When things were settled thus as they thought fit,
And Nicholas had stroked her loins a bit
And kissed her sweetly, he took down his harp
And played away, a merry tune and sharp.
    It happened later she went off to church,
This worthy wife, one holiday, to search
Her conscience and to do the works of Christ.

She put her work aside and she enticed
The colour to her face to make her mark;
Her forehead shone. There was a parish clerk
Serving the church whose name was Absalon.
His hair was all in golden curls and shone;
Just like a fan it strutted outwards, starting
To left and right from an accomplished parting.
Ruddy his face, his eyes as grey as goose,
His shoes cut out in tracery, as in use
In old St Paul's. The hose upon his feet
Showed scarlet through, and all his clothes were neat
And proper. In a jacket of light blue,
Flounced at the waist and tagged with laces too,
He went, and wore a surplice just as gay
And white as any blossom on the spray.
God bless my soul, he was a merry knave!
He knew how to let blood, cut hair and shave,
And draw up legal deeds; at other whiles
He used to dance in twenty different styles
(After the current school at Oxford though,
Casting his legs about him to and fro).
He played a two-stringed fiddle, did it proud,
And sang a high falsetto rather loud;
And he was just as good on the guitar.
There was no public-house in town or bar
He didn't visit with his merry face
If there were saucy barmaids round the place.
He was a little squeamish in the matter
Of farting, and satirical in chatter.
   This Absalon, so jolly in his ways,
Would bear the censer round on holy days
And cense the parish women. He would cast
Many a love-lorn look before he passed,
Especially at this carpenter's young wife;
Looking at her would make a happy life
He thought, so neat, so sweet, so lecherous,
And I dare say if she had been a mouse
And he a cat, she'd have been pounced upon.
   In taking the collection Absalon
Would find his heart was set in such a whirl
Of love he would take nothing from a girl,
For courtesy, he said, it wasn't right.

That evening, when the moon was shining bright
He ups with his guitar and off he starts
Doing his rounds and looking out for tarts.
Larky and amorous, away he strode
Until he reached the carpenter's abode
A little after cock-crow, took his stand
Beside the casement window close at hand
(It was set low upon the cottage-face)
And started singing softly and with grace,
 'Now dearest lady, if thy pleasure be
 In thoughts of love, think tenderly of me!'
On his guitar he plucked a tuneful string.
 This carpenter awoke and heard him sing
And turning to his wife said, 'Alison!
Wife! Do you hear him? There goes Absalon
Chanting away under our chamber wall.'
And she replied, 'Yes, John, I hear it all.'
If she thought more of it she didn't tell.
 So things went on. What's better than 'All's well'?
From day to day this jolly Abasalon
Wooing away became quite woe-begone;
He lay awake all night, and all the day
Combed his thick locks and tried to pass for gay,
Wooed her by go-between and wooed by proxy,
Swore to be page and servant to his doxy,
Trilled and rouladed like a nightingale,
Sent her sweet wine and mead and spicy ale,
And wafers piping hot and jars of honey,
And, as she lived in town, he offered money.
For there are some a money-bag provokes
And some are won by kindness, some by strokes.
 Once, in the hope his talent might engage,
He played the part of Herod on the stage.
What was the good? Were he as bold as brass,
She was in love with dandy Nicholas;
However Absalon might blow his horn
His labour won him nothing but her scorn.
She looked upon him as her private ape
And held his earnest wooing all a jape.
 There is a proverb—and it is no lie—
You'll often hear repeated: 'Nigh and Sly
Wins against Fair and Square who isn't there.'
For much as Absalon might tear his hair

DORSET COUNTY LIBRARY

And rage at being seldom in her sight,
Nicholas, nigh and sly, stood in his light.
Now show your paces, Nicholas the Spark,
And leave lamenting to the parish clerk.
    And so it happened that one Saturday,
When the old carpenter was safe away
At Osney, Nicholas and Alison
Agreed at last in what was to be done.
Nicholas was to exercise his wits
On her suspicious husband's foolish fits,
And if so be the trick worked out all right
She then would sleep with Nicholas all night,
For such was his desire and hers as well;
And even quicker than it takes to tell,
Young Nicholas, who simply couldn't wait,
Went to his room on tip-toe with a plate
Of food and drink, enough to last a day
Or two, and Alison was told to say,
In case her husband asked for Nicholas,
That she had no idea where he was,
And that she hadn't set eyes on him all day
And thought he must be ill, she couldn't say;
And more than once the maid had given a call
And shouted but no answer came at all.
    So things went on the whole of Saturday
Without a sound from Nicholas, who lay
Upstairs, and ate or slept as pleased him best
Till Sunday when the sun went down to rest.
    This foolish carpenter was lost in wonder
At Nicholas; what could have got him under?
He said, 'I can't help thinking, by the Mass,
Things can't be going right with Nicholas.
What if he took and died? God guard his ways!
A ticklish place the world is, nowadays.
I saw a corpse this morning borne to kirk
That only Monday last I saw at work.
Run up,' he told the serving-lad, 'be quick,
Shout at his door, or knock it with a brick.
Take a good look and tell me how he fares.'
    The serving-boy went sturdily upstairs,
Stopped at the door and, standing there, the lad
Shouted away and, hammering like mad,
Cried, 'Ho! What's up? Hi! Master Nicholay!

How can you lie up there asleep all day?'
      But all for nought, he didn't hear a soul.
He found a broken panel with a hole
Right at the bottom, useful to the cat
For creeping in; he took a look through that,
And so at last by peering through the crack
He saw this scholar gaping on his back
As if he'd caught a glimpse of the new moon.
Down went the boy and told his master soon
About the state in which he found the man.
      On hearing this the carpenter began
To cross himself and said, 'St Frideswide bless us!
We little know what's coming to distress us.
The man has fallen, with this here astromy,
Into a fit, or lunacy maybe.
I always thought that was how it would go.
God has some secrets that we shouldn't know.
How blessed are the simple, aye, indeed,
That only know enough to say their creed!
Happened just so with such another student
Of astromy and he was so imprudent
As to stare upwards while he crossed a field
Busy foreseeing what the stars revealed;
And what should happen but he fell down flat
Into a marl-pit. No foreseeing that!
But by the Saints we've reached a sorry pass;
I can't help worrying for Nicholas.
He shall be scolded for his studying
If I know how to scold, by Christ the King!
Get me a staff to prise against the floor.
Robin, you put your shoulder to the door.
We'll shake the study out of him, I guess!'
      The pair of them began to heave and press
Against the door. Happened the lad was strong
And so it didn't take them very long
To heave it off its hinges; down it came.
Still as a stone lay Nicholas, with the same
Expression, gaping upwards into air.
The carpenter supposed it was despair
And shook him by the shoulders with a stout
And purposeful attack, and gave a shout:
'What, Nicholas! Hey! Look down! Is that a fashion

To act? Wake up and think upon Christ's passion.
I sign you with the cross from elves and sprites!'
And he began the spell for use at nights
In all four corners of the room and out
Across the threshold too and round about:
  Jesu Christ and Benedict Sainted
  Bless this house from creature tainted,
  Drive away night-hags, white Pater-noster,
  Where did you go St Peter's soster?
  And in the end the dandy Nicholas
Began to sigh, 'And must it come to pass?'
He said, 'Must all the world be cast away?'
The carpenter replied, 'What's that you say?
Put trust in God as we do, working men.'
  Nicholas answered, 'Fetch some liquor then,
And afterwards, in strictest secrecy,
I'll speak of something touching you and me,
But not another soul must know, that's plain.'
  This carpenter went down and came again
Bringing some powerful ale—a largeish quart.
When each had had his share of this support
Young Nicholas got up and shut the door
And, sitting down beside him on the floor,
Said to the carpenter, 'Now, John, my dear,
My excellent host, swear on your honour here
Not to repeat a syllable I say,
For here are Christ's intentions, to betray
Which to a soul puts you among the lost,
And vengeance for it at a bitter cost
Shall fall upon you. You'll be driven mad!'
'Christ and His holy blood forbid it, lad!'
The silly fellow answered. 'I'm no blab,
Though I should say it. I'm not given to gab.
Say what you like, for I shall never tell
Man, woman or child by Him that harrowed Hell!'
  'Now, John,' said Nicholas, 'believe you me,
I have found out by my astrology,
And looking at the moon when it was bright,
That Monday next, a quarter way through night,
Rain is to fall in torrents, such a scud
It will be twice as bad as Noah's Flood.
This world,' he said, 'in just about an hour,

Shall all be drowned, it's such a hideous shower,
And all mankind, with total loss of life.'
   The carpenter exclaimed, 'Alas, my wife!
My little Alison! Is she to drown?'
And in his grief he very near fell down.
'Is there no remedy,' he said, 'for this?'
'Thanks be to God,' said Nicholas, 'there is,
If you will do exactly what I say
And don't start thinking up some other way.
In wise old Solomon you'll find the verse
"Who takes advice shall never fare the worse,"
And so if good advice is to prevail
I undertake with neither mast nor sail
To save her yet, and save myself and you.
Haven't you heard how Noah was saved too
When God forewarned him and his sons and daughters
That all the world should sink beneath the waters?'
'Yes,' said the carpenter, 'a long time back.'
'Haven't you heard,' said Nicholas, 'what a black
Business it was, when Noah tried to whip
His wife (who wouldn't come) on board the ship?
He'd have been better pleased, I'll undertake,
With all that weather just about to break,
If she had had a vessel of her own.
Now, what are we to do? We can't postpone
The thing; it's coming soon, as I was saying,
It calls for haste, not preaching or delaying.
   'I want you, now at once, to hurry off
And fetch a shallow tub or kneading-trough
For each of us, but see that they are large
And such as we can float in, like a barge.
And have them loaded with sufficient victual
To last a day—we only need a little.
The waters will abate and flow away
Round nine o'clock upon the following day.
Robin the lad mayn't know of this, poor knave,
Nor Jill the maid, those two I cannot save.
Don't ask me why; and even if you do
I can't disclose God's privity to you.
You should be satisfied, unless you're mad,
To find as great a grace as Noah had.
And I shall save your wife, you needn't doubt it,

Now off you go, and hurry up about it.
　'And when the tubs have been collected, three,
That's one for her and for yourself and me,
Then hang them in the roof below the thatching
That no one may discover what we're hatching.
When you have finished doing what I said
And stowed the victuals in them overhead,
Also an axe to hack the ropes apart,
So, when the water rises, we can start,
And, lastly, when you've broken out the gable,
The garden one that's just above the stable,
So that we may cast free without delay
After the mighty shower has gone away,
You'll float as merrily, I undertake,
As any lily-white duck behind her drake.
And I'll call out, "Hey, Alison! Hey, John!
Cheer yourselves up! The flood will soon be gone."
And you'll shout back, "Hail, Master Nicholay!
Good morning! I can see you well. It's day!"
We shall be lords for all the rest of life
Of all the world, like Noah and his wife.
　'One thing I warn you of; it's only right.
We must be very careful on the night,
Once we have safely managed to embark,
To hold our tongues, to utter no remark,
No cry or call, for we must fall to prayer.
This is the Lord's dear will, so have a care.
　'Your wife and you must hang some way apart,
For there must be no sin before we start,
No more in longing looks than in the deed.
Those are your orders. Off with you! God speed!
Tomorrow night when everyone's asleep
We'll all go quietly upstairs and creep
Into our tubs, awaiting Heaven's grace.
And now be off. No time to put the case
At greater length, no time to sermonize;
The proverb says, "Say nothing, send the wise."
You're wise enough, I do not have to teach you.
Go, save our lives for us, as I beseech you.'
　This silly carpenter then went his way
Muttering to himself, 'Alas the day!'
And told his wife in strictest secrecy.

She was aware, far more indeed than he,
What this quaint stratagem might have in sight,
But she pretended to be dead with fright.
'Alas!' she said. 'Whatever it may cost,
Hurry and help, or we shall all be lost.
I am your honest, true and wedded wife,
Go, dearest husband, help to save my life!'
    How fancy throws us into perturbation!
People can die of mere imagination,
So deep is the impression one can take.
This silly carpenter began to quake,
Before his eyes there verily seemed to be
The floods of Noah wallowing like the sea
And drowning Alison his honey-pet.
He wept and wailed, his features were all set
In grief, he sighed with many a doleful grunt.
He went and got a tub, began to hunt
For kneading-troughs, found two, and had them sent
Home to his house in secret; then he went
And, unbeknowns, he hung them from a rafter.
With his own hands he made three ladders after,
Uprights and rungs, to help them in their scheme
Of climbing where they hung upon the beam.
He victualled tub and trough, and made all snug
With bread and cheese, and ale in a large jug,
Enough for three of them to last the day,
And, just before arranging this display,
Packed off the maid and his apprentice too
To London on a job they had to do.
And on the Monday when it drew to night
He shut his door and dowsed the candle-light
And made quite sure all was as it should be.
And shortly, up they clambered, all the three,
Silent and separate. They began to pray
And 'Pater Noster mum', said Nicholay,
And 'mum' said John, and 'mum' said Alison.
The carpenter's devotions being done
He sat quite still, then fell to prayer again
And waited anxiously to hear the rain.
    The carpenter, with all the work he'd seen,
Fell dead asleep—round curfew, must have been,
Maybe a little later on the whole.

310

He groaned in sleep for travail of his soul
And snored because his head was turned awry.
   Down by their ladders, stalking from on high
Came Nicholas and Alison, and sped
Softly downstairs without a word to bed,
And where this carpenter was wont to be
The revels started and the melody.
And thus lay Nicholas and Alison
At busy play in eager quest of fun,
Until the bell for lauds had started ringing
And in the chancel Friars began their singing.
   This parish clerk, this amorous Absalon,
Love-stricken still and very woe-begone,
Upon the Monday was in company
At Osney with his friends for jollity,
And chanced to ask a resident cloisterer
What had become of John the carpenter.
The fellow drew him out of church to say,
'Don't know; not been at work since Saturday.
I can't say where he is; I think he went
To fetch the Abbot timber. He is sent
Often enough for timber, has to go
Out to the Grange and stop a day or so;
If not he's certainly at home today,
But where he is I can't exactly say.'
   Absalon was a jolly lad and light
Of heart; he thought, 'I'll stay awake tonight;
I'm certain that I haven't seem him stirring
About his door since dawn; it's safe inferring
That he's away. As I'm alive I'll go
And tap his window softly at the crow
Of cock—the sill is low-set on the wall.
I shall see Alison and tell her all
My love-longing, and I can hardly miss
Some favour from her, at the least a kiss.
I'll get some satisfaction anyway;
There's been an itching in my mouth all day
And that's a sign of kissing at the least.
And all last night I dreamt about a feast.
I think I'll go and sleep an hour or two,
Then wake and have some fun, that's what I'll do.'
   The first cock crew at last, and thereupon

Up rose this jolly lover Absalon
In gayest clothes, garnished with that and this;
But first he chewed a grain of liquorice
To charm his breath before he combed his hair.
Under his tongue the comfit nestling there
Would make him gracious. He began to roam
To where old John and Alison kept home
And by the casement window took his stand.
Breast-high it stood, no higher than his hand.
He gave a cough, no more than half a sound:
'Alison, honey-comb, are you around?
Sweet cinnamon, my little pretty bird,
Sweetheart, wake up and say a little word!
You seldom think of me in all my woe,
I sweat for love of you wherever I go!
No wonder if I do, I pine and bleat
As any lambkin hungering for the teat,
Believe me, darling, I'm so deep in love
I croon with longing like a turtle-dove,
I eat as little as a girl at school.'
'You go away,' she answered, 'you Tom-fool!
There's no come-up-and-kiss-me here for you.
I love another and why shouldn't I too?
Better than you, by Jesu, Absalon!
Take yourself off or I shall throw a stone.
I want to get some sleep. You go to Hell!'
'Alas!' said Absalon. 'I knew it well;
True love is always mocked and girded at;
So kiss me, if you can't do more than that,
For Jesu's love and for the love of me!'
'And if I do, will you be off?' said she.
'Promise you, darling,' answered Absalon.
'Get ready then; wait, I'll put something on,'
She said, and then she added under breath
To Nicholas, 'Hush . . . we shall laugh to death!'
   This Absalon went down upon his knees;
'I am a lord at least, and by degrees
I hope,' he said, 'there may be more to come.
Your mouth, my pretty bird, and drop a crumb!'
   She flung the window open then in haste
And said, 'Have done, come on, no time to waste,
The neighbours here are always on the spy.'

Absalon started wiping his mouth dry.
Dark was the night as pitch, as black as coal,
And at the window out she put her hole,
And Absalon, so fortune framed the farce,
Put up his mouth and kissed her naked arse
Most savorously before he knew of this.
　　And back he started. Something was amiss;
He knew quite well a woman has no beard,
Yet something rough and hairy had appeared.
'What have I done?' he said. 'Can that be you?'
'Teehee!' she cried and clapped the window to.
Off went poor Absalon sadly through the dark.
'A beard! a beard!' cried Nicholas the Spark.
'God's body, that was something like a joke!'
And Absalon, overhearing what he spoke,
Bit on his lips and nearly threw a fit
In rage and thought, 'I'll pay you back for it!'
　　Who's busy rubbing, scraping at his lips
With dust, with sand, with straw, with cloth, with chips,
But Absalon? He thought, 'I'll bring him down!
I wouldn't let this go for all the town.
I'd take my soul and sell it to the Devil
To be revenged upon him! I'll get level.
O God, why did I let myself be fooled?'
　　The fiery heat of love by now had cooled,
For from the time he kissed her hinder parts
He didn't give a tinker's curse for tarts;
His malady was cured by this endeavour
And he defied all paramours whatever.
　　So, weeping like a child that has been whipped,
He turned away; across the road he slipped
And called on Gervase. Gervase was a smith;
His forge was full of things for ploughing with
And he was busy sharpening a share.
　　Absalon knocked, and with an easy air
Called, 'Gervase! Open up the door, come on!'
'What's that? Who's there?' 'It's me, it's Abasalon.'
'What, Absalon? By Jesu's blessed tree
You're early up! Hey, *benedicite*,
What's wrong? Some jolly girl as like as not
Has coaxed you out and set you on the trot.
Blessed St Neot! You know the thing I mean.'

But Absalon, who didn't give a bean
For all his joking, offered no debate.
He had a good deal more upon his plate
Than Gervase knew, and said, 'Would it be fair
To borrow that coulter in the chimney there,
The hot one, see it? I've a job to do;
It won't take long, I'll bring it back to you.'
Gervase replied, 'Why, if you asked for gold,
A bag of sovereigns or for wealth untold,
It should be yours, as I'm an honest smith.
But, Christ, why borrow that to do it with?'
'Let that,' said Absalon, 'be as it may;
You'll hear about it all some other day.'
    He caught the coulter up — the haft was cool—
And left the smithy softly with the tool,
Crept to the little window in the wall
And coughed. He knocked and gave a little call
Under the window as he had before.
    Alison said, 'There's someone at the door.
Who's knocking there? I'll warrant it's a thief.'
'Why, no,' said he, 'my little flower-leaf,
It's your own Absalon, my sweety-thing!
Look what I've brought you—it's a golden ring.
My mother gave me, as I may be saved.
It's very fine, and prettily engraved;
I'll give it to you, darling, for a kiss.'
    Now Nicholas had risen for a piss,
And thought he could improve upon the jape
And make him kiss his arse ere he escape,
And opening the window with a jerk,
Stuck out his arse, a handsome piece of work,
Buttocks and all, as far as to the haunch.
    Said Absalon, all set to make a launch,
'Speak, pretty bird, I know not where thou art!'
This Nicholas at once let fly a fart
As loud as if it were a thunder-clap.
He was near blinded by the blast, poor chap,
But his hot iron was ready; with a thump
He smote him in the middle of the rump.
    Off went the skin a hand's-breadth round about
Where the hot coulter struck and burnt it out.
Such was the pain, he thought he must be dying

314

And, mad with agony, he started crying,
'Help! Water! Water! Help! For Heaven's love!'
   The carpenter, startled from sleep above,
And hearing shouts for water and a thud,
Thought, 'Heaven help us! Here comes Nowel's Flood!'
And up he sat and with no more ado
He took his axe and smote the ropes in two
And down went everything. He didn't stop
To sell his bread and ale, but came down flop
Upon the floor and fainted right away.
   Up started Alison and Nicholay
And shouted, 'Help!' and 'Murder!' in the street.
The neighbours all came running up in heat
And stood there staring at the wretched man.
He lay there fainting, pale beneath his tan;
His arm in falling had been broken double.
But still he was obliged to face his trouble,
For when he spoke he was at once borne down
By Nicholas and his wife. They told the town
That he was mad, there'd got into his blood
Some sort of nonsense about 'Nowel's Flood',
That vain imaginings and fantasy
Had made him buy the kneading-tubs, that he
Had hung them in the rafters up above
And that he'd begged them both for heaven's love
To sit up in the roof for company.
   All started laughing at this lunacy
And streamed upstairs to gape and pry and poke,
And treated all his sufferings as a joke.
No matter what the carpenter asserted
It went for nothing, no one was converted;
With powerful oaths they swore the fellow down
And he was held for mad by all the town;
Even the learned said to one another,
'The fellow must be crazy, my dear brother.'
So to a general laughter he succumbed.
   That's how the carpenter's young wife was plumbed
For all the tricks his jealousy could try,
And Absalon has kissed her nether eye
And Nicholas is branded on the bum
And God bring all of us to Kingdom Come.

GEOFFREY CHAUCER *translated by* NEVILL COGHILL

The Reviewing of Poetry

So your new book's just out? You should splash wine
  about—for this must be a joyful occasion?
Not at all! you reply to that questioning eye, for the
  critical gift of 'abrasion'
is the one that's most favoured—you're salt that's not
  savoured; reviewers must be *entertaining*
(readers must have their fun)—though they're in a bright
  sun, they will tell their dim public it's raining
if this makes a good story, for a journalist's glory is to stir
  up those somnolent morons
who have much less idea of the art we have here than a
  tribe of illiterate Hurons!
Circulation's shoe pinches—they waste column inches on
  mocking the innocent photos
of the authors on jackets (like flowers on seed packets)—
  then proceed with andante con motos
to lament with a tear how it doesn't appear, although *their*
  attempts are so gallant,
that a person could find, unless out of his mind, the
  slightest small vestige of talent
in this tedious verbiage that runs wild like herbage all
  over the pitiful pages.
But if Truth's what you want, from an unsullied font,
  you should know that it isn't for ages
or possibly ever that he's been so clever (although he's
  devoted to Culture)
to sort out in his head what's worthwhile that he's read or
  to tell a good verse from a vulture!
It's so safe, though, mock-sad, to call everything bad; no
  one then can say you were a sucker
if the fashion should change and you had to arrange to
  revive that young lad Tommy Tucker
as inspired 'Nursery Folk'—and this isn't a joke—it could
  happen and maybe tomorrow
(and with no thought of merit—a rabbit's a ferret for *them*
  and a Cotman a Corot)
that for Gunn and Ted Hughes we read 'Rhythm and
  Blues' in half-with-it, half-in school anthologies

where a bad word like 'bed', if it raises its head, is quite
   stifled at once with apologies—
for as everyone knows from his head to his toes (or her
   toes) there is no animality
in a teenager's heart. They are pure in each part, and the
   word they've not heard's 'sexuality'!
What they don't understand, critics blast out of hand—
   they're spectators who don't know the rules well
in a whole lot of cases, but they don't hide their faces!
   They will say that they don't suffer fools well
and with no hint of shame they will go on to blame the
   poor writer; it's very much harder
to produce wholesome food than to write something
   rude pointing out that there's zilch in the larder!

For its hard to create. And it's Art that they hate. It's not
   newsworthy—nobody cares much,
readers don't want to know; it seems baiting a poet's just
   fun—as it once was with bears, much
less exciting perhaps, more like throwing of craps—but it
   raises *your* temperature highly,
paranoia is throbbing, there's sighing and sobbing, and
   those darts have gone home, oh, so slyly—

for you can't bear to look at your miserable book, and a
needless bad line drills a hole in your spine, and you feel
you would like someone's head on a spike and—of true
SF size, just to kick in their eyes—centipedes in big boots,
to reduce their gay hoots to a terrible scream, make their
life a bad dream, as you burn for revenge from Pitlochry
to Penge, and you feel all your efforts are wasted;

but at least the book's out (to a jeer or a shout) and
although you feel vexed, you can start on the next—
and it couldn't be *more* panned and pasted!

GAVIN EWART

Blues

Stop all the clocks, cut off the telephone,
Prevent the dog from barking with a juicy bone,
Silence the pianos and with muffled drum
Bring out the coffin, let the mourners come.

Let aeroplanes circle moaning overhead
Scribbling on the sky the message He Is Dead,
Put crepe bows round the white necks of the public doves,
Let the traffic policemen wear black cotton gloves.

He was my North, my South, my East, and West,
My working week and my Sunday rest,
My noon, my midnight, my talk, my song;
I thought that love would last for ever: I was wrong.

The stars are not wanted now; put out every one,
Pack up the moon and dismantle the sun,
Pour away the ocean and sweep up the wood;
For nothing now can ever come to any good.

W. H. AUDEN

Balliol Rhymes

J. L. Strachan Davidson

STRACHAN DAVIDSON am I, the lean
Unbuttoned, cigaretted Dean,
Brother numismatists, you see a
Historian in a Dahabeeah.

J. A. HAMILTON

R. L. Nettleship

Roughly, so to say, you know,
I am NETTLESHIP or so;
You are gated after Hall,
That's all. I mean that's nearly all.

H. C. BEECHING

Variants on the above

I

So to say—at least—you know
I am NETTLESHIP or so,
Or—in other words—I mean
What they call the Junior Dean.
You are gated after Hall:
That's all: at least that's nearly all.

II

Just roughly, so to speak, you know,
My name is NETTLESHIP or so;
I'm what they call the Junior Dean.
At least I think that's what I mean.
If you cut Chapel, you'll be gated.
I don't think that is overstated.

J. W. Mackail

I am rather tall and stately
And I care not very greatly
What you say or what you do:
I'm MACKAIL—and who are you?

ANON

S. L. Lee

I am featly-tripping LEE,
Learned in modern history,
My gown, the wonder of beholders
Hangs like a foot-note from my shoulders.

                              H. C. BEECHING

J. B. B. Nichols

Mark the subtle smile that trickles
Down the sphinx-like face of NICHOLS;
My hair is black, my china blue,
My Botticellis fifty-two.

                              J. W. MACKAIL

A. C. K. Nasserl-Moulk

I am ABOUL CASSEM KHAN,
In my grave sweet way I scan
Western life. My thoughts would fill a
Book if written out. Bismillah.

                              J. W. MACKAIL

H. G. Liddell

I am the Dean of Christ Church, Sir,
This is my wife—look well at her.
She is the Broad; I am the High:
We are the University.

                              C. A. SPRING-RICE

G. N. Curzon

I am a most superior person, Mary,
My name is GEORGE NATHANIEL CURZON, Mary,
I'll make a speech on any political question of the day, Mary,
Provided you'll not say me nay, Mary.

H. C. BEECHING

Variant on the above

My name is GEORGE NATHANIEL CURZON,
I am a most superior person.
My hair is soft, my face is sleek,
I dine at Blenheim once a week.

B. Jowett

First come I. My name is JOWETT.
There's no knōwledge but I know it.
I am Master of this College,
What I don't know isn't knōwledge.

H. C. BEECHING

London Rurality

or Miss Bunn and Mrs Bunt

'Contiguas tenuêre domos.'—*Ovid*
'Thin partitions do their bounds divide.'—*Dryden*

Stretching round England's chief emporium far
(No rage for building quenched by raging war),
What would-be villas, ranged in dapper pride,
Usurp the fields and choke the highway side!

321

Thither the *small-folk* of two sorts repair;
The first, as constant dwellers stagnate there;
The second sojourn, wasting cash, to come
On visits to their vulgar Tusculum.

These folly lures to gape in broad retreat,
And lease a cake-house for a country seat;
Those prudence prompts to shrink from London rents,
In sprucer but less costly tenements.

Thither the secondary Cit, in haste
To show he thrives in trade and fails in taste,
From London jogs hebdomadally down,
And rusticates in London out of town.
Thither the scribe whom government retains
(A self-important drudge with slender gains),
Vain of his furnished floor, *genteelly* cheap,
Six evenings out of seven plods home to sleep;
But all the sabbath while his goose-quill lies
Inactive at the Customs or Excise,
He worships the *suburban picturesque*,
To ease his lungs with brick-kilns from the desk.

And there the haberdasher with his wife,
His ledger closed, sits down to close his life.
Ale and brown stout when Sunday friends drop in,
Wash down the joint; and for a cordial—gin;
A pipe and tiff of punch succeed; and then
He fights his *counter* battles o'er again;
Exhorts the young to bustle while they can;
And proves, upon his own industrious plan,
That they in time, like him, enough may save
To smoke, like him, and muddle to a grave.

Some too for gain establish their abode
In perking mansions on the shadeless road,
Exhibiting (right rural to behold!)
The word 'Academy' in glittering gold;
Where ditches, damps, thick fog, and dense discerning,
Improve alike an infant's health and learning.

With all of these, on money-getting plans,
Mix rustic shopkeepers and publicans,
And manufacturers from London poked,
Indicted thence for having stunk and smoked.
Hail, regions of preparatory schools,
Of strict economists and squandering fools!
Hail ye, who there your various plans pursuing,
Court profit, rest, frugality, or ruin!
Ye tallow-chandlers, who *retired* to gaze
At Paul's near dome, still sigh for *melting days*;
Ye demi-gentlemen, whose fingers ache
With posting duties for the nation's sake;
Or ye, as *demi*, driving pens, to live
On what the War Office and Treasury give;
Ye worn-out sea lieutenants on half-pay,
Who drop your anchors on the king's highway;
Ye careful widows who of mates bereft,
Have what ye call 'a little something' left;
Ye sour old maids, with 'somethings' much more small,
For never having had a mate at all;
Ye cockneys all, who pastorally shoot
Your brickwork scions from the City's root,
Which form but branches, branch what way they will,
From that old trunk the Standard in Cornhill;
Be ye old, young, or feminine, or male,
Or rich, or poor—whate'er ye be, all hail!

Peace to each swain who rural rapture owns
As soon as passed a toll, and off the stones!
Whose joy, if buildings solid bliss bestow,
Cannot for miles an interruption know;
Save when a gap of some half-dozen feet
Just breaks the continuity of street;
Where the prig architect with style in view,
Has doled his houses forth in two by two;
And reared a row upon the plan no doubt,
Of old men's jaws, with every third tooth out.
Or where, still greater lengths in taste to go,
He warps his tenements into a bow;
Nails a scant canvas, propped on slight deal sticks,

Nicknamed *verandah*, to the first floor bricks;
Before the whole in one snug segment drawn,
Claps half a rood of turf he calls a lawn;
Then chuckling at his lath-and-plaster bubble,
Dubs it 'The Crescent', and the rents are double.
Sometimes indeed an acre's breadth, half green
And half strewed o'er with rubbish, may be seen;
When lo! a board with quadrilateral grace,
Stands stiff in the phenomenon of space;
Proposing still the neighbourhood's increase,
By—'Ground to Let upon a Building Lease'.

And here and there thrown back a few yards deep,
Some staring coxcombry pretends to peep;
Low paled in front and shrubbed with laurels in,
That sometimes flourish higher than your chin.
Here modest ostentation sticks a plate,
Or daubs Egyptian letters on the gate,
Informing passengers 'tis 'Cowslip Cot',
Or 'Woodbine Lodge', or 'Mr Pummock's Grot'.
Oh! why not, vanity! since dolts bestow
Such names on dog-holes squeezed out from a row,
The title of Horn Hermitage entail
Upon the habitation of a snail?
Why not inscribe ('twould answer quite as well)
'Marine Pavilion' on an oyster-shell?

See in these roads, scarce conscious of a field,
What uniform varieties they yield!
Row smirks at row, each bandbox has a brother,
And half the causeway just reflects the other.*
To beautify each close-wedged neighbour's door,
A strip of garden aims at length before;
Gritty in sunshine; yet in showers 'twill do,
Between a coach and house to wet you through;
But soon the public path in envious sort
Crosses, and cuts it at right angles short;
Then up the jemmy rail, with tenters topped,
Like virtue from necessity, is popped;
Behind it pine, to decorate the grounds,

* *'Grove nods at grove'*, etc. – *Pope*.

324

DORSET COUNTY LIBRARY

And mark with greater elegance their bounds,
Three thin aquatic poplars, parched with drought,
Vying with lines of lamp-posts, fixed without.

Still may the scene some rustic thoughts supply,
When sounds and objects strike the ear and eye;
For here the gardener bawls his greens and leeks,
And (jostling funerals) the wagon creaks;
Oxen, though pastureless, each hour appear,
And bellow, though with drovers in the rear;
While flocks of sheep enrich the turnpike trust,
And bleat their way to Smithfield through the dust.

Blest neighbourhood! but three times blest! thrice three!
When neighbours (as 'twill happen) disagree;
When grievances break forth and deadly spite,
'Twixt those whom fate and bricklayers would unite;
When sharp epistles like the following prove
A lack of style, of grammar, and of love.

Miss Bunn to Mrs Bunt

Miss Bunn sends compliments to Mrs Bunt;
Requests she'll cover up her drain in front;
Which looks so ungenteel, and smells so strong,
It makes Miss Bunn go backward all day long.
Also regrets to be obliged to state
That Mrs Bunt's deal safe fixed up of late
Has caused a very ugly nail to run
Some inches in the passage of Miss Bunn.
Is sorry their partitions aren't of brick;
Only thin paper—wishes it was thick,
Especially as Mrs Bunt thinks right
To heat her washing-copper over night;
And Mrs Bunt's new maid is quite a stranger;
Hopes she'll be careful, for we're both in danger.
Such heavy washes, usen't to be so
Till you came down to live at Prospect Row.

The former tenants were all married men,
With large young families, at Number Ten,
But never while they dwelt within the walls
Got up their great things, nothing but their smalls.
Can't wonder Mrs Bunt so seldom stays
At Prospect Row upon her drying days;
For then her garden is disfigured quite,
And so is Miss Bunn's garden, to her right;
Because the maid, which is extreme improper,
Hangs out upon *both sides*—request she'll stop her.
She must (while wishing nuisances was fewer)
Excuse her mentioning her donkey to her;
For once, as their hind gate was left unbarred,
She dropped her scissors in her back grass yard,
When stooping to restore them to her case,
A nose as cold as *marvel* touched her face;
And jumping up quite startled from the grass,
She saw that monster, Mrs Bunt's huge ass.
She screamed, and her maids heard her, every one.
Madam, your humble servant, Bridget Bunn.

Mrs Bunt to Miss Bunn

Mrs Bunt's compliments—informs Miss Bunn
That her front drain shall speedily be done,
Provided that Miss Bunn will be so kind
To put her ball-cock in repair behind,
Which lets all Miss Bunn's water overflow
All Mrs Bunt's back premises below.
Wonders how anything of hers can run
So far into the passage of Miss Bunn.
The man who does her jobs shall see what's wrong,
But thinks Miss Bunn won't find his nails too long.
Knows their partitions are exceeding slight,
From Miss Bunn's parrot calling *Pots* all night;
It fidgets Mrs Bunt in bed, and wakes her,
And then her poodle howls, your parrot makes her.
Surprised to learn that great things washed of mine
At Number Ten surprises Number Nine;
Or that clean sheets and table-cloths should be
Sights so uncommon for Miss Bunn to see.
I'm always used to have my linen got

Well up; which it should seem Miss Bunn is *not*;
But she may rest henceforward satisfied
That Betty shall hang all upon one side.
Is shocked to find Miss Bunn, when on the grass,
Was so alarmed at seeing of my ass;
Thought she had seen it frequently—can't dream
How it should touch her face, and make her scream!
The harmless creature is entirely blind,
And makes no noise, as all the neighbours find.
'Twas never called a monster till Miss Bunn
Was pleased by letter to baptize it one.
But, Madam, notwithstanding the affront,
I rest your humble servant, Rachael Bunt.

GEORGE COLMAN THE YOUNGER

A Receipt for Stewing Veal

Take a knuckle of veal,
You may buy it or steal.
In a few pieces cut it,
In a stewing pan put it.
Salt, pepper and mace,
Must season this knuckle;
Then what's joined to a place[1]
With other herbs muckle,—
That which killed king Will,[2]
And what never stands still;[3]
Some springs of that bed
Where children are bred,[4]
Which, much you will mend, if
Both spinach and endive,
And lettuce and beet,
With marigolds meet.
Put no water at all
For it maketh things small,
Which, lest it should happen,
A close cover clap on,
Put this pot of Wood's metal[5]
In a hot boiling kettle,

And there let it be
(Mark the doctrine I teach)
About,—let me see,—
Thrice as long as you preach.[6]
So skimming the fat off,
Say grace with your hat off.
Oh, then, with what rapture
Will it fill dean and chapter!

This piece was sent by Gay to Swift with the following notes:
[1] Vulgo Salary.
[2] Supposed sorrel.
[3] This is by Dr Bentley thought to be time or thyme.
[4] Parsley.
[5] Of this composition see the works of the copper-farthing Dean.
[6] Which we suppose to be near four hours.

JOHN GAY

The Abbé Liszt

The Abbé Liszt
Hit the piano with his fist.
That was the way
He used to play.

E. CLERIHEW BENTLEY

The Art of Biography

The Art of Biography
Is different from Geography.
Geography is about Maps,
But Biography is about Chaps.

E. CLERIHEW BENTLEY

Ballad

I

The auld wife sat at her ivied door,
    (*Butter and eggs and a pound of cheese*)
A thing she had frequently done before;
    And her spectacles lay on her aproned knees.

The piper he piped on the hill-top high,
    (*Butter and eggs and a pound of cheese*)
Till the cow said 'I die,' and the goose asked 'Why?'
    And the dog said nothing, but searched for fleas.

The farmer he strode through the square farmyard;
    (*Butter and eggs and a pound of cheese*)
His last brew of ale was a trifle hard—
    The connection of which with the plot one sees.

The farmer's daughter hath frank blue eyes;
    (*Butter and eggs and a pound of cheese*)
She hears the rooks caw in the windy skies,
    As she sits at her lattice and shells her peas.

The farmer's daughter hath ripe red lips;
    (*Butter and eggs and a pound of cheese*)
If you try to approach her, away she skips
    Over tables and chairs with apparent ease.

The farmer's daughter hath soft brown hair;
    (*Butter and eggs and a pound of cheese*)
And I met with a ballad, I can't say where,
    Which wholly consisted of lines like these.

II

She sat, with her hands 'neath her dimpled cheeks,
    (*Butter and eggs and a pound of cheese*)
And spake not a word. While a lady speaks
    There is hope, but she didn't even sneeze.

She sat, with her hands 'neath her crimson cheeks,
   (*Butter and eggs and a pound of cheese*)
She gave up mending her father's breeks,
   And let the cat roll in her new chemise.

She sat, with her hands 'neath her burning cheeks,
   (*Butter and eggs and a pound of cheese*)
And gazed at the piper for thirteen weeks;
   Then she followed him out o'er the misty leas.

Her sheep followed her, as their tails did them.
   (*Butter and eggs and a pound of cheese*)
And this song is considered a perfect gem,
   And as to the meaning, it's what you please.

CHARLES STUART CALVERLEY

Etiquette

The *Ballyshannon* foundered off the coast of Cariboo,
And down in fathoms many went the captain and the crew;
Down went the owners—greedy men whom hope of gain allured:
Oh, dry the starting tear, for they were heavily insured.

Besides the captain and the mate, the owners and the crew,
The passengers were also drowned excepting only two:
Young PETER GRAY, who tasted teas for BAKER, CROOP, AND CO.,
And SOMERS, who from Eastern shores imported indigo.

These passengers, by reason of their clinging to a mast,
Upon a desert island were eventually cast.
They hunted for their meals, as ALEXANDER SELKIRK used,
But they couldn't chat together—they had not been introduced.

For PETER GRAY, and SOMERS too, though certainly in trade,
Were properly particular about the friends they made;
And somehow thus they settled it without a word of mouth—
That GRAY should take the northern half, while SOMERS took the
   south.

On PETER's portion oysters grew—a delicacy rare,
But oysters were a delicacy PETER couldn't bear.
On SOMERS' side was turtle, on the shingle lying thick,
Which SOMERS couldn't eat, because it always made him sick.

GRAY gnashed his teeth with envy as he saw a mighty store
Of turtle unmolested on his fellow-creature's shore:
The oysters at his feet aside impatiently he shoved,
For turtle and his mother were the only things he loved.

And SOMERS sighed in sorrow as he settled in the south,
For the thought of PETER's oysters brought the water to his
    mouth.
He longed to lay him down upon the shelly bed, and stuff:
He had often eaten oysters, but had never had enough.

How they wished an introduction to each other they had had
When on board the *Ballyshannon!* And it drove them nearly mad
To think how very friendly with each other they might get,
If it wasn't for the arbitrary rule of etiquette!

One day, when out a-hunting for the *mus ridiculus*,
GRAY overheard his fellow-man soliloquizing thus:
'I wonder how the playmates of my youth are getting on,
M'CONNELL, S. B. WALTERS, PADDY BYLES, and ROBINSON?'

These simple words made PETER as delighted as could be,
Old chummies at the Charterhouse were ROBINSON and he!
He walked straight up to SOMERS, then he turned extremely red,
Hesitated, hummed and hawed a bit, then cleared his throat, and
    said:

'I beg your pardon—pray forgive me if I seem too bold,
But you have breathed a name I knew familiarly of old.
You spoke aloud of ROBINSON—I happened to be by—
You know him?' 'Yes, extremely well.' 'Allow me—so do I!'

It was enough: they felt they could more sociably get on,
For (ah, the magic of the fact!) they each knew ROBINSON!
And MR SOMERS' turtle was at PETER's service quite,
And MR SOMERS punished PETER's oyster-beds all night.

They soon became like brothers from community of wrongs:
They wrote each other little odes and sang each other songs;
They told each other anecdotes disparaging their wives;
On several occasions, too, they saved each other's lives.

They felt quite melancholy when they parted for the night,
And got up in the morning soon as ever it was light;
Each other's pleasant company they reckoned so upon,
And all because it happened that they both knew ROBINSON!

They lived for many years on that inhospitable shore,
And day by day they learned to love each other more and more.
At last, to their astonishment, on getting up one day,
They saw a vessel anchored in the offing of the bay!

To PETER an idea occurred. 'Suppose we cross the main?
So good an opportunity may not occur again.'
And SOMERS thought a minute, then ejaculated, 'Done!
I wonder how my business in the City's getting on?'

'But stay,' said MR PETER: 'when in England, as you know,
I earned a living tasting teas for BAKER, CROOP, AND CO.,
I may be superseded—my employers think me dead!'
'Then come with me,' said SOMERS, 'and taste indigo instead.'

But all their plans were scattered in a moment when they found
The vessel was a convict ship from Portland, outward bound!
When a boat came off to fetch them, though they felt it very kind,
To go on board they firmly but respectfully declined.

As both the happy settlers roared with laughter at the joke,
They recognized an unattractive fellow pulling stroke:
'Twas ROBINSON—a convict, in an unbecoming frock!
Condemned to seven years for misappropriating stock!!!

They laughed no more, for SOMERS thought he had been rather
    rash
In knowing one whose friend had misappropriated cash;
And PETER thought a foolish tack he must have gone upon
In making the acquaintance of a friend of ROBINSON.

At first they didn't quarrel very openly, I've heard;
They nodded when they met, and now and then exchanged a
    word:
The word grew rare, and rarer still the nodding of the head,
And when they meet each other now, they cut each other dead.

To allocate the island they agreed by word of mouth,
And PETER takes the north again, and SOMERS takes the south;
And PETER has the oysters which he loathes with horror grim,
And SOMERS has the turtle—turtle disagrees with him.

W. S. GILBERT

The Welsh Mutton

The Cambrian Welsh or Mountain Sheep
        Is of the Ovine race,
His conversation is not deep,
        But then—observe his face!

HILAIRE BELLOC

The Cheese-Mites

The cheese-mites asked how the cheese got there,
And warmly debated the matter;
The orthodox said it came from the air,
And the heretics said from the platter.

ANON

Sincere Flattery

(Walt Whitman)

The clear cool note of the cuckoo which has ousted the
                                    legitimate nest-holder,
The whistle of the railway guard dispatching the train to
                                    the inevitable collision,
The maiden's monosyllabic reply to a polysyllabic proposal,
The fundamental note of the last trump, which is presumably
                                    D natural;
All of these are sounds to rejoice in, yea to let your very
                                    ribs re-echo with:
But better than all of them is the absolutely last chord of
            the apparently inexhaustible pianoforte player.

                                    J. K. STEPHEN

The Common Cormorant

The common cormorant or shag
Lays eggs inside a paper bag
The reason you will see no doubt
It is to keep the lightning out.
But what these unobservant birds
Have never noticed is that herds
Of wandering bears may come with buns
And steal the bags to hold the crumbs.

                        CHRISTOPHER ISHERWOOD

Lady Acheson Weary of the Dean

The Dean would visit Market Hill,
    Our invitation was but slight;
I said, 'Why let him, if he will,'
    And so I bid Sir Arthur write.

334

His manners would not let him wait,
   Lest we should think ourselves neglected,
And so we saw him at our gate
   Three days before he was expected.

After a week, a month, a quarter,
   And day succeeding after day,
Says not a word of his departure,
   Though not a soul would have him stay.

I've said enough to make him blush,
   Methinks, or else the devil's in't,
But he cares not for it a rush,
   Nor for my life will take the hint.

But you, my life, may let him know,
   In civil language, if he stays,
How deep and foul the roads may grow,
   And that he may command the chaise.

Or you may say, 'My wife intends,
   Though I should be exceeding proud,
This winter to invite some friends,
   And, sir, I know you hate a crowd.'

Or, 'Mr Dean, I should with joy
   Beg you would here continue still,
But we must go to Aghnacloy,
   Or Mr Moore will take it ill.'

The house accounts are daily rising,
   So much his stay does swell the bills;
My dearest life, it is surprising
   How much he eats, how much he swills.

His brace of puppies how they stuff,
   And they must have three meals a day,
Yet never think they get enough;
   His horses too eat all our hay.

Oh! if I could, how I would maul
    His tallow face and wainscot paws,
His beetle brows and eyes of wall,
    And make him soon give up the cause.

Must I be every moment chid
    With skinny, boney, snip and lean,
Oh! that I could but once be rid
    Of that insulting tyrant Dean.

JONATHAN SWIFT

The Digestion of Milton

The digestion of Milton
Was unequal to Stilton.
He was only feeling so-so
When he wrote *Il Penseroso*.

E. CLERIHEW BENTLEY

The Undertaker's Horse

'To-tschin-shu is condemned to death. How can he drink tea with
    the Executioner?'— *Japanese Proverb*

The eldest son bestrides him,
And the pretty daughter rides him,
And I meet him oft o' mornings on the Course;
And there kindles in my bosom
An emotion chill and gruesome
As I canter past the Undertaker's Horse.

Neither shies he nor is restive,
But a hideously suggestive
Trot, professional and placid, he affects;
And the cadence of his hoof-beats
To my mind this grim reproof beats:—
'Mend your pace, my friend. I'm coming. Who's the
    next?'

Ah! stud-bred of ill-omen,
I have watched the strongest go—men
Of pith and might and muscle—at your heels,
Down the plantain-bordered highway,
(Heaven send it ne'er be my way!)
In a lacquered box and jetty upon wheels.

Answer, sombre beast and dreary,
Where is Brown, the young, the cheery?
Smith, the pride of all his friends and half the Force?
You were at that last dread _dak_★
We must cover at a walk,
Bring them back to me, O Undertaker's Horse!

With your mane unhogged and flowing,
And your curious way of going,
And that businesslike black crimping of your tail,
E'en with Beauty on your back, Sir,
Pacing as a lady's hack, Sir,
What wonder when I meet you I turn pale?

It may be you wait your time, Beast,
Till I write my last bad rhyme, Beast—
Quit the sunlight, cut the rhyming, drop the glass—
Follow after with the others,
Where some dusky heathen smothers
Us with marigolds in lieu of English grass.

Or, perchance, in years to follow,
I shall watch your plump sides hollow,
See Carnifex (gone lame) become a corse—
See old age at last o'erpower you,
And the Station Pack devour you,
I shall chuckle then, O Undertaker's Horse!

★ _Stage of a journey._

But to insult, jibe, and quest, I've
Still the hideously suggestive
Trot that hammers out the unrelenting text,
And I hear it hard behind me
In what place soe'er I find me:—
' 'Sure to catch you soon or later. Who's the next?'

RUDYARD KIPLING

Ten Types of Hospital Visitor

I

The first enters wearing the neon armour
Of virtue.
Ceaselessly firing all-purpose smiles
At everyone present
She destroys hope
In the breasts of the sick,
Who realize instantly
That they are incapable of surmounting
Her ferocious goodwill.

Such courage she displays
In the face of human disaster!

Fortunately, she does not stay long.
After a speedy trip round the ward
In the manner of a nineteen-thirties destroyer
Showing the flag in the Mediterranean,
She returns home for a week
—With luck, longer—
Scorched by the heat of her own worthiness.

II

The second appears, a melancholy splurge
Of theological colours;
Taps heavily about like a healthy vulture
Distributing deep-frozen hope.

The patients gaze at him cautiously.
Most of them, as yet uncertain of the realities
Of heaven, hell-fire, or eternal emptiness,
Play for safety
By accepting his attentions
With just-concealed apathy,
Except one old man, who cries
With newly sharpened hatred,
'Shove off! Shove off!
'Shove . . . shove . . . shove . . . shove
Off!
Just you
Shove!'

III

The third skilfully deflates his weakly smiling victim
By telling him
How the lobelias are doing,
How many kittens the cat had,
How the slate came off the scullery roof,
And how no one has visited the patient for a fortnight
Because everybody
Had colds and feared to bring the jumpy germ
Into hospital.

The patient's eyes
Ice over. He is uninterested
In lobelias, the cat, the slate, the germ.
Flat on his back, drip-fed, his face
The shade of a newly dug-up Pharaoh,
Wearing his skeleton outside his skin,
Yet his wits as bright as a lighted candle,
He is concerned only with the here, the now,
And requires to speak
Of nothing but his present predicament.

It is not permitted.

IV

The fourth attempts to cheer
His aged mother with light jokes
Menacing as shell-splinters.
'They'll soon have you jumping round
Like a gazelle,' he says.
'Playing in the football team.'
Quite undeterred by the sight of kilos
Of plaster, chains, lifting-gear,
A pair of lethally designed crutches,
'You'll be leap-frogging soon,' he says.
'Swimming ten lengths of the baths.'

At these unlikely prophecies
The old lady stares fearfully
At her sick, sick offspring
Thinking he has lost his reason—

Which, alas, seems to be the case.

V

The fifth, a giant from the fields
With suit smelling of milk and hay,
Shifts uneasily from one bullock foot
To the other, as though to avoid
Settling permanently in the antiseptic landscape.
Occasionally he looses a scared glance
Sideways, as though fearful of what intimacy
He may blunder on, or that the walls
Might suddenly close in on him.

He carries flowers, held lightly in fingers
The size and shape of plantains,
Tenderly kisses his wife's cheek
—The brush of a child's lips—
Then balances, motionless, for thirty minutes
On the thin chair.

At the end of visiting time
He emerges breathless,
Blinking with relief, into the safe light.

He does not appear to notice
The dusk.

VI

The sixth visitor says little,
Breathes reassurance,
Smiles securely.
Carries no black passport of grapes
And visa of chocolate. Has a clutch
Of clean washing.

Unobtrusively stows it
In the locker; searches out more.
Talks quietly to the Sister
Out of sight, out of earshot, of the patient.
Arrives punctually as a tide.
Does not stay the whole hour.

Even when she has gone
The patient seems to sense her there:
An upholding
Presence.

VII

The seventh visitor
Smells of bar-room after-shave.
Often finds his friend
Sound asleep: whether real or feigned
Is never determined.

He does not mind; prowls the ward
In search of second-class, lost-face patients
With no visitors
And who are pretending to doze
Or read paperbacks.

He probes relentlessly the nature
Of each complaint, and is swift with such
Dilutions of confidence as,
'Ah! You'll be worse
Before you're better.'

Five minutes before the bell punctuates
Visiting time, his friend opens an alarm-clock eye.
The visitor checks his watch.
Market day. The Duck and Pheasant will be still open.

Courage must be refuelled.

VIII
The eighth visitor looks infinitely
More decayed, ill and infirm than any patient.
His face is an expensive grey.
He peers about with antediluvian eyes
As though from the other end
Of time.
He appears to have risen from the grave
To make this appearance.
There is a whiff of white flowers about him;
The crumpled look of a slightly used shroud.
Slowly he passes the patient
A bag of bullet-proof
Home-made biscuits,
A strong, death-dealing cake—
'To have with your tea,'
Or a bowl of fruit so weighty
It threatens to break
His glass fingers.

The patient, encouraged beyond measure,
Thanks him with enthusiasm, not for
The oranges, the biscuits, the cake,
But for the healing sight
Of someone patently worse
Than himself. He rounds the crisis-corner;
Begins a recovery.

IX
The ninth visitor is life.

X
The tenth visitor
Is not usually named.

CHARLES CAUSELEY

A Ballade of Suicide

The gallows in my garden, people say,
Is new and neat and adequately tall.
I tie the noose on in a knowing way
As one that knots his necktie for a ball;
But just as all the neighbours—on the wall—
Are drawing a long breath to shout 'Hurray!'
The strangest whim has seized me. . . . After all
I think I will not hang myself today.

Tomorrow is the time I get my pay—
My uncle's sword is hanging in the hall—
I see a little cloud all pink and grey—
Perhaps the Rector's mother will *not* call—
I fancy that I heard from Mr Gall
That mushrooms could be cooked another way—
I never read the works of Juvenal—
I think I will not hang myself today.

The world will have another washing day;
The decadents decay; the pedants pall;
And H. G. Wells has found that children play,
And Bernard Shaw discovered that they squall;
Rationalists are growing rational—
And through thick woods one finds a stream astray,
So secret that the very sky seems small—
I think I will not hang myself today.

Envoi
Prince, I can hear the trumpet of Germinal,
The tumbrils toiling up the terrible way;
Even today your royal head may fall—
I think I will not hang myself today.

G. K. CHESTERTON

A Country House Party

The gentlemen got up betimes to shoot
   Or hunt: the young, because they liked the sport
The very first thing boys like after play and fruit;
   The middle-aged to make the day more short;
For *ennui* is a growth of English root,
   Though nameless in our language:—we retort
The fact for words, and let the French translate
That awful yawn which sleep cannot abate.

The elderly walked through the library,
   And tumbled books, or criticized the pictures,
Or sauntered through the gardens piteously,
   And made upon the hothouse several strictures;
Or rode a nag which trotted not too high,
   Or on the morning papers read their lectures;
Or on the watch their longing eyes would fix,
Longing, at sixty, for the hour of six.

But none were *gêné*: the great hour of union
   Was rung by dinner's knell; till then all were
Masters of their own time—or in communion,
   Or solitary, as they chose to bear
The hours, which how to pass is but to few known.
   Each rose up at his own, and had to spare
What time he chose for dress, and broke his fast
When, where, and how he chose for that repast.

The ladies—some rouged, some a little pale—
   Met the morn as they might. If fine, they rode,
Or walked; if foul, they read, or told a tale,
   Sung, or rehearsed the last dance from abroad;
Discussed the fashion which might next prevail,
   And settled bonnets by the newest code;
Or crammed twelve sheets into one little letter,
To make each correspondent a new debtor.

DORSET COUNTY LIBRARY

For some had absent lovers, all had friends.
   The earth has nothing like a she-epistle,
And hardly heaven—because it never ends.
   I love the mystery of a female missal,
Which, like a creed, ne'er says all it intends,
   But, full of cunning as Ulysses' whistle
When he allured poor Dolon:—You had better
Take care what you reply to such a letter.

Then there were billiards; cards, too, but *no* dice;—
   Save in the clubs, no man of honour plays;—
Boats when 'twas water, skating when 'twas ice,
   And the hard frost destroyed the scenting days:
And angling, too, that solitary vice,
   Whatever Izaak Walton sings or says:
The quaint, old, cruel coxcomb, in his gullet
Should have a hook, and a small trout to pull it.

With evening came the banquet and the wine;
   The conversazione; the duet,
Attuned by voices more or less divine
   (My heart or head aches with the memory yet).
The four Miss Rawbolds in a glee would shine;
   But the two youngest loved more to be set
Down to the harp—because to music's charms
They added graceful necks, white hands and arms.

Sometimes a dance (though rarely on field-days,
   For then the gentlemen were rather tired)
Displayed some sylph-like figures in its maze:
   Then there was small-talk ready when required;
Flirtation—but decorous; the mere praise
   Of charms that should or should not be admired.
The hunters fought their fox-hunt o'er again,
And then retreated soberly—at ten.

The politicians, in a nook apart,
  Discussed the world, and settled all the spheres:
The wits watched every loophole for their art,
  To introduce a *bon mot*, head and ears.
Small is the rest of those who would be smart;
  A moment's good thing may have cost them years
Before they find an hour to introduce it;
And then, even *then*, some bore may make them lose it.

But all was gentle and aristocratic
  In this our party; polished, smooth, and cold,
As Phidian forms cut out of marble Attic.
  There now are no Squire Westerns, as of old;
And our Sophias are not so emphatic,
  But fair as then, or fairer to behold.
We have no accomplished blackguards, like Tom Jones,
But gentlemen in stays, as stiff as stones.

They separated at an early hour;
  That is, ere midnight—which is London's noon:
But in the country, ladies seek their bower
  A little earlier than the waning moon.
Peace to the slumbers of each folded flower—
  May the rose call back its true colour soon!
Good hours of fair cheeks are the fairest tinters,
And lower the price of rouge—at least some winters.

LORD BYRON

Golf Links

The golf links lie so near the mill
That almost every day
The labouring children can look out
And see the men at play.

SARAH CLEGHORN

The Hen

The Hen is a ferocious fowl,
She pecks you till she makes you howl.

And all the time she flaps her wings,
And says the most insulting things.

And when you try to take her eggs,
She bites large pieces from your legs.

The only safe way to get these,
Is to creep on your hands and knees.

In the meanwhile a friend must hide,
And jump out on the other side.

And then you snatch the eggs and run,
While she pursues the other one.

The difficulty is, to find
A trusty friend who will not mind.

ALFRED DOUGLAS

Beauty Parlour

The homeliest folks of either sex,
Are those with a crease in the back of their necks.

CHRISTOPHER MORLEY

A Mild Drinking Song

The horrid men who live on beer,
   And swear in public bars,
Have no digestion left except
   For fourpenny cigars.

They stumble home at break of day,
   And often end their lives
Beneath a lorry or a 'bus—
   Unmindful of their wives.

The millionaire who sips his port
   Gets gout in all his toes,
And children pass remarks about
   The colour of his nose.

The sailor with his breezy air
   Is sodden through with rum,
And always meets a sordid death
   In some revolting slum.

The whisky drinker rots his brain
   And rots his liver too,
And ends by making faces like
   The creatures at the Zoo.

I like my little glass of milk
   Before I go to bed,
For then I know that I shall wake
   Without a splitting head.

J. B. MORTON

Liquor and Longevity

The horse and mule live thirty years
And nothing know of wines and beers.
The goat and sheep at twenty die
And never taste of Scotch or Rye.
The cow drinks water by the ton
And at eighteen is mostly done.
The dog at fifteen cashes in
Without the aid of rum and gin.
The cat in milk and water soaks
And then in twelve short years it croaks.
The modest, sober, bone-dry hen
Lays eggs for nogs, then dies at ten.
All animals are strictly dry:
They sinless live and swiftly die;
But sinful, ginful rum-soaked men
Survive for three score years and ten.
And some of them, a very few,
Stay pickled till they're ninety-two.

ANON

The New Ballad of Sir Patrick Spens
(Old border ballad)

The King sits in Dumferline toun
  Drinking the blude-red wine:
'O wha will rear me an equilateral triangle
  Upon a given straight line?'

O up and spake an eldern knight
  Sat at the King's right knee—
'Of a' the clerks by Granta side
  Sir Patrick bears the gree.

' 'Tis he was taught by the Tod-huntère
    Tho' not at the tod-hunting;
Yet gif that he be given a line
    He'll do as brave a thing.'

Our King has written a braid letter
    To Cambrigge or thereby
And there it found Sir Patrick Spens
    Evaluating π

He hadna warked his quotient
    A point but barely three,
There stepped to him a little foot-page
    And louted on his knee.

The first word that Sir Patrick read
    'Plus X' was a' he said:
The neist word that Sir Patrick read
    'Twas *'plus* expenses paid'.

The last word that Sir Patrick read
    The tear blinded his e'e:
'The pound I most admire is not
    In Scottish currencie.'

Stately stepped he east the wa'
    And stately stepped he north;
He fetched a compass frae his ha'
    And stood beside the Forth.

Then gurly grew the waves o' Forth
    And gurlier by-and-bye—
'O never yet was sic a storm
    Yet it isna sic as I!'

Syne he had crossed the Firth o' Forth
    Until Dumferline toun
And tho' he came with a kittle wame
    Fu' low he louted down.

'A line, a line, a gude straight line,
  O King, purvey me quick!
And see it be of thilka kind
  That's neither braid nor thick.'

'Nor thick nor braid?' King Jamie said,
  'I'll eat my gude hatband
If arra line as ye define
  Be found in our Scotland.'

'Tho' there be nane in a' thy rule
 , It sall be ruled by me';
And lichtly with his little pencil
  He's ruled the line A B.

Stately stepped he east the wa',
  And stately stepped he west;
'Ye touch the button,' Sir Patrick said,
  'And I sall do the rest.'

And he has set his compass foot
  Until the centre A,
From A to B he's stretched it oot—
  'Ye Scottish carles, give way!'

Syne he has moved his compass foot
  Until the centre B,
From B to A he's stretched it oot,
  And drawn it viz-a-vee.

The ane circle was B C D,
  And A C E the tither.
'I rede ye well,' Sir Patrick said,
  'They interseck ilk ither.

'See here, and where they interseck—
  To wit with yon point C—
Ye'll just obsairve that I conneck
  The twa points A and B.

'And there ye have a little triangle
    As bonny as e'er was seen;
The whilk is not isosceles,
    Nor yet it is scalene.'

'The proof! the proof!' King Jamie cried:
    'The how and eke the why!'
Sir Patrick laughed within his beard—
    ' 'Tis *ex hypothesi*—

'When I ligg'd in my mither's wame
    I learned it frae my mither,
That things was equal to the same
    Was equal ane to t'ither.

'Sith in the circle first I drew
    The lines B A, B C,
Be radii true, I wit to you
    The baith maun equal be.

'Likewise and in the second circle
    Whilk I drew widdershins
It is nae skaith the radii baith
    A B, A C, be twins.

'And sith of three a pair agree
    That ilk suld equal ane,
By certes they maun equal be
    Ilk unto ilk by-lane.'

'Now by my faith!' King Jamie saith,
    'What *plane* geometrie!
If only Potts had written in Scots,
    How loocid Potts would be!'

'Now, wow's my life!' saith Jamie the King,
    And the Scots lords said the same,
For but it was that envious knicht
    Sir Hughie o' the Graeme.

'Flim-flam, flim-flam!' and 'Ho-indeed?'
  Quod Hughie o' the Graeme;
' 'Tis I could better upon my heid
  This prabblin prablem-game.'

Sir Patrick Spens was nothing laith
  When as he heard 'flim-flam',
But syne he's ta'en a silken claith
  And wiped his diagram.

'Gif my small feat may better'd be;
  Sir Hew, by thy big head,
What I hae done with an A B C
  Do thou with X Y Z.'

Then sairly sairly swore Sir Hew,
  And loudly laucht the King;
But Sir Patrick tuk the pipes and blew,
  And *played* that eldritch thing!

He's play'd it reel, he's play'd it jig,
  And the baith alternative;
And he's danced Sir Hew to the Asses' Brigg.
  That's Proposition Five.

And there they've met and there they've fet,
  Forenenst the Asses' Brigg,
And waefu', waefu' was the fate
  That gar'd them there to ligg.

For there Sir Patrick's slain Sir Hew
  And Sir Hew, Sir Patrick Spens.
Now was not that a fine to-do
  For Euclid's Elemen's?

But let us sing Long live the King!
  And his foes the Deil attend 'em:
For he has gotten his little triangle,
  Quod erat faciendum!

ARTHUR QUILLER-COUCH

The Lady McTaggart

The Lady McTaggart preferred to recline
(Not to sit on a chair) when she went out to dine;
And, if she approved of the victuals, she would,
When she sank on the sofa, sigh, 'So far, so good.'

WALTER DE LA MARE

There's Money in Mother and Father

The lamp burns long in the cottage,
　The light shines late in the shop,
Their beams disclosing the writers composing
　Memories of Mom and Pop.

　　Oh don't write a book about Father!
　　　Don't write a book about Dad!
　　Better not bother to tell how Father
　　　Went so amusingly mad.
　　Better pass over the evening
　　　Father got locked in the zoo—
　　For your infant son has possibly begun
　　　A funny little book about you.

The author broods in his study,
　The housewife dreams in her flat:
Since Mommer and Popper were most improper,
　There ought to be a book in that.

　　But don't write a book about Mother!
　　　Don't write a book about Mum!
　　We all know Mumsy was vague and clumsy,
　　　Dithering, drunken and dumb.
　　There may be money in Mother,
　　　And possibly a movie, too—
　　But some little mite is learning how to write
　　　To write a little book about you.

MORRIS BISHOP

A Glass of Beer
(From the Irish)

The lanky hank of a she in the inn over there
Nearly killed me for asking the loan of a glass of beer;
May the devil grip the whey-faced slut by the hair,
And beat bad manners out of her skin for a year.

That parboiled ape, with the toughest jaw you will see
On virtue's path, and a voice that would rasp the dead,
Came roaring and raging the minute she looked at me,
And threw me out of the house on the back of my head!

If I asked her master he'd give me a cask a day;
But she, with the beer at hand, not a gill would arrange!
May she marry a ghost and bear him a kitten, and may
The High King of Glory permit her to get the mange.

JAMES STEPHENS

The Lion

The Lion comes to meet you
  With a bland emollient smile;
He says: 'I'm going to eat you
  If I think it worth my while.'
    (Which he very frequently does.)

He then becomes a party
  With a rough and ready air;
He says: 'Come on, my hearty,
  For I think I've room to spare.'
    (He is really most accommodating.)

But, if you have a rifle,
  And your knees will let you aim,
You may count the risk a trifle—
  'Just a little bit o' game.'
    (And of course you'll write a book.)

JOHN JOY BELL

Graduate Student

The loveliest pupil I ever had
Was my little Samoyed Soubrette
Who used to cry, after every lecture,
'When does the drinking begin?'
And declared Bosanquet's *Essentials of Logic*
Was more fun than Sherlock Holmes.

CHRISTOPHER MORLEY

The Spectre

The moment I glanced at the mirk-windowed mansion
    that lifts from the woodlands of Dankacre, Lincs.,
To myself I said softly: 'Confide in me, pilgrim, why
    is it the heart in your bosom thus sinks?
What's amiss with this region? It's certainly England;
    the moon, there, is rising, and there Vega blinks.'

A drear wind sighed bleakly; it soughed in the silence;
    it sobbed as if homesick for Knucklebone, Notts.;
The moon with her mountains showed spectral and
    sullen; the corn-crake and nightjar craked, jarred,
    from their grots;
And aloft from its mistletoe nest in an oak-tree, a
    scritch-owlet's scritch froze my blood into clots.

I called on my loved one asleep 'neath the myrtles
    whose buds turn to berries in Willowlea, Herts.;
I mused on sweet innocent scenes where in summer
    the deer browse, the doves croon, the butterfly
    darts;
But, alas! these devices proved vain, horror loured,
    my terror was such as no metre imparts.

For afar o'er the marshes the booming of bitterns, like
    the bitterns that boomed once from Bootle in
    Lancs.,
Came mingled with wailings from Dowsing and
    Dudgeon of sea-gulls lamenting o'er Bluddi-
    thumbe Banks—
My bowels turned to water; my knees shook; my skin
    crept; and the hairs on my cranium rose up in
    hanks.

And lo! from an attic, there peered out a visage, with
    eyes like brass bed-knobs and beak like a hawk's;
And it opened the casement, and climbed down the
    ivy, with claws like a trollop's, on legs like a
    stork's;
And I screamed and fled inland, from mansion and
    moonshine, till I saw the sun rising on Pen-y-gent,
    Yorks.

WALTER DE LA MARE

The Newt

The Newt, the Newt is a strange little brute!
    No creature I know of is 'cuter—
Tho', when he is living he's only a Newt,
    Yet, when he is dead he is neuter.

JOHN JOY BELL

Charles Augustus Fortescue

Who always Did what was Right, and so accumulated an
Immense Fortune

The nicest child I ever knew
Was Charles Augustus Fortescue.
He never lost his cap, or tore
His stockings or his pinafore:
In eating Bread he made no Crumbs,
He was extremely fond of sums,
To which, however, he preferred
The Parsing of a Latin Word—
He sought, when it was in his power,
For information twice an hour,
And as for finding Mutton-Fat
Unappetizing, far from that!
He often, at his Father's Board,
Would beg them, of his own accord,
To give him, if they did not mind,
The Greasiest Morsels they could find—
His Later Years did not belie
The Promise of his Infancy.
In Public Life he always tried
To take a judgment Broad and Wide;
In Private, none was more than he
Renowned for quiet courtesy.
He rose at once in his Career,
And long before his Fortieth Year
Had wedded Fifi, Only Child
Of Bunyan, First Lord Aberfylde.
He thus became immensely Rich,
And built the Splendid Mansion which
Is called 'The Cedars, Muswell Hill',
Where he resides in Affluence still,
To show what Everybody might
Become by
    SIMPLY DOING RIGHT.

HILAIRE BELLOC

Ma, What's a Banker?

or
Hush, my child

The North wind doth blow,
And we shall have snow,
And what will the banker do then, poor thing?
Will he go to the barn
To keep himself warm,
And hide his head under his wing?
Is he on the spot, poor thing, poor thing?
Probably not, poor thing.

For when he is good,
He is not very good,
And when he is bad he is horrider,
And the chances are fair
He is taking the air
Beside a cabaña in Florida.
But the wailing investor, mean thing, mean thing.
Disturbs his siesta, poor thing.

He will plunge in the pool,
But he makes it a rule
To plunge with his kith and his kin,
And whisper about
That it's time to get out
When the widows and orphans get in.
He only got out, poor thing, poor thing,
Yet they call him a tout, poor thing.

His heart simply melts
For everyone else;
By love and compassion he's ridden;
The pay of his clerks
To reduce, how it irks!
But he couldn't go South if he didden.
I'm glad there's a drink within reach, poor thing,
As he weeps on the beach, poor thing.

May he someday find peace
In a temple in Greece,
Where the Government harbors no rancor;
May Athens and Sparta
Play host to the martyr,
And purchase a bond from the banker.
With the banker in Greece, poor thing, poor thing,
We can cling to our fleece, Hot Cha!

OGDEN NASH

Hot Lemonade

The Old Mandarin
Sneezing fiercely in an attack of flu
Said, 'If I die tell Henry Wallace
This was the Century
Of the Common Cold.'

CHRISTOPHER MORLEY

The Danger of Queer Hats

The only hat that suited him—
Or so he fancied—had a brim
Of quite enormous size; the crown
Was lofty, and a seedy brown.
He held an unimportant post
In the Home Office, but his boast
Was 'One day I shall get promotion.'
A rather optimistic notion,
And one his chief would never share.
And so he toiled on humbly there,
Until—ah, cruel, hapless day!—
He heard a Secretary say,
'Promote a man with such a hat!
Good Lord! We really can't do that!'

Then, in despair, he cut his throat,
Leaving a tactful little note,
Saying, 'Here lies a man whose brim
Was his undoing. Pity him!'

And Smith, who wears a common bowler,
Has risen to be Birth Controller.

J. B. MORTON

The Puritan

The Puritan through Life's sweet garden goes
To pluck the thorn and cast away the rose,
And hopes to please by this peculiar whim
The God who fashioned it and gave it him.

KENNETH HARE

A Nurseryman

The Queen was in the garden,
A-smelling of a rose.
She started for to pick one,
To please her royal nose;
When up speaks the gardener:
'You can't have none of those.'

The Queen was in the greenhouse,
A-looking at a grape.
She started to admire one:
Its colour, bloom and shape.
When up comes the gardener,
Before she could escape.

361

The Queen is in the parlour
A-slamming of the door;
And writing of a letter
Because she feels so sore:
'I don't want no gardener;
    So don't come back no more.'

REGINALD ARKELL

A Gallop of False Analogies
'The chavender or chub' – *Izaak Walton*

There is a fine stuffed chavender,
    A chavender or chub,
That decks the rural pavender,
    The pavender or pub,
Wherein I eat my gravender,
    My gravender or grub.
How good the honest gravender!
How snug the rustic pavender!
From sheets as sweet as lavender,
    As lavender or lub,
I jump into my tavender,
    My tavender or tub.

Alas, for town and clavender,
    For business and my club!
They call me from my pavender
Tonight—ay, there's the ravender,
    Alas, there comes the rub!

To leave each blooming shravender,
    Each spring-bedizened shrub,
And meet the horsey savender,
    The very forward sub,
At dinner in the clavender,
And then at billiards dravender,
    At billiards soundly drub
The self-sufficient cavender,

The not ill-meaning cub,
Who me a bear will davender
A bear unfairly dub,
Because I sometimes snavender,
Not too severely snub,
His setting right the clavender,
His teaching all the club.

Farewell to peaceful pavender,
My river-dreaming pub,
To bed as sweet as lavender,
To homely, wholesome gravender,
And you, inspiring chavender,
Stuffed chavender or chub.

W. ST LEGER

Just Keep Quiet and Nobody Will Notice

There is one thing that ought to be taught in all the colleges,
Which is that people ought to be taught not to go around always
        making apologies.
I don't mean the kind of apologies people make when they run
        over you or borrow five dollars or step on your feet,
Because I think that kind is sort of sweet;
No, I object to one kind of apology alone,
Which is when people spend their time and yours apologizing for
        everything they own.
You go to their house for a meal,
And they apologize because the anchovies aren't caviar or the
        partridge is veal;
They apologize privately for the crudeness of the other guests,
And they apologize publicly for their wife's housekeeping or their
        husbands jests;
If they give you a book by Dickens they apologize because it isn't
        by Scott,
And if they take you to the theater, they apologize for the acting
        and the dialogue and the plot;
They contain more milk of human kindness than the most capa-
        cious dairy can,

But if you are from out of town they apologize for everything local
        and if you are a foreigner they apologize for everything
        American.
I dread these apologizers even as I am depicting them,
I shudder as I think of the hours that must be spent in contradict-
        ing them.
Because you are very rude if you let them emerge from an argu-
        ment victorious,
And when they say something of theirs is awful, it is your duty to
        convince them politely that it is magnificent and glori-
        ous,
And what particularly bores *me* with them,
Is that half the time you have to politely contradict them when
        you rudely agree with them,
So I think there is one rule every host and hostess ought to keep
        with the comb and nail file and bicarbonate and aromatic
        spirits on a handy shelf,
Which is don't spoil the denouement by telling the guests every-
        thing is terrible, but let them have the thrill of finding it
        out for themself.

OGDEN NASH

The Waif

There lived a small hermaphrodite beside the silver Brent,
A stream meandering not in maps of Surrey, Bucks, or Kent;
Yet jealous elves from these sweet parts, this tiny mite to vex,
Would tease, torment, and taunt, and call him, 'Master
      Middlesex!'

He lived on acorns, dewdrops, cowslips, bilberries, and snow—
A small, shy, happy, tuneful thing, and innocent of woe;
Except when these malignant imps, his tenderness to vex,
Would tease, torment, and taunt, and call him, 'Master
      Middlesex!'

He ran away; he went to sea; to far Peru he came.
There where the Ataquipa flows and odorous cinchona
    blows and no one knows his name,
He nests now with the humming-bird that sips but never pecks;
And silent slides the silver Brent, and mute is Middlesex.

WALTER DE LA MARE

The Characters of Shakespeare

There once was a king named Macbeth;
A better king never drew breath;
    The faults of his life
    Were all due to his wife,
The notorious *Lady* Macbeth.

No doubt you have heard of Othello—
An African sort of a fellow.
    When they said 'You are black!'
    He cried 'Take it back!
I am only an exquisite yellow.'

I cannot help feeling that Lear
At the end of his splendid career,
    When he strolled in the teeth
    Of that storm on that heath,
Was—well, just a little bit 'queer'.

Hamlet, I'm sorry to find,
Was unable to make up his mind;
    He shillied, he shallied,
    He dillied, he dallied—
In fact, he was over-refined.

Then Cymbeline. How about Cymbeline?
You could hold in a cup—in a thimble, e'en—
    All that is not
    Sheer downright *rot*
In Shakespeare's presentment of Cymbeline.

The doings of Coriolanus
Shall not for one moment detain us.
    It's clear that we can't
    And we won't and we shan't
Be bothered with Coriolanus.

Hats off, however, to Romeo—
One o' the Montagues, don't-you-know;
    And we mustn't forget
    That dear little pet
    Of the Capulet set,
        Juliet,
Who asked him *why* he was Romeo.

The other Shakespearean characters
Are deadly damned dullards and dodderers.
    I would warn you to shun
    Every one
Of the other Shakespearean characters.

MAX BEERBOHM

It Makes a Change

There's nothing makes a Greenland whale
Feel half so high and mighty
As sitting on a mantlepiece
In Aunty Mabel's nighty.

It makes a change from Freezing Seas,
(Of which a whale can tire),
To warm his weary tail at ease
Before an English fire.

For this delight he leaves the seas
(Unknown to Aunty Mabel),
Returning only when the dawn
Lights up the Breakfast Table.

MERVYN PEAKE

Bishop Winterbourne

The Reverend William Winterbourne,
When walking in the Mall,
Tired of genteel pedestrians,
Much yearned to meet a *pal*,
Or, failing an old crony,
      His best gal.

Beelzebub decoyed that wish up.
The Reverend William's now a bishop.
Now, when he fares down Piccadilly,
His blameless Conscience—willy-nilly—
So archiepiscopally staid is,
He never gives a thought to ladies.
Heedless of impious scrutinies
The curious fix on all DD's,
His gaiters 'neath his apron wend;
His steps in one direction bend;
His heart, as right as reverend,
Has for desire one only end—

To wit, to join the wild Te Deum
That echoes through the Athenaeum.

WALTER DE LA MARE

The Gem-like Flame

There was a chap—I forget his name—
Who burned with a hard and gem-like flame;
His spirit was pure, his spirit was white,
And it shone like a candle in the night.

This singular state that chap achieved
By living up to the things he believed;
He spurned the Better, pursued the Best,
He wedded the Form to the Thing Expressed,

He strove for Beauty with all his heart,
And worshipped Life as a form of Art;
And everything Vulgar he flung aside
Till his soul was perfectly purified.

And that explains how the poor chap came
To burn with a hard and gem-like flame;
And that explains why my old friend Mike
Laid him out with a marline-spike.

R. P. LISTER

The Wife of Carcassone

There was a man of Carcassone
Who put his buxom wife upon
A diet whereon lunch and dinner
Did not appear: so she grew thinner,
As thin, in fact, as any lath.
And one sad evening, in her bath
She slipped and slithered down the vent
Calling her husband as she went.
But he, alas, not understanding,
Stood wavering upon the landing,
Until a final gurgling noise
Disturbed his normal equipoise.
Then rushing round in fierce despair
He tried to find her everywhere.
He tapped the pipes, and then at once
Called down the sinks, without response:
He even dug the garden drain
And pushed the whole thing back again.
But nothing was the slightest use.

For she, now well adown the sluice
Beyond the clay-beds and the gravel
Without a vestige of apparel
But with an undulating motion,
Was heading swiftly for the ocean.
So nothing obvious could be done
For that poor wife of Carcassone.

Her husband, in strong sorrow pent,
Then knew he should have been content
To love her as the Lord had built her:
(Or fitted some safe bathroom filter
To meet the needs of her condition
As well he might, in his position.)

So now upon his lone verandah
He sits and muses on Miranda,
A charming wife whose tragic slimming
Was not offset by skill in swimming.

A. E. PRYS-JONES

There was a Naughty Boy

There was a naughty Boy,
    And a naughty Boy was he,
He ran away to Scotland
    The people for to see—

        Then he found
        That the ground
        Was as hard,
        That a yard
        Was as long,
        That a song
        Was as merry,
        That a cherry
        Was as red—
        That lead
        Was as weighty,
        That fourscore
        Was as eighty,
        That a door
        Was as wooden
        As in England—

So he stood in his shoes
And he wondered,
He wondered,
He stood in his shoes
And he wondered.

JOHN KEATS

Green

There was an old grocer of Goring
Had a butter assistant named Green,
Who sank through a hole in the flooring
And never was afterwards seen.
　　Did he look in his cellar?
　　Did he miss the poor fellow?
　　Not at all. Quite phlegmatic,
　　He retired to an attic,
And there watched the moon in her glory o'er Goring—
A sight not infrequently seen.

WALTER DE LA MARE

Buttons

There was an old skinflint of Hitching
Had a cook, Mrs Casey, of Cork;
There was nothing but crusts in the kitchen,
　　While in parlour was sherry and pork.
So at last, Mrs Casey, her pangs to assuage,
Having snipped off his buttonses, curried the page;
And now, while that skinflint gulps sherry and pork
　　In his parlour adjacent to Hitching,
To the tune blithe and merry of knife and of fork,
　　Anthropophagy reigns in the kitchen.

WALTER DE LA MARE

370

Very

There was a young lady of Bow,
A dandy there was, too, of Derry;
'How sweetly the hawthorn trees blow!'
    He murmured. And she replied, 'Very.'
    Then she glanced, and she smiled,
    And she tapped with her shoe;
    Then slid her eyes sidelong,
    And both were pure blue;
    And the longer the silence,
    The deeper it grew:
    Till he said, 'If 'twere kissing,
    I'd like to kiss *you*.
Would it be very naughty to do—well—like—so?'
She thought him a goose, yet she didn't cry, 'Bo!'
But blushed, tittered, sighed, and said, 'Very!'

WALTER DE LA MARE

The Bonnet

There was a young man in a hat,
And by went Miss B. in a bonnet;
When he saw her, he smiled at the lat-
ter: ay, and the roses upon it.
    But when, by and by—
    As blue as the sky—
    He detected her eye
    'Neath its brim; well, oh my!
He wished that fair cheek was well under his hat.
    And his own half-concealed in her bonnet.

WALTER DE LA MARE

The Ape

The sacred ape, now, children, see,
He's searching for the modest flea.
If he should turn around we'd find
He has no hair on his behind.

ROLAND YOUNG

A Morning with the Royal Family

The shades of night were falling fast,
And the rain was falling faster,
When through an Alpine village passed,
An Alpine village pastor.
A youth, who bore 'mid snow and ice
A bird that wouldn't chirrup,
And a banner with the strange device—
'Mrs Winslow's Soothing Syrup'.

Oh, stay, the maiden said, and rest,
For the wind blows from the nortward,
With thy weary head upon this breast:
And please don't think I'm forward.
A tear stood in his bright blue eye,
And he gladly would have tarried;
But still he answered, with a sigh,
'Unhappily, I'm married.'

'Try not the pass,' the old man said,
'My bold, my desperate fellow;
Dark lowers the tempest overhead,
And you'll want an umb(e)rella;
And the roaring torrent is deep and wide:
You can hear how loud it washes';
But loud that clarion voice replied—
'I've got my old galoshes.'

A. E. HOUSMAN

Two Minutes with the Poets

The busy man's 'Excelsior'

'The shades of night were falling fast',
Thro' snow a youth with flag went past;
An old man warned, a young girl vamped him,
But neither one nor t'other damped him:

He climbed a mountain in the dark,
By morning he was stiff and stark:
An avalanche fell from a height,
The fool was caught and serve him right.

Moral
Don't carry flags when climbing ice
And don't flout females or advice,
But if you *must* go on that way
Take guides and ropes and climb by day.

PS
(I think that saves you all the bore
Of ploughing through 'Excelsior'.)

H. S. MACKINTOSH

The Walrus and the Carpenter

The sun was shining on the sea,
   Shining with all his might:
He did his very best to make
   The billows smooth and bright—
And this was odd, because it was
   The middle of the night.

The moon was shining sulkily,
  Because she thought the sun
Had got no business to be there
  After the day was done—
'It's very rude of him,' she said,
  'To come and spoil the fun!'

The sea was wet as wet could be,
  The sands were dry as dry.
You could not see a cloud, because
  No cloud was in the sky:
No birds were flying overhead—
  There were no birds to fly.

The Walrus and the Carpenter
  Were walking close at hand;
They wept like anything to see
  Such quantities of sand:
'If this were only cleared away,'
  They said, 'it *would* be grand!'

'If seven maids with seven mops
  Swept it for half a year,
Do you suppose,' the Walrus said,
  'That they could get it clear?'
'I doubt it,' said the Carpenter,
  And shed a bitter tear.

'O Oysters, come and walk with us!'
  The Walrus did beseech.
'A pleasant walk, a pleasant talk,
  Along the briny beach:
We cannot do with more than four,
  To give a hand to each.'

The eldest Oyster looked at him,
  But never a word he said:
The eldest Oyster winked his eye,
  And shook his heavy head—
Meaning to say he did not choose
  To leave the oyster-bed.

But four young Oysters hurried up,
   All eager for the treat:
Their coats were brushed, their faces washed,
   Their shoes were clean and neat—
And this was odd, because, you know,
   They hadn't any feet.

Four other Oysters followed them,
   And yet another four;
And thick and fast they came at last,
   And more, and more, and more—
All hopping through the frothy waves,
   And scrambling to the shore.

The Walrus and the Carpenter
   Walked on a mile or so,
And then they rested on a rock
   Conveniently low:
And all the little Oysters stood
   And waited in a row.

'The time has come,' the Walrus said,
   'To talk of many things:
Of shoes—and ships—and sealing-wax—
   Of cabbages—and kings—
And why the sea is boiling hot—
   And whether pigs have wings.'

'But wait a bit,' the Oysters cried,
   'Before we have our chat;
For some of us are out of breath,
   And all of us are fat!'
'No hurry!' said the Carpenter.
   They thanked him much for that.

'A loaf of bread,' the Walrus said,
   'Is what we chiefly need:
Pepper and vinegar besides
   Are very good indeed—
Now if you're ready, Oysters dear,
   We can begin to feed.'

375

'But not on us!' the Oysters cried,
  Turning a little blue.
'After such kindness, that would be
  A dismal thing to do!'
'The night is fine,' the Walrus said.
  'Do you admire the view?

'It was so kind of you to come!
  And you are very nice!'
The Carpenter said nothing but
  'Cut us another slice:
I wish you were not quite so deaf—
  I've had to ask you twice!'

'It seems a shame,' the Walrus said,
  'To play them such a trick,
After we've brought them out so far,
  And made them trot so quick!'
The Carpenter said nothing but
  'The butter's spread too thick!'

'I weep for you,' the Walrus said:
  'I deeply sympathize.'
With sobs and tears he sorted out
  Those of the largest size,
Holding his pocket-handkerchief
  Before his streaming eyes.

'O Oysters,' said the Carpenter,
  'You've had a pleasant run!
Shall we be trotting home again?'
  But answer came there none—
And this was scarcely odd, because
  They'd eaten every one.

LEWIS CARROLL

Every Doggerel Has Its Day

'The sun winks back from the back of the blade' – John Arlott,
BBC commentary on the Second Test Match, England v.
Australia, 11 July 1977

The sun winks back from the back of the blade,
the commentators sit in the shade
and, however many runs are made,

it's a funny old game—sentimental too,
a ritual practised for me and you—
and Youth is the cause of the hullabaloo.

When the arm is strong and the eye is keen
the idea of old age is quite obscene.
But the County Cap (and the might-have-been)

lose the throwing arm and the timing sense,
however clever, however dense,
and the past, at last, is the only tense—

even the legendary W. G. Grace
at the very end couldn't stand the pace.
He vanished too—though not without trace—

and even a batsman as great as Hobbs
when he lay dead couldn't handle lobs—
this is what causes our sighs and sobs.

Old men with MCC-striped ties
lament lost vigour with watery eyes—
the active stroking of balls (and thighs).

Cricket for them's an escape from Life,
the worries of business, children, wife;
as Death stands by with his surgeon's knife

each fancies himself as a Peter Pan,
a young attractive cricketing man,
one of the fastest who ever ran

between the wickets or in to bowl,
a batsman with genius to lift the soul,
a merrier hitter than Old King Cole.

The game, as they sit and watch for hours,
reminds them of their longlost powers
until it's over—and *Send No Flowers*.

GAVIN EWART

On the Vanity of Earthly Greatness

The tusks that clashed in mighty brawls
Of mastodons, are billiard balls.

The sword of Charlemagne the Just
Is ferric oxide, known as rust.

The grizzly bear whose potent hug
Was feared by all, is now a rug.

Great Caesar's bust is on the shelf,
And I don't feel so well myself!

ARTHUR GUITERMAN

After the Ball
A Buffo lyric

The very last guest has departed,
  The lights have burnt into thin air;
The ball-room is dark and deserted,
  And silent again is the square;

378

The band, worn with playing and blowing,
   Are wishing Herr Kœnig goodnight,
And Gunter's assistants are going,
   Assured that their things are 'all right'.

The page in the study is lying
   Asleep, on the dining-room chairs,
The housemaids to slumber are trying,
   The butler is tipsy downstairs.
The love-birds, who long have been blinking,
   Quite scared by the music and light,
With all the canaries, are thinking
   At last, that it must be the night.

And She—the fair queen of the numbers,
   Who came to that beautiful ball,
Perhaps thinks now of me in her slumbers,
   And perhaps—horrid thought!—not at all.
In nights of such unalloyed pleasure
   Why cannot existence be passed?
To spend years in a polka's gay measure,
   And die of a post-horn at last?

I think I produced an impression,
   Because, in the course of the night,
Whilst polking she made a confession—
   'She liked to be held rather tight.'
And afterwards grown somewhat bolder,
   Too fluttered and breathless to speak,
I felt her fair chin on my shoulder,
   And soft scented hair on my cheek.

When Vere coarsely said she was 'stunning',
   He wanted to be in my shoes,
She gave me a *deux temps* twice running,
   And threw over one of the Blues.
And then she got rid of her brother
   So well, when the supper-time came,
And said 'We will keep by each other,'
   And, one time, our plate was the same!

She told me she loved lobster salad,
  And rode in the park every day.
And doted on Pischek's last ballad,
  And Tennyson's 'Queen of the May'.
And pulled cracker *bonbons*, and flirted,
  And laughed when I made a bad pun,
And when all my wits I exerted,
  She said I was 'capital fun!'

How dreadfully hot! I am tumbling,
  And tossing, and can't get to sleep;
And over the streets the dull rumbling
  Of wheels is beginning to creep.
And all round the room I see whirling
  The women and lights, like the wind;
And still I can hear, to their twirling,
  'The 'Olga', and 'Bridal', and 'Lind'.

I wish I could marry. 'Tis shocking,
  My income will not carry two!
Oh dear! at my door there's a knocking,
  And I have not slept the night through.
I must shake off all thoughts so entrancing,
  And fag down that horrid Whitehall,
And so there's goodbye to romancing—
  Adieu to the Belle of the Ball!

ALBERT R. SMITH

Hell in Herefordshire

('There is a great deal of secret cider-drinking in
Herefordshire'—*Evidence of Dr Weekes before the Royal
Commission on Licensing*)

The wild white rose is cankered
  Along the Vale of Lugg,
There's poison in the tankard,
  There's murder in the mug;
Through all the pleasant valleys

Where stand the white-faced kine
Men raise the Devil's chalice
And drink the lawless wine.

Unspeakable carouses
That shame the summer sky
Take place in little houses
That look towards the Wye;
And near the Radnor border
And the dark hills of Wales
Beelzebub is warder
And sorcery prevails.

For spite of church or chapel,
Ungodly folk there be
Who pluck the cider apple
From the cider apple-tree,
And squeeze it in their presses
Until the juice runs out,
At various addresses
That no one knows about.

And, maddened by the orgies
Of that unholy brew,
They slit each other's gorges
From one AM till two,
Till Ledbury is a shambles
And in the dirt and mud
Where Leominster sits and gambles
The dice are stained with blood!

But still, if strength suffices
Before my day is done
I'll go and share the vices
Of Clungunford and Clun,
And watch the red sun sinking
Across the march again
And join the secret drinking
Of outlaws at Presteign.*

E. V. KNOX

* *Presteign is really in Radnorshire, and is pronounced 'Presteen'. Never mind.*

The Director

They made me a director,
    I dreamt it in a dream;
I was a print collector
    And owned a salmon stream.

They made me a director
    Of companies one or two;
I did not fear the spectre
    Of Nemesis—would you?

They made me a director
    Of companies two or three;
I bought myself a sector
    Of Sussex, near the sea.

They made me a director
    Of companies three or four;
I had a man named Hector
    To answer the front-door.

They made me a director
    Of companies four or five;
The beams of my reflector
    Lit up the laurelled drive.

They made me a director
    Of companies five or six;
I was a stern protector
    Of meal-fed pheasant chicks.

They made me a director
    Of companies six or seven;
No shareholding objector
    Opposed my path to heaven.

They made me a director
    Of companies seven or eight;
The income-tax collector
    Knelt down before my gate.

They made me a director
    Of companies eight or nine;
I drank the golden nectar
    And had no other wine.

They made me a director
    Of companies nine or ten—

        *   *   *   *

'Hullo, police-inspector!
Good morning, plain-clothes men!'

                        E. V. KNOX

London Water

This is the water that John drinks.

This is the Thames with its cento of stinks,
That supplies the water that John drinks.

These are the fish that float in the ink-
y stream of the Thames with its cento of stinks
That supplies the water that John drinks.

This is the sewer, from cesspool and sink,
That feeds the fish that float in the ink-
y stream of the Thames with its cento of stinks
That supplies the water that John drinks.

These are the vested int'rests, that fill to the brink
The network of sewers, from cesspool and sink
That feeds the fish that float in the ink-
y stream of the Thames with its cento of stinks
That supplies the water that John drinks.

This is the price that we pay to wink
At the vested int'rests that fill to the brink
The network of sewers, from cesspool and sink
That feeds the fish that float in the ink-
y stream of the Thames with its cento of stinks
That supplies the water that John drinks.

ANON

The Ichthyosaurus

This poor beast found a doleful end—
　　It makes me weep to tell it—
One day it overheard its name,
And then it pined and died of shame
　　Because it could not spell it.

JOHN JOY BELL

The Pig

Though bald on top, the common pig
　　Will never make a fuss.
He doesn't go and buy a wig,
　　Or, like a lot of us,
Smear lotions on his hairless head,
　　Or call a masseur in
To rub his scalp when he's in bed,
　　Or monkey with his skin.

I asked a specialist I knew,
  Who lived in Harley Street,
Why pigs go bald the way they do,
  And leaping to his feet,
He yelled: 'It's wicked carelessness,
  And serves them damned well right;
I'll tell you why they're in this mess—
  Their hats are far too tight!'

J. B. MORTON

The Latest Decalogue

Thou shalt have one God only; who
Would be at the expense of two?
No graven images may be
Worshipped, except the currency:
Swear not at all; for, for thy curse
Thine enemy is none the worse:
At church on Sunday to attend
Will serve to keep the world thy friend:
Honour thy parents; that is, all
From whom advancement may befall:
Thou shalt not kill; but need'st not strive
Officiously to keep alive:
Do not adultery commit;
Advantage rarely comes of it:
Thou shalt not steal; an empty feat,
When it's so lucrative to cheat:
Bear not false witness; let the lie
Have time on its own wings to fly:
Thou shalt not covet, but tradition
Approves all forms of competition.

ARTHUR HUGH CLOUGH

Three Turkeys Fair

Three turkeys fair their last have breathed,
And now this world for ever leaved.
Their Father and their Mother too
Will sigh and weep as well as you,
Mourning for their offsprings fair
Whom they did nurse with tender care.
Indeed the rats their bones have crunched,
To eternity they are launched.
Their graceful form and pretty eyes
Their fellow fowls did not despise.
A direful death indeed they had,
That would put any parent mad—
But she was more than usual calm,
She did not give a single damn,
She is as gentle as a lamb.
Here ends this melancholy lay,
Farewell poor turkeys I must say.

MARJORIE FLEMING (aged 8)

The Shropshire Lad

'Tis Summer Time on Bredon,
And now the farmers swear;
The cattle rise and listen
In valleys far and near,
And blush at what they hear.

But when the mists in autumn
On Bredon tops are thick,
The happy hymns of farmers
Go up from fold and rick,
The cattle then are sick.

HUGH KINGSMILL

Alice's Recitation after the Lobster Quadrille

' 'Tis the voice of the Lobster; I heard him declare,
"You have baked me too brown, I must sugar my hair."
As a duck with its eyelids, so he with his nose
Trims his belt and his buttons, and turns out his toes.
When the sands are all dry, he is gay as a lark,
And will talk in contemptuous tones of the Shark:
But, when the tide rises and sharks are around,
His voice has a timid and tremulous sound.'

LEWIS CARROLL

Salad Dressing

To make this condiment your poet begs
The pounded yellow of two hard-boiled eggs;
Two boiled potatoes, passed through kitchen sieve,
Smoothness and softness to the salad give.
Let onion atoms lurk within the bowl,
And, half-suspected, animate the whole.
Of mordant mustard add a single spoon,
Distrust the condiment that bites so soon;
But deem it not, thou man of herbs, a fault
To add a double quantity of salt;
Four times the spoon with oil of Lucca crown,
And twice with vinegar procured from town;
And lastly o'er the flavoured compound toss
A magic soupçon of anchovy sauce.
Oh, green and glorious! Oh, herbaceous treat!
'Twould tempt the dying anchorite to eat;
Back to the world he'd turn his fleeting soul,
And plunge his fingers in the salad-bowl!
Serenely full, the epicure would say,
'Fate cannot harm me, I have dined today.'

SYDNEY SMITH

Archery

To place one's little boy—just *so*—
    An apple on his head,
Then loose an arrow from one's bow
    And not to shoot him dead:—

That is a feat requiring skill,
    And confidence as well;
As any archer would have told
    The man who tolled the bell.

The luck must hold; the child stand still:
    This William befell;
But just how close was core to corse
    Could only William tell.

WALTER DE LA MARE

From a Letter to My Aunt, Discussing the Correct Approach to Modern Poetry

To you, my aunt, who would explore
The literary Chankley Bore,
The paths are hard for you are not
A literary Hotentot
But just a kind and cultured dame
Who knows not Eliot (to her shame).
Fie on you, aunt, that you should see
No genius in David G.,
No elemental form and sound
In T. S. E. and Ezra Pound.
Fie on you, aunt! I'll show you how
To elevate your middle brow,
And how to scale and see the sights,
From modernist Parnassian heights.

388

First buy a hat, no Paris model
But one the Swiss wear when they yodel,
A bowler thing with one or two
Feathers to conceal the view.
And then in sandals walk the street
(All modern painters use their feet
For painting, on their canvas strips,
Their wives or mothers minus hips.)

Perhaps it would be best if you
Created something very new,
A dirty novel done in Erse
Or written backwards in Welsh verse,
Or paintings on the backs of vests,
Or Sanskrit psalms on lepers' chests.
But if this proved imposs-i-ble
Perhaps it would be just as well,
For you could then write what you please,
And modern verse is done with ease.

Do not forget that 'limpet' rhymes
With 'strumpet' in these troubled times,
And commas are the worst of crimes;
Few understand the works of Cummings,
And few James Joyce's mental slummings,
And few young Auden's coded chatter;
But then it is the few that matter.
Never be lucid, never state,
If you would be regarded great,
The simplest thought or sentiment,
(For thought, we know, is decadent);
Never omit such vital words
As belly, genitals, and ——,
For these are things that play a part
(And what a part) in all good art.
Remember this: each rose is wormy.
And every lovely woman's germy;
Remember this: that love depends
On how the Gallic letter bends;

Remember, too, that life is hell
And even heaven has a smell
Of putrefying angels who
Make deadly whoopee in the blue.
These things remembered, what can stop
A poet going to the top?

A final word: before you start
The convulsions of your art,
Remove your brains, take out your heart;
Minus these curses, you can be
A genius like David G.

Take courage, aunt, and send your stuff
To Geoffrey Grigson with my luff,
And may I yet live to admire
How well your poems light the fire.

DYLAN THOMAS

On the Death of a Favourite Cat, Drowned in a Tub of Gold Fishes

'Twas on a lofty vase's side,
Where China's gayest art had dyed
  The azure flowers that blow;
Demurest of the tabby kind,
The pensive Selima, reclined,
  Gazed on the lake below.

Her conscious tail her joy declared:
The fair round face, the snowy beard,
  The velvet of her paws,
Her coat that with the tortoise vies,
Her ears of jet, and emerald eyes—
  She saw; and purred applause.

Still had she gazed; but midst the tide
Two angel forms were seen to glide,
  The genii of the stream:
Their scaly armour's Tyrian hue
Through richest purple to the view
  Betrayed a golden gleam.

The hapless nymph with wonder saw:
A whisker first, and then a claw,
  With many an ardent wish,
She stretched, in vain, to reach the prize,
What female heart can gold despise?
  What cat's averse to fish?

Presumptuous maid! with looks intent
Again she stretched, again she bent,
  Nor knew the gulf between.
(Malignant Fate sat by, and smiled.)
The slippery verge her feet beguiled
  She tumbled headlong in.

Eight times emerging from the flood
She mewed to every watery god,
  Some speedy aid to send.
No Dolphin came, no Nereid stirred:
Nor cruel Tom, nor Susan heard—
  A favourite has no friend!

From hence ye beauties undeceived,
Know, one false step is ne'er retrieved,
  And be with caution bold:
Not all that tempts your wandering eyes
And heedless hearts is lawful prize,
  Nor all, that glisters, gold.

THOMAS GRAY

A Sonnet

Two voices are there: one is of the deep;
It learns the storm-cloud's thunderous melody,
Now roars, now murmurs with the changing sea,
Now bird-like pipes, now closes soft in sleep:
And one is of an old half-witted sheep
Which bleats articulate monotony,
And indicates that two and one are three,
That grass is green, lakes damp, and mountains steep:
And, Wordsworth, both are thine: at certain times
Forth from the heart of thy melodious rhymes,
The form and pressure of high thoughts will burst:
At other times—good Lord! I'd rather be
Quite unacquainted with the ABC
Than write such hopeless rubbish as thy worst.

J. K. STEPHEN

Ode to a Jacobin

(from Suckling's 'Ode to a Lover')

Unchristian Jacobin whoever,
If of thy God thou cherish ever
One wavering thought; if e'er His Word
Has from one crime thy soul deterred:
  Know this,
   Thou think'st amiss;
   And to think true,
Thou must renounce Him all, and think anew.

If startled at the guillotine
Trembling thou touch the dread machine;
If, leading sainted Louis to it,
Thy steps drew back, thy heart did rue it:
  Know this,
   Thou think'st amiss;
   And to think true,
Must rise 'bove weak remorse, and think anew.

If, callous, thou dost not mistake,
And murder for mild mercy's sake;
And think thou followest pity's call
When slaughtered thousands round thee fall:
     Know this,
      Thou think'st amiss;
      And to think true,
Must conquer prejudice, and think anew.

If when good men are to be slain,
Thou hear'st them plead, nor plead in vain,
Or, when thou answerest, if it be
With one jot of humanity:
     Know this,
      Thou think'st amiss;
      And to think true,
Must pardon leave to fools, and think anew.

If when all kings, priests, nobles hated,
Lie headless, thy revenge is sated,
Nor thirsts to load the reeking block
With heads from thine own murderous flock:
     Know this,
      Thou think'st amiss;
      And to think true,
Thou must go on in blood, and think anew.

If, thus, by love of executions,
Thou prov'st thee fit for revolutions;
Yet one achieved, to that art true,
Nor would'st begin to change anew:
     Know this,
      Thou think'st amiss;
      Deem, to think true,
All constitutions bad but those bran new.

GEORGE CANNING, GEORGE ELLIS, J. H. FRERE

The Village Burglar

Under a spreading gooseberry bush the village burglar lies,
The burglar is a hairy man with whiskers round his eyes
And the muscles of his brawny arms keep off the little flies.

He goes on Sunday to the church to hear the Parson shout.
He puts a penny in the plate and takes a pound note out
And drops a conscience-stricken tear in case he is found out.

ANON

A Benison on a Wartime High Tea

Upon this scanty meal, O Lord,
We ask a blessing in accord.
Pour thy grace in measure small
Lest it more than cover all.

Bless this tiny piece of ham
Bless this lonely dab of jam
Bless this sparsely-buttered toast
Father, Son and Holy Ghost.

ALAN M. LAING

Grown-up

Was it for this I uttered prayers,
And sobbed and cursed and kicked the stairs,
That now, domestic as a plate,
I should retire at half-past eight?

EDNA ST VINCENT MILLAY

Modern Language Association

'Was I too hearty? Did he think me bold?
   Should I have said, "like hell", and not "like fun"?
   Does my mustache not make me look too old?
   (He wants a man whose graduate work is done.)
Nebraska Wesleyan is probably cold,
   I'd rather get down south of Washington.
   He didn't seem to like that joke I told;
   Jeez, he's a solemn-looking son of a gun!'
Thus the young savant ponders at his ease,
   Knitting the critical brow, and on the belly
   Twirling the scholarly thumb, while Ph.D's
Deal with the manuscripts of Machiavelli,
   The intervocalic N in Portuguese,
   And the unfaithfulness of Harriet Shelley.

MORRIS BISHOP

The Sentimental Education

Wear your Thomas Hardy suit and sit with candles in the
   gloom.
Summon ghosts of years departed till they fill the empty
   room.

First of all call up the weather—heatwave 1922,
Wartime winters with the blackout, blossom on the trees
   at Kew.

Then the people. First, a nanny. Next, your father
   wearing spats.
Mummy with her pearls at evening, and her three
   amazing cats.

Childish captions fit the pictures—you were very childish
   then—
But you see it still as clearly as the present world of men.

Peter Pan was pulsing drama, green lights shone on
　　Captain Hook.
Carroll's Jabberwock caused nightmares, till you had to
　　hide the book.

You were one. Then came two sisters. They were
　　different from you.
You liked best fried bread and cocoa, loved the zebras at
　　the Zoo.

Then the schools—a bourgeois saga—we all know what
　　they were like.
Minnows in a pond, a bully swam among them like a
　　pike.

Squeeze them in? You'ld need a ballroom. Still
　　remembered, many names
Cluster round in shorts and sweaters. Latin, algebra and
　　games.

Chapel services. Then freedom, and the length of King's
　　Parade.
Dadie, Anthony—and Classics, all the dons that had it
　　made.

Cicero made ghastly speeches, elegiacs were a bore.
You had two years in the saltmines—how could you
　　come up for more?

Next was English, Richards lectures, Leavis supervising.
　　Fine.
English literature went down as stimulating as new wine.

After Cambridge—unemployment. No one wanted
　　much to know.
Good degrees are good for nothing in the business world
　　below.

In the end you were a salesman, selling lithographic
　　prints.
Trade was stagnant after Munich. Hitler frightened us
　　with hints.

War came down, a blackout curtain, shutting out the
kindly sun.
Jews went under, all the playboys somehow lost their
sense of fun.

Still, we always had the weather—freezing cold or hot as
hell—
Birds continued, flowers were rampant, life went on
through shot and shell.

Back at last to shabby London, tired and rationed, sad to
see,
With its tales of air raid wardens, siren suits and hot sweet
tea.

People, literary people, now replaced the roaring boys
Fond of vino, signorinas, dirty jokes and lots of noise.

Tambi, Nicholas and Helen. Come on in. You see them
plain.
Publishing will never, surely, be as odd as that again.

Money, said the British Council, I have money in my
hand.
Get your hair cut, keep your nose clean, live in Civil
Serviceland.

Six years later came the end game—middle grades were
axed. Goodbye!
They were victims of the Beaver's petulant persistent
cry.

Advertising. Advertising. Fatal Lady of the Lake!
No one opts for copywriting, they get in there by
mistake.

You absorbed those business ethics—not the Sermon on
the Mount—
Walked into that artful parlour, had the William Hill
account.

Let the room explode with whizz kids, dollies, every
  kind of Pop!
Only crematorium silence brings that mayhem to a stop.

Money. Children. Mortgage. Rat race. Anxious words
  that tax the brain.
Nagging fears of unemployment drive the middle class insane.

It's not pretty when they throw you, screaming, in the
  empty sack.
Filled with nothing but the cries of wives and children
  screaming back.

Does the working class get ulcers? No one worries much,
  if so.
They know jobs are hard to come by, and the pay is often low.

They're inured to thoughts of hardship and of being out
  of work.
This is life. It's no good blubbing, throwing fits or going berserk.

Moneyed men in Lloyds, the City, can't imagine what
  it's like.
To the driver of an E-type, what's the old penurious
  bike?

Workmen are a bloody nuisance—just a ROAD UP sign
  or two—
Obstacles that spoil their record from the Bank to Luton
  Hoo.

Keep your voice down. Don't start shouting. Let the
  candles burn up straight.
(Privileged and trendy diners stuff themselves with After
  Eight.)

All you learn—and from a lifetime—is that that's the way
  it goes.
That's the crumbling of the cookie, till the turning up of
  toes.

GAVIN EWART

Pun

We had a little baby girl
Who made our hearts to flutter.
We used to call her Margarine—
We hadn't any but her.

HERBERT R. ALLPORT

Mary the Cook-Maid's Letter to Dr Sheridan

Well; if ever I saw such another man, since my mother bound my
    head,
You a gentleman! Marry come up, I wonder where you were bred?
I am sure such words do not become a man of your cloth,
I would not give such language to a dog, faith and troth.
Yes, you called my master a knave. Fie, Mr Sheridan, 'tis a shame
For a parson, who should know better things, to come out with
    such a name.
Knave in your teeth, Mr Sheridan, 'tis both a shame and a sin,
And the dean my master is an honester man than you and all your
    kin:
He has more goodness in his little finger, than you have in your
    whole body,
My master is a parsonable man, and not a spindle-shanked hoddy
    doddy.
And now whereby I find you would fain make an excuse,
Because my master one day in anger called you goose.
Which, and I am sure I have been his servant four years since
    October,
And he never called me worse than sweetheart drunk or sober:
Not that I know his Reverence was ever concerned to my
    knowledge,
Though you and your come-rogues keep him out so late in your
    College.
You say you will eat grass on his grave: a Christian eat grass!
Whereby you now confess yourself to be a goose or an ass:
But that's as much as to say, that my master should die before ye,

Well, well, that's as God pleases, and I don't believe that's a true
    story,
And so say I told you so, and you may go to tell my master; what
    care I?
And I don't care who knows it, 'tis all one to Mary.
Everybody knows, that I love to tell truth and shame the Devil,
I am but a poor servant, but I think gentlefolks should be civil.
Besides, you found fault with our vittles one day that you was
    here,
I remember it was upon a Tuesday, of all days in the year.
And Saunders the man says, you are always jesting and mocking,
Mary (said he, one day as I was mending my master's stocking),
My master is so fond of that minister that keeps the school;
I thought my master a wise man, but that man makes him a fool.
Saunders, said I, I would rather than a quart of ale,
He would come into our kitchen, and I would pin a dischlout
    to his tail.

And now I must go, and get Saunders to direct this letter,
For I write but a sad scrawl, but my sister Marget she writes
    better.
Well, but I must run and make the bed before my master comes
    from prayers,
And see now, it strikes ten, and I hear him coming upstairs:
Whereof I could say more to your verses, if I could write written
    hand,
And so I remain in a civil way, your servant to command,

                              MARY

                      JONATHAN SWIFT

from The Georgiad

We poets get small chance to air our views:
But any scavenger, on the reviews
Or on the BBC, can blow his trump,
And in each column has a tub to thump,
With endless time and quantities of ink
To misinterpret what we write and think.

Small leisure for such tactics has the muse—
In my whole life I've printed twelve reviews
Mostly attacks, but all confessed and signed—
I scorn to pull the trigger from behind.
But when each dolt on whom the boot's conferred,
Punched by a line or welted by a word,
Takes half a year the buffet to divert
And half the next to prove it doesn't hurt,
Decrying, when it sends him to the floor,
The very weapon which he praised before,
What's to be thought but what I most opine—
That one has but to write, and at each line,
As lizards drop their tails for sudden dread,
A thousand philistines their foreskins shed.

ROY CAMPBELL

The Sorrows of Werther

Werther had a love for Charlotte
    Such as words could never utter;
Would you know how first he met her?
    She was cutting bread and butter.

Charlotte was a married lady,
    And a moral man was Werther,
And for all the wealth of Indies
    Would do nothing for to hurt her.

So he sighed and pined and ogled,
    And his passion boiled and bubbled,
Till he blew his silly brains out,
    And no more was by it troubled.

Charlotte, having seen his body
    Borne before her on a shutter,
Like a well-conducted person,
    Went on cutting bread and butter.

WILLIAM MAKEPEACE THACKERAY

Notting Hill Polka

We've—had—
A Body in the house
    Since Father passed away:
He took bad on
Saturday night an' he
    Went the followin' day:

Mum's—pulled—
The blinds all down
    An' bought some Sherry Wine,
An' we've put the tin
What the Arsenic's in
    At the bottom of the Ser-pen-tine!

W. BRIDGES-ADAMS

The Frog

What a wonderful bird the frog are—
When he stand he sit almost;
When he hop, he fly almost.
He ain't got no sense hardly;
He ain't got no tail hardly either.
When he sit, he sit on what he ain't got almost.

ANON

The Purist to Her Love

'Whatever its function
Like's not a conjunction.
And if you continue
Committing that sin, you
Will drive me to Reno's
Consoling casinos.'

MARGARET FISHBACK

What Happens to Women?

What happens to women
Who marry dull men?
They go into the suburbs
And never come out again.

ANON

The Motor Bus

What is this that roareth thus?
Can it be a Motor Bus?
Yes, the smell and hideous hum
Indicat Motorem Bum!
Implet in the Corn and High
Terror me Motoris Bi:
Bo Motori clamitabo
Ne Motore caedar a Bo—
Dative be or Ablative
So thou only let us live:—
Whither shall thy victims flee?
Spare us, spare us, Motor Be!
Thus I sang; and still anigh
Came in hordes Motores Bi,
Et complebat omne forum
Copia Motorum Borum.
How shall wretches live like us
Cincti Bis Motoribus?
Domine, defende nos
Contra hos Motores Bos!

A. C. GODLEY

A Threnody

'The Akhoond of Swat is dead'—*London Papers*

What, what, what,
What's the news from Swat?
   Sad news,
   Bad news,
Comes by the cable led
Through the Indian Ocean's bed,
Through the Persian Gulf, the Red
Sea and the Med-
Iterranean—he's dead;
The Ahkoond is dead!

For the Ahkoond I mourn,
   Who wouldn't?
He strove to disregard the message stern,
   But he Ahkoodn't.
Dead, dead, dead,
   (Sorrow Swats!)
Swats wha hae wi Ahkoond bled,
Swats whom he hath often led
Onward to a gory bed,
   Or to victory,
   As the case might be,
      Sorrow Swats!

Tears shed,
   Shed tears like water,
Your great Ahkoond is dead!
   That Swats the matter!

Mourn, city of Swat!
Your great Ahkoond is not,
   But laid mid worms to rot.
His mortal part alone, his soul was caught
   (Because he was a good Ahkoond)
   Up to the bosom of Mahound.
Though earthly walls his frame surround
(Forever hallowed be the ground!)
And sceptics mock the lowly mound

404

And say, 'He's now of no Ahkoond!'
  His soul is in the skies,—
The azure skies that bend above his loved
Metropolis of Swat.
He sees with larger, other eyes
Athwart all earthly mysteries—
  He knows what's Swat.

Let Swat bury the great Ahkoond
  With a noise of mourning and lamentation!
Let Swat bury the great Ahkoond
  With the noise of the mourning of the Swattish nation!

  Fallen is at length
  Its tower of strength,
Its sun is dimmed ere it had nooned;
Dead lies the great Ahkoond,
  The great Ahkoond of Swat
  Is not!

GEORGE THOMAS LANIGAN

By Windrush, Thames and Evenlode

What word-magician, more than man,
Silvanus, Faunus, Aegipan,
Or poet-godsire, unavowed,
Nameless himself, his haunts endowed
With names, delicious, quaint or queer
That sound like music in the ear
Of travellers who take the road
By Windrush, Thames and Evenlode?
I'd be contented with a hovel
At Ambrosden or Minster Lovell
Far from the flutters and the flicks,
A nook at Noke, a box at Bix.
I often ponder which would suit
Best of the Baldons, Marsh or Toot.

From Adderbury one could hop
To Adwell or to Addlestrop;
From Heythrop, Hook and Chipping Norton
There's all the Cotswolds to cavort on.
Though I aspire, when feeling lordly,
To Chastleton or Stratton Audley,
I'd be resigned to something smaller
At Filkins, Faringdon or Fawler.
At other times I set my heart on
Ewelme or Wychwood or Tadmarton
Or Duns or Great or Little Tew.
I wonder was it ever true
That folks at Oddington were *fou*?
Did men and cows at Cuddesdon chew
The cud? Was Horspath closed to cars?
Was Shotover a seat of Mars?
Seeking for slumber, one would not
Choose Nettlebed or Clattercot;
At Easington we'd sleep like logs,
And snore like pigs at Broughton Poggs.
How good to spend a summer's day
At Hampton Poyle and Hampton Gay,
Or fade and leave the world unseen
At Coombe or Weston-on-the-Green!
How sweet at Swerford-on-the-Swere
To linger for at least a year,
Or list the lazy waters lap
By Bablockhythe or Goring Gap,
Or, free from frenzy, fleet the time,
Glamoured at Glympton-on-the-Glyme!

A. H. VERNÈDE

When Adam Day by Day

When Adam day by day
    Woke up in Paradise,
He always used to say
    'Oh, this is very nice.'

406

But Eve from scenes of bliss
Transported him for life.
The more I think of this
The more I beat my wife.

A. E. HOUSMAN

Attila

When a photograph of Attila
Appeared in *The Tatler*
The Huns were all delighted
And the editor was knighted.

E. CLERIHEW BENTLEY

Upon Julia's Clothes

When as in silks my Julia goes,
Then, then, methinks, how sweetly flows
That liquefaction of her clothes.

Next, when I cast my eyes, and see
That brave vibration each way free;
O how that glittering taketh me!

ROBERT HERRICK

When Autumn Mists were Falling Dank

When autumn mists were falling dank
   And autumn days were waning,
Alone beside a river bank
   I heard a nymph complaining.
She sang in accents high and strange
   Beside the sighing river
Of Mutability and Change,
   Of Life and of her Liver.
She recognized me as I passed;
   'It was in nineteen-ten,'
She said, 'I think, I saw you last;
   You were a stripling then.
To think what merry songs were sung
   And what good things were said!
When I was young and you were young
   What times we had!' she said.

'When I was young and you were young
   And Charles was young, and Fred
And Alistair and Sue were young,
   And James and Ethelred;
When Mabel Winthrop-Bligh was young,
   And Joyce and Colonel Tweed,
And you were young and I was young
   The world was young indeed!

'You used to join us in our sports
   When you were quite a lad;
Then nobody felt out of sorts,
   And ah! what times we had!
What tricks we played on Edgar's aunt,
   On Wilfred and the Plenders,
And how we chaffed Sir Arthur Grant
   About his sock-suspenders!
What mad and merry days we've seen!
   How Arthur and his mates
Applauded when we got the Dean
   On Desmond's roller-skates!

But that was many years ago,
    And since our folly faltered
The water has had far to flow
    And many things have altered.

'When I was young and you were young
    And Charles was young, and Fred
And Jane and Joyce Carew were young,
    And James and Ethelred;
When Mrs Vincent Blow was young,
    And Soames and Mrs Reid
And everyone I know was young,
    The world was young indeed!

'Now Soames is breaking stones abroad
    And Fred is broking stocks;
And Wilberforce is on a Board
    And Wilfred on the rocks;
And Desmond's deaf in both his ears,
    And bald and old and thrifty;
And James is doing forty years,
    And Charles is doing fifty.
Godolphin has a house in Kent,
    And Sue's a Lady Mayoress;
And Paul has met an accident,
    And Alistair an heiress;
And Major Twisden is in Oil,
    And George is in a fix;
And Edgar walks on foreign soil
    And Cuthbert walks on sticks.

'Now I am old and you are old
    And Charles is old, and Fred
And Alistair and Sue are old,
    And Lady Leatherhead;
And Jane is on the stage, I'm told,
    And Joyce is on the shelf;
And, though I feel no age, I'm told
    That I am old myself.

'Now Colonel Tweed has lost a leg
   And Cuthbert his connections;
And Claude was wounded with an egg
   At Ilford by-elections;
Belinda's married some poor soul,
   And Mrs ffoulkes is barmy,
And Hector is in the Tyrol
   And Arthur in the Army.
What things were said! What songs were sung!
   And how we did our stuff
When I was young, and you were young——!'
   'Enough!' I said, 'Enough!'
I left the nymph to her refrain
   And home to tea went hieing;
But all along the leafy lane
   I heard the aspens sighing:—

'When I was young and you were young
   And Charles was young, and Fred
And Jane and Joyce Carew were young,
   And James and Ethelred . . .
But that was many years ago,
   And since our folly faltered
The water has had far to flow
   And many things have altered.'

PATRICK BARRINGTON

Good Gnus

(A vignette in verse)

When cares attack and life seems black,
How sweet it is to pot a yak,
   Or puncture hares and grizzly bears,
   And others I could mention:
But in my Animals 'Who's Who'
No name stands higher than the Gnu:
   And each new gnu that comes in view
   Receives my prompt attention.

410

When Afric's sun is sinking low,
And shadows wander to and fro,
    And everywhere there's in the air
        A hush that's deep and solemn;
Then is the time good men and true
With View Halloo pursue the gnu:
    (The safest spot to put your shot
        Is through the spinal column).

To take the creature by surprise
We must adopt some rude disguise,
    Although deceit is never sweet,
        And falsehoods don't attract us:
So, as with gun in hand you wait,
Remember to impersonate
    A tuft of grass, a mountain-pass,
        A kopje or a cactus.

A brief suspense, and then at last
The waiting's o'er, the vigil past:
    A careful aim. A spurt of flame.
        It's done. You've pulled the trigger,
And one more gnu, so fair and frail,
Has handed in its dinner-pail:
    (The females are all rather small,
        The males are somewhat bigger).

P. G. WODEHOUSE

Rogero's Song from 'The Rovers'

I

Whene'er with haggard eyes I view
    This dungeon that I'm rotting in,
I think of those companions true
Who studied with me at the U
        —niversity of Gottingen,—
        —niversity of Gottingen.
    (*Weeps, and pulls out a blue kerchief, with
    which he wipes his eyes; gazing tenderly at
    it, he proceeds—*)

II

Sweet kerchief, checked with heavenly blue,
  Which once my love sat knotting in!—
Alas! Matilda *then* was true!
  At least I thought so at the U—
    —niversity of Gottingen—
    —niversity of Gottingen.
(At the repetition of this line Rogero clanks his
  chains in cadence.)

III

Barbs! Barbs! alas! how swift you flew
  Her neat post-waggon trotting in!
Ye bore Matilda from my view;
  Forlorn I languished at the U—
    —niversity of Gottingen—
    —niversity of Gottingen.

IV

This faded form! this pallid hue!
  This blood my veins is clotting in,
My years are many—they were few
  When first I entered at the U—
    —niversity of Gottingen—
    —niversity of Gottingen.

V

There first for thee my passion grew,
  Sweet! sweet Matilda Pottingen!
Thou wast the daughter of my Tu—
  —tor, Law Professor at the U—
    —niversity of Gottingen—
    —niversity of Gottingen.

VI

Sun, moon, and thou vain world, adieu,
  That kings and priests are plotting in:
Here doomed to starve on water gru—
  —el never shall I see the U—
    —niversity of Gottingen—
    —niversity of Gottingen.

*(During the last stanza Rogero dashes his head
repeatedly against the walls of his prison; and,
finally, so hard as to produce a visible contusion.
He then throws himself on the floor in an agony.
The curtain drops—the music still continuing
to play, till it is wholly fallen.)*

GEORGE CANNING and GEORGE ELLIS

Hall and Knight

or

$$z + b + x = y + b + z$$

When he was young his cousins
       used to say of Mr Knight:
'This boy will write an Algebra—
       or looks as if he might.'
And sure enough, when Mr Knight
       had grown to be a man,
He purchased pen and paper
       and an inkpot, and began.

But he very soon discovered
       that he couldn't write at all,
And his heart was filled with yearnings
       for a certain Mr Hall;
Till, after many years of doubt,
       he sent his friend a card:
'Have tried to write an Algebra,
       but find it very hard.'

Now Mr Hall himself had tried
       to write a book for schools,
But suffered from a handicap:
       he didn't know the rules.
So when he heard from Mr Knight
       and understood his gist,
He answered him by telegram:
       'Delighted to assist.'

So Mr Hall and Mr Knight
          they took a house together,
And they worked away at algebra
          in any kind of weather,
Determined not to give it up
          until they had evolved
A problem so constructed
          that it never could be solved.

'How hard it is,' said Mr Knight,
          'to hide the fact from youth
That x and y are equal:
          it is such an obvious truth!'
'It is,' said Mr Hall,
          'but if we gave a b to each,
We'd put the problem well beyond
          our little victims' reach.

'Or are you anxious, Mr Knight,
          lest any boy should see
The utter superfluity
          of this repeated b?'
'I scarcely fear it,' he replied,
          and scratched his grizzled head,
'But perhaps it *would* be safer
          if to b we added z.'

'A brilliant stroke!' said Hall,
          and added z to either side;
Then looked at his accomplice
          with a flush of happy pride.
And Knight, he winked at Hall
          (a very pardonable lapse).
And they printed off the Algebra
          and sold it to the chaps.

JAMES REEVES

Reproof Deserved

or

After the lecture

When I saw the grapefruit drying, cherry in each centre
                                  lying,
  And a dozen guests expected at the table's polished oak,
Then I knew, my lecture finished, I'ld be feeling quite
                                  diminished
  Talking on, but unprotected, so that all my spirit broke.

'Have you read the last Charles Morgan?' 'Are you
                             writing for the organ
  Which is published as a vital adjunct to our cultural
                                   groups?'
'This year some of us are learning all *The Lady's Not for
                                 Burning*
  For a poetry recital we are giving to the troops.'

'Mr Betjeman, I grovel before critics of the novel,
  Tell me, if I don't offend you, have you written one your-
                                  self?
You haven't? Then the one I wrote is (not that I expect a
                                  notice)
  Something I would like to send you, just for keeping on
                                  your shelf.'

'Betjeman, I bet your racket brings you in a pretty packet
  Raising the old lecture curtain, writing titbits here and
                                  there.
But, by Jove, your hair is thinner, since you came to us in
                                  Pinner,
  And you're fatter now, I'm certain. What you need is
                                  country air.'

This and that way conversation, till I turn in desperation
  To a kind face (can I doubt it?) mercifully mute so far.
'Oh,' it says, 'I missed the lecture, wasn't it on archi-
                                  tecture?
  Do please tell me all about it, what you do and who you
                                  are.'

JOHN BETJEMAN

I Was a Bustle-maker Once, Girls

When I was a lad of twenty
    And was working in High Street, Ken.,
I made quite a pile in a very little while—
    I was a bustle-maker then.
Then there was work in plenty,
    And I was a thriving man;
But things have decayed in the bustle-making trade
    Since the bustle-making trade began.

I built bustles with a will then;
    I built bustles with a wit;
I built bustles as a Yankee hustles,
    Simply for the love of it.
I built bustles with a skill then
    Surpassed, they say, by none;
But those were the days when bustles were the craze,
    And now those days are done.

I was a bustle-maker once, girls,
    Many, many years ago;
I put my heart in the bustle-maker's art,
    And I don't mind saying so.
I may have had the brains of a dunce, girls;
    I may have had the mind of a muff;
I may have been plain and deficient in the brain,
    But I did know a bustle-maker's stuff.

I built bustles for the slender;
    I built bustles for the stout;
I built bustles for the girls with muscles
    And bustles for the girls without.
I built bustles by the thousands once
    In the good old days of yore;
But things have decayed in the bustle-making trade,
    And I don't build bustles any more.

Many were the models worn once;
    But mine were unique, 'tis said;
No rival design was so elegant as mine;
    I was a bustle-maker bred.
    I was a bustle-maker born once—
    An artist through and through;
But things have decayed in the bustle-making trade,
    And what can a bustle-maker do?

    I built bustles to enchant, girls;
    I built bustles to amaze;
I built bustles for the skirt that rustles,
    And bustles for the skirt that sways.
    I built bustles for my aunt, girls,
    When other business fled;
But a bustle-maker can't make bustles for his aunt
    When a bustle-maker's aunt is dead.

    I was a bustle-maker once, girls—
    Once in the days gone by,
I lost my heart to the bustle-maker's art,
    And that I don't deny.
    I may have had the brains of a dunce, girls,
    As many men appear to suppose;
I may have been obtuse and of little other use,
    But I could build a bustle when I chose.

    I built bustles for the bulging;
    I built bustles for the lithe;
I built bustles for the girls in Brussels
    And bustles for the girls in Hythe.
    I built bustles for all Europe once,
    But I've been badly hit.
Things have decayed in the bustle-building trade,
    And that's the truth of it.

                                   PATRICK BARRINGTON

A Memory

When I was as high as that,
I saw a poet in his hat.
I think the poet must have smiled
At such a solemn gazing child.

Now wasn't it a funny thing
To get a sight of J. M. Synge,
And notice nothing but his hat?
Yet life is often queer like that.

L. A. G. STRONG

String, in Lieu of

These melancholy lines were written when I learned that recruits to the British Territorial Army would receive a free issue of every part of their uniform, except braces, which they would have to provide for themselves

When I went into Ludlow
    The fields were full of corn,
And proud was I of fighting
    And glad that I was born.

I had my civvy things on
    But those were packed away,
Except this pair of braces
    You see me in today.

I bought my pair of braces
    At Abdon under Clee
And, oh, they'd keep the bags up
    Of larger lads than me.

I gird them on for marching
    In sunshine and in rain,
They cost me one-and-fivepence
    And well they bear the strain.

The bugle blows 'Defaulters'
    But still the buckles stand,
And when they need adjustment
    I move them up the band.

For caps and boots and tunics
    The country finds the pelf,
But holding up one's trousers
    One has to do oneself.

And long the King might whistle
    For likely lads in brown
If none of us had braces
    And all our bags came down.

E. V. KNOX

When Klopstock England Defied

When Klopstock England defied,
Uprose William Blake in his pride;
For old Nobodaddy aloft
Farted and belched and coughed;
Then swore a great oath that made heaven quake,
And called aloud to English Blake.
Blake was giving his body ease
At Lambeth beneath the poplar trees.
From his seat then started he,
And turned him round three times three.
The moon at that sight blushed scarlet red,
The stars threw down their cups and fled,
And all the devils that were in hell
Answered with a ninefold yell.
Klopstock felt the intripled turn,
And all his bowels began to churn,
And his bowels turned round three times three,
And locked in his soul with a ninefold key,
That from his body it ne'er could be parted
Till to the last trumpet it was farted.

Then again old Nobodaddy swore
He ne'er had seen such a thing before,
Since Noah was shut in the ark,
Since Eve first chose her hellfire spark,
Since 'twas the fashion to go naked,
Since the old anything was created,
And so feeling, he begged me to turn again
And ease poor Klopstock's ninefold pain.
If Blake could do this when he rose up from a shite,
What might he not do if he sat down to write?

WILLIAM BLAKE

A. E. Housman and a Few Friends

When lads have done with labour
    in Shropshire, one will cry,
'Let's go and kill a neighbour,'
    And t'other answers 'Aye!'

So this one kills his cousins,
    and that one kills his dad;
and, as they hang by dozens
    at Ludlow, lad by lad,

each of them one-and-twenty,
    all of them murderers,
the hangman mutters: 'Plenty
    even for Housman's verse.'

HUMBERT WOLFE

An Expostulation

When late I attempted your pity to move,
    What made you so deaf to my prayers?
Perhaps it was right to dissemble your love,
    But—why did you kick me downstairs?

ISAAC BICKERSTAFFE

420

The Progress of Discontent

When now mature in classic knowledge,
The joyful youth is sent to college,
His father comes, a vicar plain,
At Oxford bred—in Anna's reign,
And thus, in form of humble suitor,
Bowing accosts a reverend tutor:
'Sir, I'm a Gloucestershire divine,
And this my eldest son of nine;
My wife's ambition and my own
Was that this child should wear a gown;
I'll warrant that his good behaviour
Will justify your future favour;
And, for his parts, to tell the truth,
My son's a very forward youth;
Has Horace all by heart—you'd wonder—
And mouths out Homer's Greek like thunder.
If you'd examine—and admit him,
A scholarship would nicely fit him;
That he succeeds 'tis ten to one;
Your vote and interest, sir!'—'Tis done.
　　Our pupil's hopes, though twice defeated,
Are with a scholarship completed:
A scholarship but half maintains,
And college rules are heavy chains:
In garret dark he smokes and puns;
A prey to discipline and duns;
And now, intent on new designs,
Sighs for a fellowship—and fines.
　　When nine full tedious winters passed,
That utmost wish is crowned at last:
But the rich prize no sooner got,
Again he quarrels with his lot:
'These fellowships are pretty things,
We live indeed like petty kings:
But who can bear to waste his whole age
Amid the dullness of a college,
Debarred the common joys of life,
And that prime bliss—a loving wife!
O! what's a table richly spread,

Without a woman at its head!
Would some snug benefice but fall,
Ye feasts, ye dinners! farewell all!
To offices I'd bid adieu,
Of dean, vice-præs.—of bursar too;
Come, joys that rural quiet yields,
Come, tithes, and house, and fruitful fields!'
 Too fond of freedom and of ease
A patron's vanity to please,
Long time he watches, and by stealth,
Each frail incumbent's doubtful health;
At length, and in his fortieth year,
A living drops—two hundred clear!
With breast elate beyond expression,
He hurries down to take possession,
With rapture views the sweet retreat—
'What a convenient house! how neat!
For fuel here's sufficient wood:
Pray God the cellars may be good!
The garden—that must be new planned—
Shall these old-fashioned yew-trees stand?
O'er yonder vacant plot shall rise
The flowery shrub of thousand dyes:—
Yon wall, that feels the southern ray,
Shall blush with ruddy fruitage gay:
While thick beneath its aspect warm
O'er well-ranged hives the bees shall swarm,
From which, ere long, of golden gleam
Metheglin's luscious juice shall stream:
This awkward hut, o'ergrown with ivy,
We'll alter to a modern privy:
Up yon green slope, of hazels trim,
An avenue so cool and dim
Shall to an arbour, at the end,
In spite of gout, entice a friend.
My predecessor loved devotion—
But of a garden had no notion.'
 Continuing this fantastic farce on,
He now commences country parson.
To make his character entire,
He weds—a cousin of the squire;
Not over weighty in the purse,

But many doctors have done worse:
And though she boasts no charms divine,
Yet she can carve, and make birch wine.
    Thus fixed, content he taps his barrel,
Exhorts his neighbours not to quarrel;
Finds his church-wardens have discerning
Both in good liquor and good learning;
With tithes his barns replete he sees,
And chuckles o'er his surplice fees;
Studies to find out latent dues,
And regulates the state of pews;
Rides a sleek mare with purple housing,
To share the monthly club's carousing;
Of Oxford pranks facetious tells,
And—but on Sundays—hears no bells;
Sends presents of his choicest fruit,
And prunes himself each sapless shoot;
Plants cauliflowers, and boasts to rear
The earliest melons of the year;
Thinks alteration charming work is,
Keeps bantam cocks, and feeds his turkeys;
Builds in his copse a favourite bench,
And stores the pond with carp and tench.—
    But, ah! too soon his thoughtless breast
By cares domestic is oppressed;
And a third butcher's bill, and brewing,
Threaten inevitable ruin:
For children fresh expenses yet,
And Dicky now for school is fit.
'Why did I sell my college life,'
He cries, 'for benefice and wife?
Return, ye days, when endless pleasure
I found in reading, or in leisure!
When calm around the common-room
I puffed my daily pipe's perfume!
Rode for a stomach, and inspected,
At annual bottlings, corks selected:
And dined untaxed, untroubled, under
The portrait of our pious Founder!
When impositions were supplied
To light my pipe—or soothe my pride—
No cares were then for forward peas,

A yearly-longing wife to please;
My thoughts no christening dinners crossed,
No children cried for buttered toast;
And every night I went to bed,
Without a Modus in my head!'
　　Oh! trifling head, and fickle heart!
Chagrined at whatsoe'er thou art;
A dupe to follies yet untried,
And sick of pleasures, scarce enjoyed!
Each prize possessed, thy transport ceases,
And in pursuit alone it pleases.

　　　　　　　　　　　　THOMAS WARTON

On Certain Ladies

When other fair ones to the shades go down,
Still Chloe, Flavia, Delia, stay in town:
Those ghosts of beauty wandering here reside,
And haunt the places where their honour died.

　　　　　　　　　　　　ALEXANDER POPE

Doctrinae Sedes

When Pleasure rules in Learning's realm
　　With Heads of Houses to escort her:
And Youth directs an errant helm
　　In shorts that every year grow shorter:
When Scholars 'have their People Up'
　　(A plea that everything excuses),
And quaff the gay convivial cup
　　Where once they wooed the classic Muses:

DORSET COUNTY LIBRARY

When men who used to come at nine
    Allege (at ten) 'indisposition',
And Brown has several aunts to dine
    And cannot do his composition:
When Tomkins—once a studious lad—
    'Desires most humbly to express a
Sincere regret he has not had
    Time to complete his weekly essay':

When Lecturers have lost their use,
    Because the youth they idly prate to
Has other things whereon to muse
    Than mere Thucydides or Plato—
(You think, perhaps, he's taking notes?
    Mistaken dream! too well I know he
Is speculating on the boats,
    Or thinking of a rhyme to Chloe):—

Then seek with me some calmer scene
    Where wines are hushed, where banjoes mute are;
There—careless, though they burn the Dean
    And immolate the Senior Tutor—
I'll muse in solitude, until
    June and the Long once more disbands 'em;
Then, William, pay my washing bill
    And call at once my usual hansom.

A. C. GODLEY

The Candidate

When sly Jemmy Twitcher had smugged up his face
With a lick of court whitewash, and pious grimace,
A wooing he went, where three sisters of old
In harmless society guttle and scold.
    Lord! sister, says Physic to Law, I declare
Such a sheep-biting look, such a pick-pocket air,
Not I, for the Indies! you know I'm no prude;
But his nose is a shame, and his eyes are so lewd!

425

Then he shambles and straddles so oddly, I fear—
No; at our time of life, 'twould be silly, my dear.

I don't know, says Law, now methinks, for his look,
'Tis just like the picture in Rochester's book.
But his character, Phyzzy, his morals, his life;
When she died, I can't tell, but he once had a wife.

They say he's no Christian, loves drinking and whoring,
And all the town rings of his swearing and roaring,
His lying and filching, and Newgate-bird tricks:—
Not I,—for a coronet, chariot and six.

Divinity heard, between waking and dozing,
Her sisters denying, and Jemmy proposing;
From dinner she rose with her bumper in hand,
She stroked up her belly, and stroked down her band.

What a pother is here about wenching and roaring!
Why David loved catches, and Solomon whoring.
Did not Israel filch from th' Egyptians of old
Their jewels of silver, and jewels of gold?
The prophet of Bethel, we read, told a lie:
He drinks; so did Noah: he swears; so do I.
To refuse him for such peccadillos, were odd;
Besides, he repents, and he talks about God.

Never hang down your head, you poor penitent elf!
Come, buss me, I'll be Mrs Twitcher myself.
Damn ye both for a couple of Puritan bitches!
He's Christian enough, that repents, and that stitches.

THOMAS GRAY

When Tennyson

When Tennyson wrote 'Sir Galahad'
He was nearly driven mad
(As well as saddened)
By hints that he meant 'Sir Galahadn't'.

L. E. JONES

A Nightmare

When you're lying awake with a dismal headache, and
    repose is taboo'd by anxiety,
I conceive you may use any language you choose to indulge
    in, without impropriety;
For your brain is on fire—the bedclothes conspire of usual
    slumber to plunder you:
First your counterpane goes, and uncovers your toes, and
    your sheet slips demurely from under you;
Then the blanketing tickles—you feel like mixed pickles—
    so terribly sharp is the pricking,
And you're hot, and you're cross, and you tumble and toss
    till there's nothing 'twixt you and the ticking.
Then the bedclothes all creep to the ground in a heap, and
    you pick 'em all up in a tangle;
Next your pillow resigns and politely declines to remain
    at its usual angle!
Well, you get some repose in the form of a doze, with hot
    eyeballs and head ever aching,
But your slumbering teems with such horrible dreams that
    you'd very much better be waking;
For you dream you are crossing the Channel, and tossing
    about in a steamer from Harwich—
Which is something between a large bathing machine and
    a very small second-class carriage—
And you're giving a treat (penny ice and cold meat) to a
    party of friends and relations—
They're a ravenous horde—and they all come on board at
    Sloane Square and South Kensington Stations.
And bound on that journey you find your attorney (who
    started that morning from Devon);
He's a bit undersized, and you don't feel surprised when
    he tells you he's only eleven.
Well, you're driving like mad with this singular lad (by
    the bye the ship's now a four-wheeler),
And you're playing round games, and he calls you bad
    names when you tell him that 'ties pay the dealer',
But this you can't stand, so you throw up your hand, and
    you find you're as cold as an icicle,

In your shirt and your socks (the black silk with gold
        clocks), crossing Salisbury Plain on a bicycle:
And he and the crew are on bicycles too—which they've
        somehow or other invested in—
And he's telling the tars all the particu*lars* of a company
        he's interested in—
It's a scheme of devices, to get at low prices all goods from
        cough mixtures to cables
(Which tickled the sailors), by treating retailers as though
        they were all vege*ta*bles—
You get a good spadesman to plant a small tradesman
        (first take off his boots with a boot-tree),
And his legs will take root, and his fingers will shoot, and
        they'll blossom and bud like a fruit-tree—
From the greengrocer tree you get grapes and green pea,
        cauliflower, pineapple, and cranberries,
While the pastrycook plant cherry brandy will grant,
        apple puffs, and three-corners, and Banburys—
The shares are a penny, and ever so many are taken by
        Rothschild and Baring,
And just as a few are allotted to you, you awake with a
        shudder despairing—
You're a regular wreck, with a crick in your neck, and no
        wonder you snore, for your head's on the floor, and
        you've needles and pins from your soles to your shins,
        and your flesh is a-creep, for your left leg's asleep, and
        you've cramp in your toes, and a fly on your nose, and
        some fluff in your lung, and a feverish tongue, and a
        thirst that's intense, and a general sense that you
        haven't been sleeping in clover;
But the darkness has passed, and it's daylight at last, and
        the night has been long—ditto ditto my song—and
        thank goodness they're both of them over!

W. S. GILBERT

Lines on Thomas Warton's Poems

I

Wheresoe'er I turn my view,
All is strange, yet nothing new;
Endless labour all along,
Endless labour to be wrong;
Phrase that time has flung away,
Uncouth words in disarray:
Tricked in antique ruff and bonnet,
Ode and elegy and sonnet.

II

Hermit hoar, in solemn cell,
   Wearing out life's evening gray;
Smite thy bosom, sage, and tell,
   Where is bliss? and which the way?

Thus I spoke; and speaking sighed;
   —Scarce repressed the starting tear;—
When the smiling sage replied—
   Come, my lad, and drink some beer.

SAMUEL JOHNSON

Georgian Spring

Who does not love the spring deserves no lovers—
For peaches bloom in Georgia in the spring,
New quarterlies relume their yellow covers,
Anthologies on every bookshelf sing.
The publishers put on their best apparel
To sell the public everything it wants—
A thousand meek soprano voices carol
The loves of homosexuals or plants.
Now let the Old Cow perish, for the tune
Would turn the fatted calf to bully beef:
We know, we know, that 'silver is the Moon',
That 'skies are blue' was always our belief:

That 'grass is green' there can be no denying,
That titled whores in love can be forgot—
All who have heard poor Georgiana sighing
Would think it more surprising were they not:
As for the streams, why any carp or tench
Could tell you that they 'sparkle on their way'.
Now for the millionth time the 'country wench'
Has lost her reputation 'in the hay'.
But still the air is full of happy voices,
All bloody: but no matter, let them sing!
For who would frown when all the world rejoices,
And who would contradict when, in the spring,
The English Muse her annual theme rehearses
To tell us birds are singing in the sky?
Only the poet slams the door and curses,
And all the little sparrows wonder why!

ROY CAMPBELL

Dooleysprudence

Who is the man when all the gallant nations run to war
Goes home to have his dinner by the very first cablecar
And as he eats his cantelope contorts himself in mirth
To read the blatant bulletins of the rulers of the earth?
    It's Mr Dooley,
    Mr Dooley,
    The coolest chap our country ever knew
    'They are out to collar
    The dime and dollar'
    Says Mr Dooley-ooley-ooley-oo.

Who is the funny fellow who declines to go to church
Since pope and priest and parson left the poor man in the lurch
And taught their flocks the only way to save all human souls
Was piercing human bodies through with dumdum bulletholes?
    It's Mr Dooley,
    Mr Dooley,
    The mildest man our country ever knew
    'Who will release us

From Jingo Jesus'
Prays Mr Dooley-ooley-ooley-oo.

Who is the meek philosopher who doesn't care a damn
About the yellow peril or problem of Siam
And disbelieves that British Tar is water from life's fount
And will not gulp the gospel of the German on the Mount?
    It's Mr Dooley,
    Mr Dooley,
    The broadest brain our country ever knew
    'The curse of Moses
    On both your houses'
    Cries Mr Dooley-ooley-ooley-oo.

Who is the cheerful imbecile who lights his long chibouk
With pages of the pandect, penal code and Doomsday Book
And wonders why bald justices are bound by law to wear
A toga and a wig made out of someone else's hair?
    It's Mr Dooley,
    Mr Dooley,
    The finest fool our country ever knew
    'They took that toilette
    From Pontius Pilate'
    Thinks Mr Dooley-ooley-ooley-oo.

Who is the man who says he'll go the whole and perfect hog
Before he pays the income tax or license for a dog
And when he licks a postage stamp regards with smiling scorn
The face of king or emperor or snout of unicorn?
    It's Mr Dooley,
    Mr Dooley,
    The wildest wag our country ever knew
    'O my poor tummy
    His backside gummy!'
    Moans Mr Dooley-ooley-ooley-oo.

Who is the tranquil gentleman who won't salute the State
Or serve Nebuchadnezzar or proletariat
But thinks that every son of man has quite enough to do
To paddle down the stream of life his personal canoe?
    It's Mr Dooley,
    Mr Dooley,

The wisest wight our country ever knew
'Poor Europe ambles
Like sheep to shambles'
Sighs Mr Dooley-ooley-ooley-oo.

All, All are Gone, the Old Familiar Quotations

Who was born too soon? I will tell you who was born too soon:
    Francis Bacon, Baron Verulam.
Therefore he could not ask his friends, *Why is Charles Lamb like*
    Baltimore, and supply his own answer, *Because he is deep in*
    the heart of Mary Lamb.
Who was born too late? I will tell you without further parley:
It was I, because I cannot remember whether it was Charles Lamb
    or who, who on the death of his last nearest and dearest pa-
    thetically exclaimed, *Now there is no one left to call me*
    Charlie.
I am always getting entangled in such mnemonic snarls,
But from internal evidence it was obviously someone named
    Charles,
So it couldn't have been Scrooge or Marley.
Nor could it have been Charles II, because there was always some-
    body to call him Charlie.
It would have been duck soup or pie or jam
If he had said, *There is no one left to call me Elia*, then I would
    have known it was Lamb.
If I could but spot a conclusion, I should race to it,
But Charles is such a simple name that I can't put a face to it.
Still, I shouldn't complain, since it is its simplicity that gives it its
    pathos;
There would be no poignancy in saying, *There is no one left to call*
    me Charlemagne or Lancelot or Athos.
People prefer the simple to the grandiose,
And I do not believe that even in an antique land anybody would
    sympathize with anybody who went around saying, *There is*
    no one left to call me Ozymandias.

OGDEN NASH

[Chesterton was piqued – as many another reader has been – by the middle-class complacency of a verse by Frances Cornford called:]

To a Fat Lady Seen from a Train

O why do you walk through the fields in gloves,
    Missing so much and so much?
O fat white woman whom nobody loves
Why do you walk through the fields in gloves,
When the grass is soft as the breast of doves
    And shivering-sweet to the touch?
O why do you walk through the fields in gloves,
    Missing so much and so much?

The Fat White Woman Speaks

Why do you rush through the fields in trains,
Guessing so much and so much;
Why do you flash through the flowery meads,
Fat headed poet whom nobody reads;
And how do you know such a frightful lot
About people in gloves as such?

And how the devil can you be sure,
Guessing so much and so much,
How do you know but what someone who loves
Always to see me in nice white gloves
At the end of the field you are rushing by,
Is waiting for his Old Dutch?

G. K. CHESTERTON

433

After Dilettante Concetti

D. G. Rossetti

'Why do you wear your hair like a man,
      Sister Helen?
This week is the third since you began.'
'I'm writing a ballad; be still if you can,
      Little brother.
    (O Mother Carey, mother!
What chickens are these between sea and heaven!)'

'But why does your figure appear so lean,
      Sister Helen?
And why do you dress in sage, sage green?'
'Children should never be heard, if seen,
      Little·brother!
    (O Mother Carey, mother!
What fowls are a-wing in the stormy heaven!)'

'But why is your face so yellowy white,
      Sister Helen?
And why are your skirts so funnily tight?'
'Be quiet, you torment, or how can I write,
      Little brother?
    (O Mother Carey, mother!
How gathers thy train to the sea from the heaven!)'

'And who's Mother Carey, and what is her train,
      Sister Helen?
And why do you call her again and again?'
'You troublesome boy, why that's the refrain,
      Little brother.
    (O Mother Carey, mother!
What work is toward in the startled heaven?)'

'And what's a refrain? What a curious word,
      Sister Helen!
Is the ballad you're writing about a sea-bird?'
'Not at all; why should it be? Don't be absurd,
      Little brother.

(O Mother Carey, mother!
Thy brood flies lower as lowers the heaven.)'

(A big brother speaketh:)
'The refrain you've studied a meaning had,
      Sister Helen!
It gave strange force to a weird ballad.
But refrains have become a ridiculous "fad",
      Little brother.
      And *Mother Carey, mother,*
Has a bearing on nothing in earth or heaven.

'But the finical fashion has had its day,
      Sister Helen.
And let's try in the style of a different lay
To bid it adieu in poetical way,
      Little brother.
      So Mother Carey, mother!
Collect your chickens and go to—heaven.'

(A pause. Then the big brother singeth, accompany-
*   ing himself in a plaintive wise on the triangle)*:
   'Look in my face. My name is Used-to-was;
   I am also called Played-out and Done-to-death,
   And It-will-wash-no-more. Awakeneth
Slowly, but sure awakening it has,
The common sense of man; and I, also!
   The ballad-burden trick, now known too well,
   Am turned to scorn, and grown contemptible—
A too transparent artifice to pass.

H. D. TRAILL

William I, 1066

William the first was the first of our kings,
Not counting Ethelreds, Egberts and things,
And he had himself crowned and anointed and blest
In Ten-Sixty-I-Needn't-Tell-You-The-Rest.

But being a Norman, King William the First
By the Saxons he conquered was hated and cursed,
And they planned and they plotted far into the night,
Which William could tell by the candles alight.

Then William decided these rebels to quell
By ringing the Curfew, a sort of a bell,
And if any Saxon was found out of bed
After eight o'clock sharp, it was Off With His Head!

So at BONG NUMBER ONE they all started to run
Like a warren of rabbits upset by a gun;
At BONG NUMBER TWO they were all in a stew,
Flinging cap after tunic and hose after shoe;
At BONG NUMBER THREE they were bare to the knee,
Undoing the doings as quick as could be;
At BONG NUMBER FOUR they were stripped to the core,
And pulling on nightshirts the wrong side before;
At BONG NUMBER FIVE they were looking alive,
And bizzing and buzzing like bees in a hive;
At BONG NUMBER SIX they gave themselves kicks,
Tripping over the rushes to snuff out the wicks;
At BONG NUMBER SEVEN, from Durham to Devon,
They slipped up a prayer to Our Father in Heaven;
And at BONG NUMBER EIGHT it was fatal to wait,
So with hearts beating all at a terrible rate,
In the deuce of a state, I need hardly relate,
They jumped BONG into bed like a bull at a gate.

ELEANOR FARJEON

In Memoriam

Willie had a purple monkey climbing on a yellow
    stick,
And when he had sucked the paint all off it made him
    deadly sick;
And in his latest hours he clasped that monkey in his
    hand,
And bade goodbye to earth and went into a better
    land.

Oh no more he'll shoot his sister with his little wooden
    gun;
And no more he'll twist the pussy's tail and make her
    yowl for fun.
The pussy's tail now stands out straight; the gun is
    laid aside;
The monkey doesn't jump around since little Willie
    died.

MAX ADELER

To R. K.

As long I dwell on some stupendous
And tremendous (Heaven defend us!)
Monstr'-inform'-ingens-horrendous
Demoniaco-seraphic
Penman's latest piece of graphic.

BROWNING

Will there never come a season
Which shall rid us from the curse
Of a prose which knows no reason
And an unmelodious verse:
When the world shall cease to wonder
At the genius of an Ass,
And a boy's eccentric blunder
Shall not bring success to pass:

When mankind shall be delivered
From the clash of magazines,
And the inkstand shall be shivered
Into countless smithereens:
When there stands a muzzled stripling,
Mute, beside a muzzled bore:
When the Rudyards cease from kipling
And the Haggards Ride no more.

J. K. STEPHEN

Ancient Music

Winter is icummen in,
Lhude sing Goddamm,
Raineth drop and staineth slop,
And how the wind doth ramm!
        Sing: Goddamm.
Skiddeth bus and sloppeth us,
An ague hath my ham.
Freezeth river, turneth liver,
        Damn you, sing: Goddamm.
Goddamm, Goddamm, 'tis why I am, Goddamm,
        So 'gainst the winter's balm,
Sing goddamm, damm, sing Goddamm,
Sing goddamm, sing goddamm, DAMM.

EZRA POUND

The Character of Sir Robert Walpole

With favour and fortune fastidiously blessed,
He's loud in his laugh and he's coarse in his jest;
Of favour and fortune unmerited vain,
A sharper in trifles, a dupe in the main.
Achieving of nothing, still promising wonders,
By dint of experience improving in blunders;
Oppressing true merit, exalting the base,
And selling his country to purchase his peace.
A jobber of stocks by retailing false news;
A prater at court in the style of the stews;
Of virtue and worth by profession a giber,
Of juries and senates the bully and briber:
Though I name not the wretch you know who I mean—
'Tis the cur-dog of Britain and spaniel of Spain.

JONATHAN SWIFT

438

A Tale of Chaucer

lately found in an old manuscript

Women ben full of ragerie,
Yet swinken nat sans secresie.
Thilke moral shall ye understond,
From schoole-boy's tale of fayre Irelond;
Which to the fennes hath him betake,
To filche the grey ducke fro the lake.
Right then there passen by the way
His aunt, and eke her daughters tway.
Ducke in his trowses hath he hent,
Not to be spied of ladies gent,
'But ho! our nephew,' crieth one;
'Ho!' quoth another, 'Cozen John':
And stoppen, and lough, and callen out—
This sely clerke full low doth lout:
They asken that, and talken this.
'Lo, here is coz, and here is miss.'
But, as he glozeth with speeches soote,
The ducke sore tickleth his erse roote:
Fore-piece and buttons all to-brest
Forth thrust a white neck and red crest.
'Te-hee!' cried ladies: clerk nought spake:
Miss star'd, and grey ducke crieth 'quaake'.
'O moder, moder!' quoth the daughter,
'Be thilke same thing maids longen a'ter?
Bette is to pine on coals and chalke,
Then trust on mon whose yerde can talke.'

ALEXANDER POPE

The Belle of the Ballroom

Years—years ago—ere yet my dreams
    Had been of being wise or witty,—
Ere I had done with writing themes,
    Or yawned o'er this infernal Chitty;—
Years,—years ago,—while all my joy
    Was in my fowling-piece and filly,—
In short, while I was yet a boy,
    I fell in love with Laura Lily.

I saw her at the county ball:
    There, when the sounds of flute and fiddle
Gave signal sweet in that old hall
    Of hands across and down the middle,
Hers was the subtlest spell by far
    Of all that set young hearts romancing;
She was our queen, our rose, our star;
    And then she danced—O Heaven, her dancing!

Dark was her hair, her hand was white;
    Her voice was exquisitely tender;
Her eyes were full of liquid light;
    I never saw a waist more slender!
Her every look, her every smile,
    Shot right and left a score of arrows;
I thought 'twas Venus from her isle,
    And wondered where she'd left her sparrows.

She talked,—of politics or prayers,—
    Of Southey's prose or Wordsworth's sonnets,—
Of danglers—or of dancing bears,
    Of battles—or the last new bonnets,
By candlelight, at twelve o'clock,
    To me it mattered not a tittle;
If those bright lips had quoted Locke,
    I might have thought they murmured Little.

Through sunny May, through sultry June,
  I loved her with a love eternal;
I spoke her praises to the moon,
  I wrote them to the Sunday Journal:
My mother laughed; I soon found out
  That ancient ladies have no feeling:
My father frowned; but how should gout
  See any happiness in kneeling?

She was the daughter of a dean,
  Rich, fat and rather apoplectic;
She had one brother, just thirteen,
  Whose colour was extremely hectic;
Her grandmother for many a year
  Had fed the parish with her bounty;
Her second cousin was a peer,
  And lord lieutenant of the county.

But titles, and the three per cents,
  And mortgages, and great relations,
And India bonds, and tithes, and rents,
  Oh what are they to love's sensations?
Black eyes, fair forehead, clustering locks—
  Such wealth, such honours, Cupid chooses;
He cares as little for the Stocks,
  As Baron Rothschild for the Muses.

She sketched; the vale, the wood, the beach,
  Grew lovelier from her pencil's shading:
She botanized; I envied each
  Young blossom in her boudoir fading:
She warbled Handel; it was grand;
  She made the Catalani jealous:
She touched the organ; I could stand
  For hours and hours to blow the bellows.

She kept an album, too, at home,
  Well filled with all an album's glories;
Paintings of butterflies, and Rome,
  Patterns for trimmings, Persian stories;
Soft songs to Julia's cockatoo,
  Fierce odes to Famine and to Slaughter,
And autographs of Prince Leboo,
  And recipes for elder-water.

And she was flattered, worshipped, bored;
  Her steps were watched, her dress was noted;
Her poodle dog was quite adored,
  Her sayings were extremely quoted;
She laughed, and every heart was glad,
  As if the taxes were abolished;
She frowned, and every look was sad,
  As if the Opera were demolished.

She smiled on many, just for fun,—
  I knew that there was nothing in it;
I was the first—the only one
  Her heart had thought of for a minute.—
I knew it, for she told me so,
  In phrase which was divinely moulded;
She wrote a charming hand,—and oh!
  How sweetly all her notes were folded.

Our love was like most other loves;—
  A little glow, a little shiver,
A rose-bud, and a pair of gloves,
  And 'Fly not yet'—upon the river;
Some jealousy of some one's heir,
  Some hopes of dying broken-hearted,
A miniature, a lock of hair,
  The usual vows,—and then we parted.

We parted; months and years rolled by;
    We met again four summers after:
Our parting was all sob and sigh;
    Our meeting was all mirth and laughter:
For in my heart's most secret cell
    There had been many other lodgers;
And she was not the ballroom's Belle,
    But only—Mrs Something Rogers!

                              W. M. PRAED

Ye Flags of Piccadilly

Ye flags of Piccadilly,
    Where I posted up and down,
And wished myself so often
    Well away from you and Town,—

Are the people walking quietly
    And steady on their feet,
Cabs and omnibuses plying
    Just as usual in the street?

Do the houses look as upright
    As of old they used to be,
And does nothing seem affected
    By the pitching of the sea?

Through the Green Park iron railings
    Do the quick pedestrians pass?
Are the little children playing
    Round the plane-tree in the grass?

This squally wild north-wester
    With which our vessel fights,
Does it merely serve with you to
    Carry up some paper kites?

443

Ye flags of Piccadilly,
    Which I hated so, I vow
I could wish with all my heart
    You were underneath me now!

ARTHUR HUGH CLOUGH

The British Journalist

You cannot hope
    To bribe or twist
(Thank God!) the British
    Journalist;
But, seeing what
    The man will do
Unbribed, there's no
    Occasion to.

HUMBERT WOLFE

Obstruction

You know Lord's? Well, once I played there,
And a ball I hit to leg
Struck the umpire's head and stayed there,
As a nest retains an egg.

Hastily the wicket-keeper
Seized a stump and prized about.

Had it gone two inches deeper
He would ne'er have run me out.

This I minded all the more,
As my stroke was well worth four.

HARRY GRAHAM

from The Famous Ballad of the Jubilee Cup

You may lift me in your arms, lad, and turn my face
    to the sun,
For a last look back at the dear old track where the
    Jubilee Cup was won;
And draw your chair to my side, lad—no, thank ye, I
    feel no pain—
For I'm going out with the tide, lad; but I'll tell you
    the tale again.

I'm seventy-nine or nearly, and my head it has long
    turned gray,
But it all comes back as clearly as though it was yester-
    day—
The dust, and the bookies shouting around the clerk of
    the scales,
And the clerk of the course, and the nobs in force, and
    'Is 'Ighness the Pr**ce of W*les.

'Twas a nine-hole thresh to wind'ard (but none of us
    cared for that)
With a straight run home to the service tee, and a finish
    along the flat.
'Stiff?' ah, well you may say it! Spot barred, and at
    five stone ten!
But at two and a bisque I'd ha' run the risk; for I was a
    greenhorn then.

So we stripped to the B. Race signal, the old red swallow-
    tail—
There was young Ben Bolt and the Portland Colt, and
    Aston Villa and Yale;
And W. G. and Steinitz, Leander and The Saint,
And the G*rm*n Emp*r*r's Meteor, a-looking as fresh
    as paint;

John Roberts (scratch), and Safety Match, The Lascar,
    and Lorna Doone,
Oom Paul (a bye), and Romany Rye, and me upon
    Wooden Spoon;

445

And some of us cut for partners, and some of us strung
    for baulk,
And some of us tossed for stations—But there, what use
    to talk?

Three-quarter-back on the Kingsclere crack was station
    enough for me,
With a fresh jackyarder blowing and the Vicarage goal
    a-lee!
And I leaned and patted her centre-bit and eased the
    quid in her cheek,
With a 'Soh my lass!' and a 'Woa you brute!'—for
    she could do all but speak.

She was geared a thought too high perhaps; she was
    trained a trifle fine;
But she had the grand reach forward! I never saw such
    a line!
Smooth-bored, clean run, from her fiddle head with its
    dainty ear half-cock,
Hard-bit, *pur sang*, from her overhang to the heel of her
    off hind sock.

Sir Robert he walked beside me as I worked her down
    to the mark;
'There's money on this, my lad,' said he, 'and most of
    'em's running dark;
But ease the sheet if you're bunkered, and pack the
    scrummages tight,
And use your slide at the distance, and we'll drink to
    your health tonight!'

But I bent and tightened my stretcher. Said I to myself,
    said I—
'John Jones, this here is the Jubilee Cup, and you have
    to do or die.'
And the words weren't hardly spoken when the umpire
    shouted 'Play!'
And we all kicked off from the Gasworks End with a
    'Yoicks!' and a 'Gone Away!'

446

And at first I thought of nothing, as the clay flew by in
    lumps,
But stuck to the old Ruy Lopez, and wondered who'd
    call for trumps,
And luffed her close to the cushion, and watched each
    one as it broke,
And in triple file up the Rowley Mile we went like a
    trail of smoke.

We were running as strong as ever—eight knots—but it
    couldn't last;
For the spray and the bails were flying, the whole field
    tailing fast;
And the Portland Colt had shot his bolt, and Yale was
    bumped at the Doves,
And The Lascar resigned to Steinitz, stalemated in fifteen
    moves.

It was bellows to mend with Roberts—starred three for a
    penalty kick:
But he chalked his cue and gave 'em the butt, and Oom
    Paul marked the trick—
'Offside—No Ball—and at fourteen all! Mark Cock!
    and two for his nob!'
When W. G. ran clean through his lee and beat him
    twice with a lob.

He yorked him twice on a crumbling pitch and wiped
    his eye with a brace,
But his guy-rope split with the strain of it and he dropped
    back out of the race;
And I drew a bead on the Meteor's lead, and challenging
    none too soon,
Bent over and patted her garboard strake, and called
    upon Wooden Spoon.

But none of the lot could stop the rot—nay, don't ask
    me to stop!
The Villa had called for lemons, Oom Paul had taken
    his drop,

And both were kicking the referee. Poor fellow! he
    done his best;
But, being in doubt, he'd ruled them out—which he
    always did when pressed.

So, inch by inch, I tightened the winch, and chucked
    the sandbags out—
I heard the nursery cannons pop, I heard the bookies
    shout:
'The Meteor wins!' 'No, Wooden Spoon!' 'Check!'
    'Vantage!' 'Leg Before!'
'Last Lap!' 'Pass Nap!' At his saddle-flap I put
    up the helm and swore.

Had I lost at that awful juncture my presence of mind?
    . . . but no!
I leaned and felt for the puncture, and plugged it there
    with my toe . . .
Hand over hand by the Members' Stand I lifted and
    eased her up,
Shot—clean and fair—to the crossbar there, and landed
    the Jubilee Cup!

ARTHUR QUILLER-COUCH

The Giraffe

You must not chaff
The tall Giraffe
About his size of collars,
    Nor watch him drink
    And rudely wink
And ask him how he swallers.

When at the Zoo
It will not do
To criticize his spots,
    Nor ask him when
    You pass his pen
To tie his neck in knots.

Nor is it nice
To give advice
On troubles of the spine—
The tall Giraffe
Enjoys a laugh,
But there he draws the line.

JOHN JOY BELL

Algernon

*who played with a loaded gun, and, on missing his sister, was
reprimanded by his father*

Young Algernon, the Doctor's Son,
Was playing with a Loaded Gun.
He pointed it towards his sister,
Aimed very carefully, but Missed her!
His Father, who was standing near,
The Loud Explosion chanced to Hear,
And reprimanded Algernon
For playing with a Loaded Gun.

HILAIRE BELLOC

The Cock and the Bull

(Browning)

You see this pebble-stone? It's a thing I bought
Of a bit of a chit of a boy i' the mid o' the day—
I like to dock the smaller parts-o'-speech,
As we curtail the already cur-tail'd cur
(You catch the paronomasia, play 'po' words?)
Did, rather, i' the pre-Landseerian days.
Well, to my muttons. I purchased the concern,
And clapt it i' my poke, having given for same

By way o' chop, swop, barter or exchange—
'Chop' was my snickering dandiprat's own term—
One shilling and fourpence, current coin o' the realm.
O-n-e one and f-o-u-r four
Pence, one and fourpence—you are with me, sir?—
What hour it skills not: ten or eleven o' the clock,
One day (and what a roaring day it was
Go shop or sight-see—bar a spit o' rain!)
In February, eighteen sixty-nine,
Alexandrina Victoria, Fidei
Hm—hm—how runs the jargon? being on throne.

Such, sir, are all the facts, succinctly put,
The basis or substratum—what you will—
Of the impending eighty thousand lines.
'Not much in 'em either,' quoth perhaps simple Hodge.
But there's a superstructure. Wait a bit.
Mark first the rationale of the thing:
Hear logic rivel and levigate the deed.

That shilling—and for matter o' that, the pence—
I had o' course upo' me—wi' me say—
(*Mecum*'s the Latin, make a note o' that)
When I popp'd pen i' stand, scratch'd ear, wiped snout,
(Let everybody wipe his own himself)
Sniff'd—tch!—at snuffbox; tumbled up, he-heed,
Haw-haw'd (not hee-haw'd, that's another guess thing:)
Then fumbled at, and stumbled out of, door,
I shoved the timber ope wi' my omoplat;
And *in vestibulo*, i' the lobby to wit,
(Iacobi Facciolati's rendering, sir,)
Donn'd galligaskins, antigropeloes,
And so forth; and, complete with hat and gloves,
One on and one a-dangle i' my hand,
And ombrifuge (Lord love you!) case o' rain,
I flopp'd forth, 'sbuddikins! on my own ten toes,
(I do assure you there be ten of them),
And went clump-clumping up hill and down dale
To find myself o' the sudden i' front o' the boy.
Put case I hadn't 'em on me, could I ha' bought
This sort-o' kind-o'-what-you-might-call toy,
This pebble-thing, o' the boy-thing? QED.

That's proven without aid from mumping Pope,
Sleep porporate or bloated Cardinal.
(Isn't it, old Fatchaps? You're in Euclid, now.)
So, having the shilling—having i' fact a lot—
And pence and halfpence, ever so many o' them,
I purchased, as I think I said before,
The pebble (lapis, lapidis, -di, -dem, -de—
What nouns 'crease short i' the genitive, Fatchaps, eh?)
O' the boy, a bare-legg'd beggarly son of a gun,
For one-and-fourpence. Here we are again.

Now Law steps in, bigwigg'd, voluminous-jaw'd
Investigates and re-investigates.
Was the transaction illegal? Law shakes head.
Perpend, sir, all the bearings of the case.

At first the coin was mine, the chattel his.
But now (by virtue of the said exchange
And barter) *vice versa* all the coin,
Per juris operationem, vests
I' the boy and his assigns till ding o' doom;
In *sœcula sœculo-o-o-orum;*
(I think I hear the Abate mouth of that.)
To have and hold the same to him and then . . .
Confer some idiot on Conveyancing.
Whereas the pebble and every part thereof,
And all that appertaineth thereunto,
Quodcunque pertinet ad eam rem,
(I fancy, sir, my Latin's rather pat)
Or shall, will, may, might, can, could, would or should,
(*Subandi cœtera*—clap me to the close——
For what's the good of law in a case o' the kind?)
Is mine to all intents and purposes.
This settled, I resume the thread o' the tale.

Now for a touch o' the vendor's quality.
He says a gen'lman bought a pebble of him,
(This pebble i' sooth, sir, which I hold i' my hand)—
And paid for't *like* a gen'lman, on the nail.
'Did I o'ercharge him a ha'penny? Devil a bit
Fiddlepin's end! Get out, you blazing ass!
Gabble o' the goose. Don't bugaboo-baby *me*!

451

Go double or quits? Ya! tittup! what's the odds?'
—There's the transaction view'd i' the vendor's light.

Next ask that dumpled hag, stood snuffling by,
With her three frowsy blowsy brats o' babes,
The scum o' the kennel, cream o' the filth-heap— Faugh!
Aie, aie, aie, aie! *ototototot*
('Stead which we blurt out Hoighty toighty now)—
And the baker and the candlestickmaker, and Jack and Jill,
Blear'd Goody this and queasy Gaffer that.
Ask the schoolmaster. Take schoolmaster first.

He saw a gentleman purchase from a lad
A stone, and pay for it *rite*, on the square,
And carry it off *per saltum*, jauntily,
Propria quae maribus, gentleman's property now
(Agreeably to the law explain'd above),
In proprium usum, for his private ends.
The boy he chuck'd a brown i' the air, and bit
I' the face the shilling: heaved a thumping stone
At a lean hen that ran cluck clucking by,
(And hit her, dead as nail i' post o' door,)
Then abiit—what's the Ciceronian phrase?—
Excessit, evasit, erupit—off slogs boy;
Off like bird, *avi similis*—(you observed
The dative? Pretty i' the Mantuan!)—*Anglice*,
Off in three flea skips. *Hactenus*, so far,
So good, *tam bene. Bene, satis, male*—,
Where was I with my trope 'bout one in a quag?
I did once hitch the syntax into verse:
Verbum personale, a verb personal,
Concordat—ay, 'agrees', old Fatchaps—*cum
Nominativo*, with its nominative,
Genere, i' point o' gender, *numero*,
O' number, *et persona*, and person. *Ut*,
Instance: *Sol ruit*, down flops sun, *et* and
Montes umbrantur, out flounce mountains. Pah!
Excuse me, sir, I think I'm going mad.
You see the trick on 't though, and can yourself
Continue the discourse *ad libitum*.
It takes up about eighty thousand lines,
A thing imagination boggles at:

And might, odd-bobs, sir! in judicious hands,
Extend from here to Mesopotamy.

CHARLES STUART CALVERLEY

A Letter of Advice

From Miss Medora Trevilian, at Padua, to Miss Araminta Vavasour,
in London

You tell me you're promised a lover,
    My own Araminta, next week;
Why cannot my fancy discover
    The hue of his coat and his cheek?
Alas! if he look like another,
    A vicar, a banker, a beau,
Be deaf to your father and mother,
    My own Araminta, say 'No!'

Miss Lane, at her Temple of Fashion,
    Taught us both how to sing and to speak,
And we loved one another with passion,
    Before we had been there a week:
You gave me a ring for a token;
    I wear it wherever I go;
I gave you a chain,—is it broken?
    My own Araminta, say 'No!'

O think of our favourite cottage,
    And think of our dear Lalla Rookh!
How we shared with the milkmaids their pottage,
    And drank of the stream from the brook;
How fondly our loving lips faltered
    'What further can grandeur bestow?'
My heart is the same;—is yours altered?
    My own Araminta, say 'No!'

Remember the thrilling romances
   We read on the bank in the glen;
Remember the suitors our fancies
   Would picture for both of us then.
They wore the red cross on their shoulder,
   They had vanquished and pardoned their foe—
Sweet friend, are you wiser or colder?
   My own Araminta, say 'No!'

You know, when Lord Rigmarole's carriage
   Drove off with your cousin Justine,
You wept, dearest girl, at the marriage,
   And whispered 'How base she has been!'
You said you were sure it would kill you,
   If ever your husband looked so;
And you will not apostatize,—will you?
   My own Araminta, say 'No!'

When I heard I was going abroad, love,
   I thought I was going to die;
We walked arm in arm to the road, love,
   We looked arm in arm to the sky;
And I said 'When a foreign postillion
   Has hurried me off to the Po,
Forget not Medora Trevilian:
   My own Araminta, say "No!" '

We parted! but sympathy's fetters
   Reach far over valley and hill;
I muse o'er your exquisite letters,
   And feel that your heart is mine still;
And he who would share it with me, love,—
   The richest of treasures below,—
If he's not what Orlando should be, love,
   My own Araminta, say 'No!'

If he wears a top-boot in his wooing,
　If he comes to you riding a cob,
If he talks of his baking or brewing,
　If he puts up his feet on the hob,
If he ever drinks port after dinner,
　If his brow or his breeding is low,
If he calls himself 'Thompson' or 'Skinner',
　My own Araminta, say 'No!'

If he studies the news in the papers
　While you are preparing the tea,
If he talks of the damps or the vapours
　While moonlight lies soft on the sea,
If he's sleepy while you are capricious,
　If he has not a musical 'Oh!'
If he does not call Werther delicious,
　My own Araminta, say 'No!'

If he ever sets foot in the City
　Among the stockbrokers and Jews,
If he has not a heart full of pity,
　If he don't stand six feet in his shoes,
If his lips are not redder than roses,
　If his hands are not whiter than snow,
If he has not the model of noses,—
　My own Araminta, say 'No!'

If he speaks of a tax or a duty,
　If he does not look grand on his knees,
If he's blind to a landscape of beauty,
　Hills, valleys, rocks, waters, and trees,
If he dotes not on desolate towers,
　If he likes not to hear the blast blow,
If he knows not the language of flowers,—
　My own Araminta, say 'No!'

He must walk—like a god of old story
  Come down from the home of his rest;
He must smile—like the sun in his glory
  On the buds he loves ever the best;
And oh! from its ivory portal
  Like music his soft speech must flow!—
If he speak, smile, or walk like a mortal,
  My own Araminta, say 'No!'

Don't listen to tales of his bounty,
  Don't hear what they say of his birth,
Don't look at his seat in the county,
  Don't calculate what he is worth;
But give him a theme to write verse on,
  And see if he turns out his toe;
If he's only an excellent person,—
  My own Araminta, say 'No!'

W. M. PRAED

Jenny on D. G. Rossetti

('I wonder what you're thinking of' – *D. G. R. on Jenny*)

You think I'm sleeping, Mr R.
That only shows how wrong you are!
Not likely I'd drop off, myself,
Before your guinea's on the shelf.
A girl must live; and who's to blame
If there's no credit in this game?
Still writing? You're *that* kind of man?
Well, let's be cosy while we can.
Though I must say I do not care
For all these poets with long hair,
And painters with their rings and cloaks;
I never really like their jokes.
Look what they done to poor Miss S.
She's like a living ghost, I guess.
Just for a painting, so they say,
They lay her in her bath all day.

456

There's Mr Swinburne—you should see
The verses what he wrote for me.
They really are—well, not quite nice.
I wouldn't care to read them twice.
Some pictures I could take to. Once
I saw a show of Mr Hunt's,
And Mr Millais' and Rossetti's
At least aren't rude like Mr Etty's.

At last. He's closed his little book.
I've half a mind to take a look.
What, going now?
    Well, there's a ninny!
I never earned an easier guinea!

        PONTIFEX

Notes

Mac Flecknoe

The notes that follow are based on those to be found in *Dryden's Satire*, edited by D. R. Elloway and published by Macmillan.

Mac Flecknoe   Richard Flecknoe, a skinny Irishman and writer of feeble verse, had long been the butt of the literary set. *Mac* means 'son of', hence the title.

Shadwell   Writer of knockabout farce – fat, dissolute, but very successful.

business   Sex.

Heywood/Shirley   Prolific hacks.

Epsom blankets   Allusion to high jinks in one of Shadwell's comedies.

Arion   A Greek musician – Shadwell was also a musician.

Pissing-Alley   London street.

Aston Hall   The home of another dull poet.

toast   Toast of the town, female.

St André   A noted dancing-master.

Singleton   John Singleton was leader of the Royal musicians.

Augusta   One of the Roman names for London.

a Nursery   This was a theatre in Golden Lane for the training of child actors.

Maximin   A tyrant.

Simkin   A simpleton.

clinch   A pun.

Panton   A notorious punster.

Psyches . . . Bruce   These are allusions to various plays by Shadwell.

Martyrs of pies and reliques of the bum   The works of the neglected authors are now so much waste paper, and are put to sundry uses, the lining of pie-dishes being the least undignified.

Herringman   Shadwell's publisher.

Love's Kingdom   A play by Flecknoe.

George   Sir George Etherege, Restoration playwright.

false flowers of rhetoric   Shadwell was a notable plagiarist.

Sir Formal   A character in *The Virtuoso*, one of Shadwell's plays.

northern dedications   Shadwell dedicated four plays to the ducal family of Newcastle.

sell bargains   To 'sell bargains' was to answer innocent questions with coarse expressions such as those quoted.

tympany   Swollen flatulence.

kilderkin   A small barrel.

Irish   To be stupid.

458

Verses on the Death of Dr Swift

The notes below are based on those to be found in *The Complete Poems*, edited by Pat Rogers and published by the Yale University Press.

I'm glad the medals were forgot   Swift had given the Queen (Anne), who was then the princess, some Irish poplin and in return she had promised him medals which he hadn't received.

Chartres   He was a moneylender, and spy to Walpole.

Sir Robert   Walpole, Prime Minister.

dead without his shoes   A cant term for being hanged.

Will   Sir William Pulteney, once Walpole's ally.

Bolingbroke   Henry St John, Viscount Bolingbroke, Secretary of State, and Walpole's rival.

Curll   The publisher, who did not scruple to put Swift's name to works he hadn't written.

Tibbalds, Moore and Cibber   'Three stupid verse writers.'

vole   To win all the tricks at the card-game quadrille.

Lintot   Bernard Lintot, the bookseller.

Duck Lane   It was where second-hand books were sold.

the pastry-cook's   More waste-paper lining pudding-basins.

Henly   'An absolute dunce.'

Woolston   A fashionable theologian.

Had set a price upon his head   Rewards had been offered both in England and Ireland for the name of the author of two pamphlets written anonymously by Swift.

Was all destroyed by one event   This was the death of Queen Anne.

Far to the land of slaves and fens   Swift retired to Dublin upon the Queen's death.

An infamous destructive cheat   Wood, of Wood's Halfpence – he had a licence to make copper coin in Ireland, a scheme to which Swift was implacably opposed.

A wicked monster on the bench   Whitshed, Chief Justice of Ireland, attempted to browbeat juries when the printers of certain of Swift's pamphlets were being prosecuted.

Scroggs, Tressilian   Corrupt judges.

topics   Legalistic debating points.

biennial squires   The Irish parliament met once every two years.

go snacks   To share.

rapparees   Banditti.

keep the peace   To act as magistrates.

job   A racket.

to build a house for fools and mad   Swift's bequest for the founding of a madhouse in Dublin.

To Mrs Martha Blount

The coronation was that of George I.

Loo

Loo was a game not unlike whist.

Pam   The over-riding trump.

Fielding   Sir John Fielding, Bow Street magistrate, and half-brother of Henry Fielding, the novelist.

quinto Elizabeth   The Act of Elizabeth I under which pickpockets were arraigned.

mobs   Mob caps.

Ephibol on My Dear Love Isabella

By Marjorie Fleming, born in 1803 at Kirkaldy, died 1811. Marjorie Fleming's diary, from which these and other verses are taken, was a schoolroom task set by her cousin Isabella. Marjorie suffered a bout of measles from which she seemed to recover, but she fell ill again, possibly with meningitis, and died in her ninth year. Her journal remained in the Fleming family until 1858, when it was published as a sixpenny pamphlet.

Two Sonnets Composed by a Computer

Dr J. R. Partington tells me: 'The machine was provided with a large list of fairly vivid words, classified by their part of speech, number of syllables and (in some cases) rhyme type. In addition a reasonable number of skeleton sonnets (often modelled on Shakespeare) were provided from which the programme could choose, proceeding then to flesh it out with the appropriate words. . . . In fact, over two million different sonnets are possible, but the sense of novelty wears off rather earlier.'

Cancer's a Funny Thing

As originally printed in the *New Statesman* the poem does not contain lines 11.5/8. I have ventured to include them, since Haldane himself felt the generally bracing object of the poem might have been better served with them than without them.

Twelve Articles

break no squares   Do no harm.

One-and-Twenty

Of the young man who is the subject of this poem Johnson once said 'Sir, when I heard of him last, he was running about town shooting cats' (Boswell's *Life of Johnson*).

Lunching One Day with Morgan

It may be necessary to point out that this is Charles Morgan, author of the novel *Sparkenbroke*.

Daily Trials

gutter-roker Roker was a poor sort of fish, food of the working-classes (according to the *NED*.) Hence, food of the gutter.

Molly Bloom

Joyce had been dreaming of the character he had 'limned for Ireland's gamest daughter' – 'I . . . strode up to her and delivered the one speech of my life. It was very long, eloquent and full of passion, explaining all the last episode of *Ulysses* to her. She wore a black opera cloak or *sortie de bal*, had become slightly grey and looked like *la Duse*. She smiled when I ended on an astronomical climax, and then, bending, picked up a tiny snuffbox in the form of a little black coffin and tossed it towards me, saying "And I have done with you, too, Mr Joyce . . ." ' (Richard Ellmann, *James Joyce*).

Epigram

The peer in question is said to have been Lord Radnor. Pope had lopped three of his walnut trees to improve the view from his own garden.

To Mrs Thrale

'I went into his room the morning of my birthday once', writes Hester Thrale, 'and said to him, "Nobody sends me any verses now, because I am five-and-thirty years old".' Whereat Johnson extemporized the verses instantly 'without having entertained the smallest intention towards it half a minute before'. ' "And now" (said he, as I was writing the verses down), "you may see what it is to come for poetry to a Dictionary-maker; you may observe that the rhymes run in alphabetical order exactly." '

A Valentine

Quoted in *James Joyce* by Richard Ellmann.

Lines on an Envelope Addressed to Clive Bell Esq

'For the benefit of the author I may say that this pleasantry gave satisfaction to the postman invoked. He considered it "clever". He was not quite sure about the "spinet", but knew that I was fond of shooting: it was not true about the "virginals" he hoped' (Clive Bell).

To the Brothers Fay

These lines are reprinted from *James Joyce* by Richard Ellmann.

To Mr Thomas Southern

sent down to raise

The price of prologues and of plays Southern wanted a prologue from Dryden, and Dryden charged him six guineas when hitherto the price had been four.

A Letter to Harriet Weaver
Quoted in Richard Ellmann, *James Joyce*.

from Epistle to Dr Arbuthnot
Arbuthnot was Queen Anne's physician and a man much esteemed in contemporary literary circles.
good John   John Serle, his servant.
high in Drury Lane   i.e. in a garret.

Balliol Rhymes
These were all written by undergraduates of the college, and first appeared in 1881 entitled *The Masque of B—ll—l*. Those I include (together with the following notes) come from *The Balliol Rhymes*, edited by, and printed for, W. G. Hiscock, in 1955.
Strachan-Davidson   He collected Graeco-Roman coins.
dahabeah   A Nile boat.
Nettleship   Celebrated for his tentative manner.
Mackail   'This rhyme must be recited in a soft Highland accent.'
Liddell   'The rhyme with "High" must not be avoided.'
Jowett   'Jowett pronounced "Knowledge" with a long "o".'

London Rurality
The author notes: 'The correspondence which closes the subsequent poem is founded on two prose letters in manuscript, which, it is asserted, actually passed between two ladies who were neighbours, out of town. Some of the passages are almost literally given from the original epistles. It is an irony that Colman's snooty verse preamble to the corresponding hits just the note of cockney pretentiousness that he is presuming to sneer at.
jemmy rail   A smart railing.
tenter   A stretcher.

Lady Acheson Weary of the Dean
eyes of wall   Rolling eyes.
skinny, boney, snip and lean   These were roguish names bestowed by Swift on his hostess. *Snip* = a little scrap, a little bit of a thing.

From a Letter to My Aunt
David G.   Presumably the poet David Gascoyne.
Chankley Bore   Fanciful region of hills (Edward Lear).

Ode to a Jacobin

The 'three caricaturists of false sentiment' who founded the journal, *The Anti-Jacobin*, at the time of the French Revolution, were George Canning, George Ellis and John Hookham Frere. Their poems, parodies and squibs were often joint productions, and though it's on record that Canning and Frere were responsible for *The Knife Grinder* (see page 236) and Canning and Ellis wrote *Rogero's Song* (see page 411), *Ode to a Jacobin* has not been ascribed.

Mary the Cook-maid's Letter

concerned   Drunk.
come-rogues   Fellow rogues.
Saunders   Swift's servant.
pin a dishclout to his tail   Said of men who fuss in the kitchen.
written hand   Handwriting.

When Klopstock England Defied

Klopstock, author of the epic *Messias*, was known as 'the German Milton'. He criticized English verse for its supposed coarseness.
Nobodaddy   The Devil.

The Progress of Discontent

Modus   Money payment in lieu of a tithe.

The Candidate

Jemmy Twitcher is John Montague, 4th Earl of Sandwich who – even though well-known to be a libertine – was supported for the post of High Steward of Cambridge University by the Divinity Faculty. As James Reeves (editor of *Thomas Gray: Complete English Poems*) points out, this is the central irony of the poem.
guttle   Guzzle.
stitches   Fornicates.

Lines on Thomas Warton's Poems

'He observed that a gentleman of eminence in literature (Tom Warton) had got into a bad style of poetry of late. "He puts" (said he) "a very common thing in a strange dress till he does not know it himself, and thinks other people do not know it."
Boswell: "That is owing to his being versant in old English Poetry."
Johnson: "What is that to the purpose, Sir? If I say a man is drunk, and you tell me that is owing to his taking too much drink, the matter is not mended. No, Sir, Warton has taken to an odd mode. For example, he'd write thus:

> *Hermit hoar, in solemn cell,*
> *Wearing out life's evening gray.*

Gray evening is common enough; but *evening gray* he'd think fine. Stay — we'll make out the stanza:

> *Hermit hoar, in solemn cell,*
> *Wearing out life's evening gray;*
> *Smite thy bosom, sage, and tell,*
> *What is bliss? and which the way?"*

Boswell: "But why smite his bosom, Sir?"
Johnson: "Why, to shew he was in earnest," (smiling). He at an after period added the last stanza' (Boswell, *Life of Johnson*).

Dooleysprudence

Joyce wrote his version of *Mr Dooley* when he was in Zurich during the First World War, the anarchic spirit of the bloody-minded Mr Dooley being a folklorique version of his own. My source is Richard Ellmann's *James Joyce*.

464

Acknowledgments

Every conceivable effort has been made to trace copyright holders but in a few cases it has proved impossible to trace the author or his executor. We apologise for any omissions.

Kingsley Amis 'Sight Unseen' reprinted by permission of Hutchinson Books Ltd from the *Collected Poetry* of Kingsley Amis.

W. H. Auden 'Song VIII', 'Letter to Lord Byron', 'On the Circuit', 'Doggerel by a Senior Citizen', 'Blues' reprinted by permission of Faber and Faber Ltd from *Collected Poems* and from *The English Auden: Poems, Essays & Dramatic Writings 1927–1939* by W. H. Auden.

Maurice Baring 'Moan in the Form of a Ballade' reprinted by permission of A. P. Watt Ltd from *One Hundred And One Ballades* by Maurice Baring.

Max Beerbohm 'A Red Sky at Night', 'To Dr D', 'The Characters of Shakespeare', 'Ballad of a Recurring Anomaly in Berkeley Square' reprinted by permission of William Heinemann Ltd.

Hilaire Belloc 'Charles Augustus Fortesque', 'Lines to a Don', 'On Mundane Acquaintances', 'The Yak', 'The Python', 'The Welsh Mutton', 'Hildebrand', 'Algernon' reprinted by permission of Gerald Duckworth & Co Ltd.

John Betjeman 'Dorset', 'The Licorice Fields of Pontefact', 'May Day Song for North Oxford', 'Reproof Deserved', 'How to Get On in Society' reprinted by permission of John Murray (Publishers) from the *Collected Poems* of John Betjemen.

Morris Bishop from *The Best of Bishop* (Cornell University Press). © 1935, 1943, 1945, 1958 Alison Kingsbury Bishop. 'Modern Language Association' originally appeared in The Saturday Review of Literature, 'Merry Old Souls', 'There's Money in Mother and Father', 'Old Folks at the Home' originally appeared in the *New Yorker*.

Guy Boas 'Chocolates' reprinted by permission of *Punch*.

W. Bridges-Adams 'To Charlotte While Shaving', 'Blackheath', 'Notting Hill Polka', 'Ballade of No Meaning' reprinted by permission of A. D. Peters and Co Ltd from *To Charlotte While Shaving* by W. Bridges-Adams.

Roy Campbell 'The Georgiad', 'Georgian Spring' reprinted by permission of Fransisco Campbell Custodio and A. D. Donker (Pty) Ltd.

Melville Cane 'Askew, We Ask You', 'Orchestra Notes' from *Poems: New and Selected* and 'After Reading the Reviews of Finnegans

Wake' from *A Wider Arc* reprinted by permission of Harcourt Brace
Jovanovich Inc.

Charles Causley 'Ballad of the Bread Man', 'Ten Types of Hospital
Visitor' reprinted by permission of David Higham Ltd from the
Collected Poems by Charles Causley.

Geoffrey Chaucer 'The Miller's Tale' trans Nevill Coghill reprinted by
permission of Penguin Books Ltd.

G. K. Chesterton 'The Fat White Woman Speaks', 'A Ballade of
Suicide', 'Antichrist, or the Reunion of Christendom', 'Commercial
Candour' reprinted by permission of A. P. Watt Ltd from *The
Collected Poems of G. K. Chesterton*.

E. Clerihew Bentley 'Henry VIII', 'Mr Maxton', 'Karl Marx', 'When a
Photograph of Attila', 'Bunyan', 'The Art of Biography', 'Liszt',
'Milton' reprinted by permission of Oxford University Press from
The Complete Clerihews Of E. Clerihew Bentley. © The Estate of
E. C. Bentley.

Walter de la Mare 'The Bards', 'The Spectre', 'The Waif', 'Archery',
'Bishop Winterbourne', 'Fish', 'The Lady McTaggart', 'Buttons',
'Green', 'The Bonnet', 'Very' reprinted by permission of The
Literary Trustees of Walter de la Mare and The Society of Authors as
their representative.

Alfred Douglas 'The Hen', 'The Antelope' reprinted by permission of
Edward Colman from *The Duke of Happiness* by Alfred Douglas.

John Drinkwater 'Mamble' reprinted by permission of Sidgwick &
Jackson from *The Poems Of John Drinkwater*.

Max Ehrmann 'A Tradesman and a Poet' reprinted by permission of
Robert L. Bell, Melrose, Mass.02176 USA. © 1948 by Bertha
K. Ehrmann. All rights reserved. Copyright renewed 1976 by
Robert L. Bell.

T. S. Eliot 'There's No One Left to Press My Pants' printed by
permission of Mrs Valerie Eliot and Faber and Faber Ltd from
previously unpublished verse by T. S. Eliot. © Valerie Eliot 1984
'Letter to Clive Bell' reprinted by permission of Mrs Valerie Eliot
and Faber and Faber Ltd from *T.S.Eliot: A Symposium (1948)*. ©
T. S. Eliot 1948.
'Lines to Ralph Hodgson Esq' reprinted by permission of Faber and
Faber Ltd from *Collected Poems 1906–1962* by T. S. Eliot.
'Billy M'Caw; The Remarkable Parrot' reprinted by permission of
Faber and Faber Ltd: first published in *The Queen's Book Of The Red
Cross (1939)* and subsequently reprinted in *Cats*; the book of the
musical based on *Old Possum's Book Of Practical Cats* by T. S. Eliot.
Permission to reprint in the USA from Harcourt Brace Jovanovich
Inc.

Gavin Ewart 'The Reviewing of Poetry', 'The Sentimental Education',

'Every Doggerel Has Its Day', 'Miss Twye', reprinted by permission of Hutchinson Books Ltd.

Eleanor Farjeon 'William I' reprinted by permission of David Higham Associates Ltd from *Kings and Queens* by Eleanor Farjeon.

Margaret Fishback 'The Purist to Her Love' reprinted by permission of E. P. Dutton from *One to a Customer, Collected Poems of Margaret Fishback*, copyright 1937 by E. P. Dutton, 1965 by M. F. Antolini.

Roy Fuller 'A Portrait of the Author' reprinted by permission of André Deutsch from *Poor Roy* by Roy Fuller.

Stephen Gaselee 'Grace During a Meal' reprinted by permission of *The International Wine and Food Society*.

Phoebe Fenwick Gaye 'The Plaint of the Middlebrow Novelist' reprinted by permission of André Deutsch from *Time And Tide Anthology 1957*.

Oliver St John Gogarty 'Ringsend', 'Time, Gentlemen, Time!' reprinted by permission of Oliver D. Gogarty from *Collected Poems* of Oliver St John Gogarty and by permission of the Devin Adair Publishers, Greenwich, CT, USA.

Harry Graham 'Inconsiderate Hannah', 'Lord Gorbals', 'The Cockney of the North', 'My First Love', 'Obstruction' reprinted by permission of Edward Arnold Ltd.

Robert Graves 'The Traveller's Curse After Misdirection' reprinted by permission of A. P. Watt Ltd.

Arthur Guiterman 'On the Vanity of Earthly Greatness' reprinted by permission of Mrs Louise Sclove.

J. B. S. Haldane 'Cancer's a Funny Thing' reprinted by permission of *New Statesman*.

G. Rostrevor Hamilton 'Don's Holiday', 'A Window Cleaner', 'On a Distant Prospect of an Absconding Bookmaker' reprinted by permission of William Heinemann Ltd.

A. E. Housman 'Amelia Mixed the Mustard', 'When Adam Day by Day', 'O Have You Caught the Tiger', 'On the Death of a Female Officer of the Salvation Army', 'As I Was Walking Backwards', 'Let us Play on the Pianner', 'The Elephant', 'Infant Innocence', 'Fragment of a Greek Tragedy', 'A Morning with the Royal Family' reprinted by permission of The Society of Authors as the literary representative of the Estate of A. E. Housman, and Jonathan Cape Ltd, publishers of A. E. Housman's *Collected Poems*.

Christopher Isherwood 'The Common Cormorant or Shag' reprinted by permission of Curtis Brown Ltd on behalf of Christopher Isherwood.

L. E. Jones 'A Clerical Error', 'A Novel', 'Journalism', 'Food', 'Literary Party 1949', 'When Tennyson' reprinted by permission of Secker & Warburg Ltd from *A La Carte* by L. E. Jones.

James Joyce 'Dooleysprudence', 'Molly Bloom', 'Gas from a Burner', 'The Fays', 'A Letter to Harriet Weaver in the Style of the Wasteland' reprinted by permission of The Society of Authors as the literary representative of the Estate of James Joyce.

Hugh Kingsmill 'The Shropshire Lad' reprinted by permission of Curtis Brown Ltd, London from *The Dawn's Delay* (Elkin Matthews 1924).

E. V. Knox 'So Many Caesars', 'The Everlasting Percy', 'The Three Calenders', 'Hell in Herefordshire', 'The Director', 'String, in Lieu Of' reprinted by permission of Mrs M. E. Knox. All appeared first in *Punch* apart from 'The Three Calenders' first published in *The New Statesman* by E. V. Knox (Evoe).

A. M. Laing 'A Benison on a Wartime High Tea' reprinted by permission of George Allen & Unwin from *Bank Holiday On Parnassus*.

Philip Larkin 'I Remember' reprinted by permission of The Marvell Press, from *The Less Deceived*.

R. P. Lister 'The Gem-Like Flame', 'Mr Bluefrock Considers It All', 'Plumber-Song at Evening', 'Defenestration', reprinted by permission of R. P. Lister from *The Idle Demon*.

Malcolm Lowry 'Eye-Opener', 'Strange Type', 'Epitaph' reprinted by permission of City Lights Books. © Margerie Lowry 1962.

Louis MacNeice 'Bagpipe Music' reprinted by permission of Faber and Faber Ltd from *The Collected Poems of Louis MacNeice*.

Edna St Vincent Millay 'First Fig', 'Grown-up', 'To the Not Impossible Him' reprinted by permission of Harper & Row from *Collected Poems*. Copyright 1922, 1950 by Edna St Vincent Millay.

Christopher Morley 'Studies in Dry Vermouth', 'Hot Lemonade', 'Graduate Student', 'Beauty Parlor' from *The Middle Kingdom* reprinted by permission of Harcourt Brace Jovanovich Inc.

Ogden Nash 'All, All Are Gone', 'Peekaboo, I Almost See You', 'The Private Dining Room', 'Just Keep Quiet and Nobody Will Notice', 'Ma, What's a Banker?' reprinted by permission of André Deutsch from *I Wouldn't Have Missed It*. Also by permission of Little, Brown and Company (USA): 'Just Keep Quiet and Nobody Will Notice' copyright 1936 by Ogden Nash. First appeared in *The New Yorker*. 'Ma, What's a Banker' copyright 1933 Ogden Nash. 'Peekaboo, I Almost See You' copyright 1949 by Ogden Nash. First appeared in *The Saturday Evening Post*.

Philip Oakes 'The Death of the Referee' reprinted by permission of André Deutsch from *In The Affirmative*.

William Plomer 'The Playboy of the Demi-World', 'The Flying Bum: 1944', 'Miss Robinson's Funeral', 'A Shot in the Park' reprinted by permission of the Estate of William Plomer and Jonathan Cape Ltd from *Collected Poems* of William Plomer.

468

Two Computer Sonnets: 'O Salamander', 'How Can the Purple Yeti Be So Red' reprinted by permission of Dr Jonathan R. Partington, Fitzwilliam College, Cambridge.

Pontifex 'Jenny On D. E. Rossetti' reprinted by permission of *The New Statesman*.

Ezra Pound 'Ancient Music' reprinted by permission of Faber and Faber Ltd from *Collected Shorter Poems* of Ezra Pound and by permission of New Directions Publishing Corporation (USA) copyright 1926 by Ezra Pound.

A. G. Prys-Jones 'A Little Nonsense' reprinted by permission of D. Brown & Sons Ltd.

A. Quiller Couch 'The New Ballad of Sir Patrick Spens', 'The Famous Ballad of the Jubilee Cup' reprinted by permission of Monro Pennefather and Co, executors of the estate of A. Quiller-Couch.

Henry Reed 'Chard Whitlow' reprinted by permission of Henry Reed and Jonathan Cape Ltd from *A Map Of Verona*.

Siegfried Sassoon 'Founder's Feast' reprinted by permission of George Sassoon. Also by permission of Viking Penguin Inc (USA): Copyright 1918, 1920 by E. P. Dutton & Co. Copyright 1936, 1946, 1947, 1948 by Siegfried Sassoon. From *Collected Poems* by Siegfried Sassoon, all rights reserved.

Stanley J. Sharpless 'Hamlet' reprinted by permission of the *New Statesman*.

Stevie Smith 'Mrs Simpkins', 'Correspondence', 'On the Death of a German Philosopher', 'Autumn' reprinted by permission of James MacGibbon as executor of the Estate of Stevie Smith from *The Collected Poems of Stevie Smith* (Allen Lane).

James Stephens 'A Glass of Beer' reprinted by permission of the Society of Authors on behalf of the copyright owner, Mrs Iris Wise.

L. A. G. Strong 'Ned', 'A Memory', 'The Roadmender', 'The Brewer's Man', 'Old Bridget Complains to the Lord', 'Jesse Welch' reprinted by permission of A. D. Peters & Co Ltd.

Dylan Thomas 'Letter To My Aunt' reprinted by permission of David Higham Ltd from *The Poems of Dylan Thomas* (Dent).

Ursula Wadey 'Sweetness and Light' printed by permission of Ursula Wadey.

Arthur Waley 'On the Birth of His Son' reprinted by permission of Constable Publishers from *170 Chinese Poems* trans Arthur Waley.

E. B. White 'A Classic Waits for Me' from *The Second Tree From The Corner* by E. B. White. Copyright 1944, 1972 by E. B. White. 'Marble-Top' from *The Lady Is Cold* by E. B. White. Copyright 1927, 1955 by E. B. White. Both selections reprinted by permission of Harper & Row, Publishers Inc.

P. G. Wodehouse 'Good Gnus', 'Printer's Error', 'Time Like An Ever Rolling Stream' reprinted by permission of Lady Ethel Wodehouse and The Hutchinson Group Ltd from *Plum Pie*.

Humbert Wolfe 'The British Journalist', 'A. E. Housman and a Few Friends', 'Queen Victoria' from *Lampoons* by Humbert Wolfe (Doubleday).

Roland Young 'The Ape' from *Not For Children* (Doubleday).

Index of Authors

471

DORSET COUNTY LIBRARY

477

478

Index of First Lines and Titles

First lines appear in italic.

481

490

498

DORSET COUNTY LIBRARY